THE FINANCIAL TIMES

A-Z
OF
INTERNATIONAL FINANCE

THE FINANCIAL TIMES

A-Z
OF
INTERNATIONAL FINANCE

The Essential Guide to Tools, Terms & Techniques

STEPHEN MAHONY

FT
PITMAN
PUBLISHING

London · Hong Kong · Johannesburg · Melbourne
Singapore · Washington DC

PITMAN PUBLISHING
128 Long Acre, London WC2E 9AN
Tel: +44 (0)171 447 2000
Fax: +44 (0)171 240 5771

A Division of Pearson Professional Limited

First published in Great Britain 1997

ISBN 0 273 62552 7

British Library Cataloguing in Publication Data
A CIP catalogue record for this book can be obtained
from the British Library.

1 3 5 7 9 10 8 6 4 2

Typeset by Northern Phototypesetting Co Ltd, Bolton
Printed and bound in Great Britain by
Biddles Ltd, Guildford and King's Lynn

*The Publishers' policy is to use paper manufactured
from sustainable forests.*

INTRODUCTION

This book has been written for all those engaged in finance and for students who need a single-volume source of reference. The book has two functions. Its first purpose is to summarize anything which is important in international finance. Its second purpose is to provoke thought about the information it conveys.

The scope of the book encompasses the practical as much as the theoretical; dealers' slang as well as put/call parity. The book has been fun to write. I hope the reader finds it enjoyable as well as useful.

Markets and institutions from many countries are included though inevitably the major markets occur most frequently. English translations are given of terms frequently used in Japan and the main European markets.

The order of entries is on a word by word basis, so that 'default interest' comes before 'defaulted receivable'; and hyphens are ignored, so that 'H-shares' appears after 'Hryvna' and 'Exercise' appears after 'Ex-date' and before 'Ex-redemption'.

Cross references are in bold in the text with sign posts to other relevant words at the end of the entry in the form 'See **Implied volatility**', for example.

Samuel Johnson was quite prepared to admit to ignorance when questioned about errors in his Dictionary. I am in good company if I say the rate of change of international financial markets is now so great that, despite my best efforts, there may be errors of commission or omission in the text. I would be particularly grateful for ideas which would extend the scope of the next edition. Readers are encouraged to send me corrections or suggestions by e-mail to mahony@broadclose.demon.co.uk, or by mail or fax c/o Pitman Publishing.

Stephen Mahony
January 1997

ACKNOWLEDGEMENTS

The team at Pitman is variously talented but uniformly excellent. They all show grace under pressure. I thank particularly Linda Dhondy and Richard Stagg.

I am grateful to the following for permission to quote material in the text:

- R. M. Austin of the Bank of England for permission to reproduce the diagram of the timetable for European Monetary Union which was originally published in the Bank of England's *Practical issues arising from the introduction of the Euro*, No. 3, 16th December 1996;
- James Dunseath of LIFFE for permission to quote examples from some of LIFFE's excellent publications;
- Graham Knibbs of IFR for permission to quote market statistics compiled by IFR Securities Data;
- Bruce Johnson and Chris Littell of ING Baring Securities Limited for permission to show the composition of the ING Baring Emerging Markets Index;
- Richard Metcalfe of *Futures and Options World*, for permission to quote trading volumes in leading government bond futures compiled by that publication, and for being such a well-informed and amusing source of information;
- Stephen Timewell, Editor of *The Banker* for permission to publish a table ranking the largest banks in the world which was originally published in that magazine;
- Transparency International, Berlin and Dr Johann Lambsdorf of Goettingen University for permission to reproduce the Transparency International Corruption Perception Index 1996;
- Goldman, Sachs & Co for permission to reproduce the table of components and weights of the Goldman Sachs Commodity Index (GSCI).

THE AUTHOR

Stephen Mahony was born in Ireland and educated at Ampleforth and Oxford University. From 1977 to 1991 he was a banker, during which time he worked for Citibank and Swiss Bank Corporation, specializing in capital markets and derivatives. He is now Director–Personal Asset Management at Battens, a leading law firm in the southwest of England. His other publications include works on securities markets, swaps, and options. In 1996 he published *Mastering Government Securities*, which is also published by Pitman Publishing. He lives in Somerset with his wife and two children.

A

AAA/Aaa

The highest credit rating awarded by the two leading US rating agencies, Standard & Poors and Moody's. See **bondrating**.

À la criée

French phrase for **open outcry**.

Abandonment

Not careless freedom, of which there is little in international finance, but allowing an option to expire without being exercised.

ABEDA

The Arab Bank for Economic Development in Africa, a development bank based in Khartoum.

Abidjan Stock Exchange

The Bourse des Valeurs d'Abidjan (BVA) in the Ivory Coast began trading in 1976. Ordinary shares and bonds are traded on the exchange. The market has three sections: the official market (*Côte officielle*), the second market (*Second Marché*) and the OTC market (*hôrs Côte*). Trading in shares is by open outcry (*à la criée*). Trading in bonds is through a computer system. The two indices are the BVA General Index and the 12VB Index, an index of the 12 most traded shares on the exchange. The BVA is expected to become a regional exchange serving seven West African countries: Burkina Faso, Benin, Niger, Togo, Senegal, Mali and the Ivory Coast.

Above par

A security whose market value is above its nominal, or par, value.

Absolute rate

Used to mean a fixed percentage in contrast to an interest rate expressed by relation to a variable rate.

Acceleration

The process by which a debt becomes due or a derivative transaction is terminated in the event of a default by the borrower or counterparty prior to its

1

originally specified maturity date. Acceleration also may be triggered by other events, such as a credit rating downgrade.

Acceptance

Short-term, trade related bill of exchange which has been accepted (i.e., guaranteed) by the financial institution on which it is drawn.

Acceptor

The institution which endorses a bill of exchange drawn on it, and is thus liable for the amount of the bill.

Accounting risk

The danger that measures which may be logical economic risk management practice may be treated in an unsatisfactory way for accounting purposes. See **risk**.

Accounting Standards Board (ASB)

The UK body with primary responsibility for accounting standards.

Accretion

The growth in the principal amount of a financial instrument or transaction (contrast with **amortization**). An accreting swap is one where the principal amount upon which each party's payment obligations are calculated increases over time.

Accrual rate

The interest rate or coupon rate used to compute accrued interest.

Accrued interest

Interest earned, but not yet due and payable. For example, the buyer of a bond pays the seller the price of the bond, plus interest accrued from the last interest payment date up to and including the value date of the bank transaction. In the case of bonds traded ex-dividend, the interest is calculated from the value date to the next coupon date and is paid effectively by the seller to the buyer.

ACG

French abbreviation for Adhérent Compensateur Général, a general clearing member of the Marché à Terme d'Instruments Financiers (MATIF).

ACI

French abbreviation for Adhérent Compensateur Individuel, an individual clearing member of the Marché à Terme d'Instruments Financiers (MATIF).

Action

French word for a share.

Action de jouissance

Form of participating share encountered in France and Belgium which does not carry ownership rights.

Action ordinaire

French phrase for ordinary share or common stock.

Action privilégiée

French phrase for preference share.

Active management

The pursuit of out performance by selection of market, segment and security. Equity fund managers will try to pick shares rather than arrange portfolios to imitate benchmark indices. Bond managers actively manage assets by changing portfolios to exploit opportunities relating to interest rate levels, the shape of the yield curve, or spreads between different markets. Contrast with **index**, **dedication**, **immunization**, and **passive management**.

Actual

Day count basis where the number of days used is the actual number of days elapsed; differs from 365-day basis in leap years, for example.

Actuals

The physical commodity which underlies a futures contract.

ADB

The Asian Development Bank, which has its headquarters in the Philippines.

ADEF

Agence d'Evaluation Financière, a French credit rating agency.

Adjustable-rate convertible securities

(1) An attempt to make dividends a tax-deductible expense. These convertible securities carry no conversion premium, and have a coupon related to the dividend payable on the underlying shares. In the USA the coupon is not an allowable expense for tax purposes.

(2) Any convertible security with a variable coupon.

Adjustable-rate preferred stock

Floating-rate preferred stock with dividend rates reset by reference to various interest-rate benchmarks, typically US Treasury bills. Many issues have had caps or collars which restrict the dividend rate.

Adjusted strike price

Most commonly refers to the change in the strike price of an equity option made necessary by a capital change affecting the underlying shares.

ADNOC prices

ADNOC is the Abu Dhabi National Oil Company which publishes retrospectively official monthly selling prices of Abu Dhabi crude oil. These prices are used as a benchmark in trading Abu Dhabi crude oil.

Advance Corporation Tax (ACT)

A tax paid by UK companies when they pay dividends. It may be offset against UK corporation tax, but not against tax paid abroad so that companies with a large proportion of foreign earnings may suffer "unrelieved ACT." The total of such unrelieved ACT is now some billions of pounds, a testament to the belief that dividend yield is the sign of a good share.

AfDB

The African Development Bank which has its headquarters in Abidjan.

AFESD

Arab Fund for Economic and Social Development, founded in 1968 in Kuwait.

After-hours dealing

Dealing after the end of mandatory trading hours on an exchange.

After-tax yield

The return on a security, net of income withholding tax and capital gains tax.

Agenti di cambio

Italian phrase for brokers.

Agents de change

French phrase for brokers.

Aggregate risk

The total exposure an institution has to another company from all the transactions between them. A key matter is whether such exposures may be netted, thus reducing the aggregate risk, or whether the exposures must be counted gross. See **risk**.

Agio

(1) The amount in percent by which a bond's market price exceeds par. (A discount to par is called a *disagio*. The terms are Swiss.)

(2) Difference in value between two currencies.

(3) The extra value of a gold coin above its gold content.

Agrarische Termijnmarkt Amsterdam (ATA)

The Agricultural Futures Market in Amsterdam has traded potato futures since 1958, live hogs futures since 1980, piglet futures since 1991, and wheat futures since 1996. Trading is through the nine brokers who trade on the exchange floor by open outcry. Settlement is through a separate clearing body (NLKKAS).

Ahmedabad Stock Exchange

Indian stock exchange which trades shares and debentures. The index is the Stock Exchange – Ahmedabad Share Price Index which is made up of 30 shares. See **National Stock Exchange of India**.

AIBOR

Amsterdam Interbank Offered Rate.

AIMR

Association for Investment Management and Research, which is based in Charlottesville, Virginia, is an international, non-profit organization which sets examinations for investment practitioners for the Chartered Financial Analyst (CFA) qualification. It has also published performance presentation standards for fund managers.

Aktie

German word for a share.

Aktiebolaget

Swedish public limited company.

Aktiengesellschaft (AG)

German joint stock company.

Alberta Stock Exchange

The Calgary Stock Exchange was founded in 1913, and changed its name in

1974. The exchange trades shares, warrants and debt instruments. Trading is by the Automated Trade Execution System (ATES). Clearing is through the West Canada Clearing Corporation.

Alexandria Stock Exchange

Operates as virtually a single market with the **Cairo Stock Exchange**. Since 1992, new legislation, reorganization and modernization of the exchanges has been undertaken. The exchanges trade shares and bonds. A central depository and delivery versus payment system were expected to become operational in late 1996.

Algorithm

A formula devised to solve a problem (e.g., the **Black–Scholes Model**)

ALIDE

Asociación Latinoamericana de Instituciónes Financieras de Desarrollo, the Latin American Association of Development Financing Institutions, based in Lima.

Alligator spread

Another name for a **butterfly spread**. Given the difficulty of executing a profitable butterfly spread when paying commissions and bid–offer spreads, this may be a better name.

All-or-nothing option

An option where the holder is paid a fixed amount if the underlying reaches or exceeds the exercise or strike price.

Allotment

The process of allocating newly issued securities to investors or underwriters. Can be controversial in the case of very successful issues, if the amount allocated to particular institutions is much less than the amount underwritten by them.

Alpha

(1) As in Alpha Stock, the most traded shares on the UK stock market

(2) As in Alpha Factor, the difference between the expected risk-adjusted yield of a portfolio and the return actually achieved.

Alternative option

An option where the holder has the choice of a payout based on two or more underlying instruments, indices, currencies or commodities.

American depository receipts (ADRs)

Certificates traded chiefly in the USA, which represent shares in a non-US company. ADRs are sometimes easier to trade for US-based investors than the underlying foreign share, settlement may be more secure, and dividends may be collected more easily. ADRs are traded and priced in US dollars and dividends are paid in US dollars. The depository bank which holds the underlying shares executes the foreign exchange transactions.

American option

An option which may be exercised on any business day during the life of the option. This is in contrast to European options which may be exercised only on a single specified date. See **Bermuda option**.

American Stock Exchange

Originally the New York Curb Exchange, which changed its name in 1953 to the American Stock Exchange. The exchange trades common and preferred stocks, rights, ADRs, warrants on stocks, currencies and foreign indices, options on indices, equities and US treasuries, corporate and government bonds. Trading is similar to the NYSE with specialists filling a dual agency/principal function and an automated order handling system, PER, equivalent in function to the NYSE's SuperDot. The exchange is known for the range of stock indices on which options are traded. These indices are the Institutional Index, the Computer Technology Index, the Oil Index, the Major Market Index, the S&P Midcap 400 Index, the Morgan Stanley Consumer Index, the Morgan Stanley Cyclical Index, the Japan Index, the Hong Kong Index, the Mexico Index, the Securities Broker-Dealer Index, the Natural Gas Index, the North-American Telecommunications Index, the Airline Index, the Biotechnology Index, the Pharmaceutical Index, the Eurotop 100 Index and Flexible Exchange Index options. Only the equity options, the Computer Technology Index and the Oil Index are American options, the others are all European options. The indices which the exchange publishes include the AMEX Market Value Index (with 16 sub-indices), the Morgan Stanley Cyclical Index, the Pharmaceutical Index and the Mexico Index.

Amman Financial Market (AFM)

Established in 1976, the AFM is a government agency. Trading is divided between the organized market and the parallel market. Trading is in common and preferred stocks. Trading is by an auction system. Settlement is directly between brokers.

Amortization

(1) The reduction of a premium over a period of time.

(2) The repayment of debt by a borrower in a series of installments, for example as in the retirement of debt by a purchase or sinking fund.

(3) The reduction of the principal amount underlying a derivative transaction such as a swap.

(4) *Or* the reduction in book value of an intangible asset such as goodwill.

Amsterdam Stock Exchange

The oldest stock exchange in the world, which began trading at the begining of the 17th century. Trading is in shares, generally bearer shares, government and mortgage bonds, and Eurobonds. The wholesale and retail parts of the market have different trading systems. There is an automated inter-dealer broker system (AIDA) for the wholesale market, a Limit Order Book for the retail segment which is both order driven and quote driven and ASSET, an advertising screen for members. There is just one jobber for each security who matches orders, and must ensure bid and offer prices are quoted at all times. Settlement of all transactions in listed securities is through Effecten-clearing, a securities clearing corporation, which is a subsidiary of the exchange. Delivery depends on the form of the security but is either through the National Securities Giro System (NECIGEF), or physically through Kas-Associatie.

The main indices are the Amsterdam EOE-Index, a weighted average of 25 actively traded stocks, the Central Bureau of Statistics (CBS)-All Share Index, the CBS-Total Return Index and the CBS-Bond Index.

Annual equivalent

The yield of a bond which does not pay interest at annual intervals expressed as an annual equivalent.

Annuity bond

A security in which the principal and interest payments are combined, in order to form a series of equal annual payments.

Antwerp Stock Exchange

Effectenbeurs van Antwerpen is the second stock exchange of Belgium and trades bearer shares. See **Brussels Stock Exchange**.

APT

Automated pit trading – a screen-based after-hours trading system at LIFFE.

Arbitrage

The simultaneous sale and purchase of different financial instruments with the intention of profiting from existing price anomalies or expected changes in price relationships. In theory, this is the process which removes market imperfections. In practice, arbitrage is sometimes supposed to cause markets to be more volatile or erratic than would otherwise be the case.

Arbitrage Pricing Theory (APT)

Developed initially by Professor Stephen Ross of Yale University, APT conforms to the basic capital asset pricing model (CAPM) assumption that investors are rewarded for systematic risk (that is, market risk which cannot be diversified away). However, unlike CAPM, which measures risk solely by the sensitivity of a security's return to movements in a broad market index, APT identifies sources of systematic risk as unanticipated changes in key economic factors such as inflation, industrial production, yield curve changes and spreads between bonds of different credit qualities. Thus if the returns of a portfolio of assets can be described by a factor model, the expected returns can be described by a combination of the covariances of the factors with the returns of the assets.

Arbitrageur

Often shortened to 'Arb' and in popular myth a demonic figure thought capable of destroying long-term prosperity in pursuit of short-term gain. In fact, arbitrageurs try to exploit price anomalies between financial instruments. By doing so, they eliminate the price differences and so make markets more effective. In the 1980s some arbs in the USA, far from helping to perfect markets, distorted them by using insider information to trade in the shares of companies susceptible to takeover bids.

Arequipa Stock Exchange

La Bolsa de Valores de Arequipa (BVA) was a Peruvian stock exchange founded in 1987 which ceased trading in December 1995. La Bolsa de Valores de Lima thus became Peru's only stock exchange.

As, if and when issued

Trading in a financial instrument (usually a bond or share) which is expected to be issued, but which has not yet been issued.

ASEAN

Association of South East Asian Nations, which are Brunei, Indonesia, Malaysia, the Philippines, Singapore and Thailand, based in Jakarta.

Asian option

An option where the payout is based on the difference between the exercise price and the average price of the underlying on specified dates during the life of the option.

ASIM

The UK Association of Solicitor Investment Managers, the professional association representing the fast-growing investment management business of UK and Scottish lawyers.

Asked price

The price at which a security is offered for sale. In the UK it is referred to as the offer price, the opposite of the bid price.

Asset allocation

Investment methodology, which specifies the proportion of funds to be invested in different asset classes.

Asset-backed securities

Debt securities which have value because of the physical or financial assets which are dedicated to their repayment. Often these underlying assets are placed in a special purpose vehicle or trust for the benefit of the investors.

With banks and corporations anxious to reduce balance sheet pressures, the use of asset-backed securities and related credit enhancement techniques have become a very large financial industry.

Assignment

(1) Notice to the writer of an option that it has been exercised by the holder, and also the process by which exercise notices are allocated among the writers of options.
(2) More generally, the transfer of contractual rights and obligations from one party to another.

Associazione Bancaria Italiana

Italian association of banks.

Associazione Tesorieri Istituzioni Creditizie (ATIC)

The Italian association of bank treasurers.

Asunción Stock Exchange

The *Bolsa de Valores y Productos de Asunción* is the only stock exchange in Paraguay. It was founded originally in 1977 but fell into inaction and was revived in 1993. The exchange trades shares, debt instruments, options and futures.

Athens Stock Exchange

Established in 1876, the exchange trades shares and bonds split between the main market and the parallel market. Trading is electronic and transfer of securities is through the Central Securities Depository SA. The main index is the Athens Stock Exchange Composite Share Price Index made up of 65 shares, with industrial sub-indices.

ATHIBOR

The Athens interbank offered rate.

At-the-money

An option with an exercise price at the current spot price of the underlying.

Auction

There are four types of auction.

(1) Multiple-price, sealed-bid auction

This is often called an "English auction," except in England where it is called an "American auction." Bids are made before a deadline. Each is known only to the bidder and the auctioneer. Each contains a price and a quantity. The auctioneer ranks the bids received, and makes awards starting at the highest price bid until the auction is covered. Winning is losing, because the highest bid carries the greatest risk of loss.

(2) Uniform-price, sealed-bid auction

The auctioneer receives sealed bids and ranks them as above, but makes awards at a single price chosen to cover the auction. The effect of this is to reduce the risk of a bidder owning bonds above the market consensus price. This method is therefore less penalizing to inexpert or badly informed bidders.

(3) Descending-price, open-outcry auction

This is called a "Dutch auction" because it was once used to auction flowers in the Netherlands. Bidders meet in one room or electronically. The auctioneer calls out prices in a descending sequence. Bids are accepted until the auction is covered. In effect, this is very similar to the first technique described above.

(4) Ascending-price, open-outcry auction

The auctioneer calls out an ascending sequence of prices. The volume of bids at each price is announced. The price is raised until until the volume of bids is less than the size of the auction. The auctioneer then knows that the previous price was the market-clearing price. Awards are made to all those who bid at the highest price, and partial awards are made to those who made lower bids at the market clearing price.

Auction-rate preferred stock

A variable-rate preferred stock, where the interest rate is reset on the basis of a Dutch auction held towards the end of the preceeding interest period. Often the interest rate is subject to a cap, and the stock may be puttable at each auction.

Audit

The inspection of a company's accounts and records by an external body, usually an accountant. The auditing of international financial businesses is difficult, given the differing tax and regulatory requirements to which it is subject. Some spectacular but quite simple frauds have not been detected by auditors, despite threatening the existence of the firm involved or running for many years. Barings Bank and Sumitomo Corporation are but two examples of companies that have suffered in this way.

Aufsichtsrat

The German word for the supervisory board of a German company. A series of failures by large companies has caused some to question the amount of effective supervision actually achieved. See *Vorstand*.

Auslandsbuchforderungen

Foreign payment rights in the Swiss debt securities markets. They are short-term book entry securities, largely exempt from stamp duty and without a secondary market.

Auslandsobligation

In the Swiss bond markets, either foreign notes with maturities of three to eight years, or foreign bonds with maturities of eight to 15 years. Foreign notes are normally private placements, while foreign bonds are normally public issues managed by a consortium of banks.

Ausserbörslicher Wertpapierhandel

German unofficial or over-the-counter market.

Australian Stock Exchange

The Australian Stock Exchange, the ASX, was founded in 1987 when the six former exchanges of Sydney, Melbourne, Brisbane, Perth, Adelaide and Hobart became subsidiaries of the ASX. The Australian Options Market and the Australian Financial Futures Market are the Derivatives Division of the ASX. The exchange trades shares, warrants options and futures. Trading of equities is by the Stock Exchange Automated Trading System (SEATS). Dealing is broker to broker without intermediaries with settlement on T+3 via the Clearing House Subregister System (CHESS). The exchange lists futures on the Twenty Leaders Index, and options on individual shares, the Twenty Leaders Index, the All-Ordinaries Index and the Gold Index. The exchange's main indices are the ASX 100 Index, a market capitalization weighted index of 100 shares, the ASX All Ordinaries Share Price Index and the Twenty Leaders Index.

Austrian Futures and Options Exchange

The *Österreichische Termin und Optionenbörse Aktiengesellschaft* (ÖTOB) began trading in 1991. The exchange trades options on certain shares quoted on the Vienna Stock Exchange, options, long-term options and futures on the Austrian Traded Index (ATX) and futures on Austrian government bonds. Trading is by automated screen-based system with market-makers. Clearing is through special accounts with the Oesterreichische Kontrollbank (OKB). ÖTOB acts as guarantor of each contract. In November 1996, it was announced that ÖTOB was to merge with the **Vienna Stock Exchange**.

Authorized share capital

The total number of shares which a company is authorized to issue. This will often be larger than the number of shares actually issued.

Auto-correlation

The idea that the size and direction of today's price changes are not independent of yesterday's price changes. This idea underlies technical analysis of price patterns. Much market theory assumes the opposite – that today's price changes are independent of what happened yesterday, and that various statistical methods may be used to value securities and to measure risk. Many market participants are happy to believe both at once. Thus they use simultaneously both charts and valuation models dependent on random distribution models.

Automatic exercise

A rule of many derivative exchanges that options which are in-the-money are exercised without a specific instruction from the holder.

Average life

The weighted average of the maturities of each cash flow arising from a particular security.

Average rate option

See **Asian Option**.

Average strike option

An option where the strike price is set as an average of the price of the underlying over the life of the option. The payoff is determined as the difference between this strike price and the price of the underlying at expiry.

Avoir fiscal

French phrase for the tax credit on dividends.

Azione

Italian word for share.

Azione ordinaria

Italian phrase for ordinary share or common stock.

Azione privilegiata

Italian phrase for preference share.

Azione risparmio

Italian phrase meaning saving share, a share which carries a right to dividend ahead of ordinary shares, but does not have voting rights.

B

Back bond

A bond created by the exercising of a warrant originally attached to another bond (which ought perhaps to be called a "front bond," but is not).

Back month

Expiry month of an exchange traded futures or option contract other than the next contract to expire.

Back office

Settlement, accounting and management information processes. It is a basic principle of proper management that the back office should be separately managed from the **front office**.

Back price

Rare event when one dealer offers a security below the bid price quoted by another dealer.

Back-to-back

The combination of two transactions on more or less equal and opposite terms. In the case of back-to-back loans, the bank in the middle may seek to establish a right of offset, so that its performance under the deposit is conditional on the performance by the borrower of his obligations under the loan. These arrangements are often seen between a parent company and an overseas subsidiary. In the case of trade finance, a back-to-back credit is where the beneficiary of one credit uses it to induce a bank to open a second credit in favour of another beneficiary. The documents required under the second credit will also satisfy the requirements of the first credit.

Back-stop

Any form of arrangement intended to supply funds in the event that another source is no longer open to the borrower. An issuer of commercial paper will have a back-stop bank loan facility to give investors peace of mind, and to fund any unexpected shortfall in sales of paper.

Backwardation

When the spot or near term price of a commodity is higher than the forward price. Since the forward price would normally be at a premium to reflect the cost of carrying the commodity until the future date, this is an unusual event sometimes caused by an artificial shortage of the commodity being traded.

Bad bank

A special entity into which a troubled bank puts all its problem non-performing loans, thus improving the asset quality of the "good" bank. The bad bank then liquidates the bad loans over time. This tactic has been used in various countries including the USA and Sweden. In Sweden, the state-owned "bad bank" Securum was formed to take some USD11 billion of problem assets from Nordbanken and Gota Bank as part of the 1992 state rescue of troubled Swedish banks.

Bad day

(1) Something all traders have occasionally.

(2) A day which is not a business day in the countries where a particular transaction is to be settled.

Bad delivery

In the settlement of a transaction, delivery of securities which are not acceptable to the counterparty or clearing house.

Badla

Indian practice of carrying over the settlement of share transactions from one settlement period to another. The Securities and Exchange Board of India banned the practice in order to curb speculation, but the practice was reintroduced in early 1996.

Baht

The national currency of Thailand.

Balance certificate

When an investor sells part of a holding of equities, the certificate given to him in respect of the unsold shares remaining is called a balance certificate.

Balboa

The national currency of Panama.

Balloon

Used to describe the amount repaid at the end of the life of an amortizing bond or loan, a balloon repayment is a large amount in relation to the amount(s) already repaid but is less than the original principal amount. Contrast with **Bullet maturity**.

Baltic Freight Index

Index compiled by the Baltic Exchange in London based on Panamax and Capesize ships and on 10 time charter routes. See **Handymax Index**.

Bangalore Stock Exchange

Indian stock exchange in Karnataka. See **National Stock Exchange of India**.

Bank Administration Institute

Non-profit making technical organization which promotes standards in bank operating practice in the USA.

Bank basis

Another name for **money-market basis**. In the calculation of interest, the interest rate is multiplied by the actual number of days elapsed in the interest period divided by 365. This method is used, for example, with **certificate of deposit** and **floating rate note**.

Bank bill

Bill of exchange which has been accepted by a bank.

Bank for International Settlements (BIS)

Founded in 1930, with headquarters in Basle, Switzerland, the BIS, which is 84 percent owned by central banks, has a number of functions in the area of international financial co-operation. These include the promotion of international monetary co-operation, the provision of research and statistical data, action as agent for the **European Monetary Institute (EMI)** in relation to the **European Monetary System (EMS)** and action as agent for the ECU clearing system. The membership of 32 was extended in 1996 to include nine new members: Banco Central do Brazil, the Hong Kong Monetary Authority, the Reserve Bank of India, the Bank of Korea, Banco de Mexico, the Central Bank of the Russian Federation, the Saudi Arabian Monetary Agency and the Monetary Authority of Singapore.

Bank holding company

These are not banks but are holding companies which own banks and may own other subsidiaries involved in non-banking activities. In the USA, any company which owns 25 percent of the voting shares of a bank, or controls a majority of a bank's directors, must register with the Federal Reserve Board of Governors under the Bank Holding Company Act.

Bankers' acceptance

American term for a bill of exchange which has been accepted by a bank. In effect the bank is promising to pay if the drawer of the bill fails to pay it.

Banks

The table in Figure B1 shows the 10 largest banks in the world, based on 1995 accounts. The merger of Bank of Tokyo and Mitsubishi Bank has formed a bank with some US$27.8 billion of capital and US$700 billion of assets.

Figure B1

	TEN LARGEST BANKS IN THE WORLD, BASED ON 1995 ACCOUNTS (AMOUNTS IN BILLIONS OF US DOLLARS)			
Ranking	Bank	Tier 1 capital	Assets	Profits
1	HSBC Holdings	21.4	351.6	5.69
2	Crédit Agricole	20.4	386.4	2.51
3	Union Bank of Switzerland	19.9	336.2	2.51
4	Citicorp	19.2	256.9	5.60
5	Dai-Ichi Kangyo Bank	19.2	498.6	1.61
6	Deutsche Bank	18.9	503.4	2.48
7	Sumitomo Bank	18.6	499.9	0.26
8	Sanwa Bank	17.7	501.0	(2.08)
9	Mitsubishi Bank	16.7	475.0	0.84
10	Sakura Bank	16.0	478.0	(3.03)

Source: *The Banker*

Bankschuldverschreibungen

German word for bearer bonds and deposit certificates issued by banks and credit institutions.

Banque Européenne d'Investissement (BEI)

The French name for the European Investment Bank (EIB).

Banque Européenne pour la Reconstruction et le Développement (BERD)

The French name for the European Bank for Reconstruction and Development (EBRD).

Banque Internationale pour la Reconstruction et le Développement (BIRD)

The French name for the International Bank for Reconstruction and Development (IBRD).

Banque pour les Réglements Internationaux (BRI)

The French name for the Bank for International Settlements (BIS).

Barcelona Stock Exchange

Spanish stock exchange founded in 1915. The exchange trades shares and debt securities. Trading is chiefly on the CATS electronic system which links the Spanish stock exchanges. Settlement is on T+5, via the Spanish Central Depository. The main indices are the Barcelona Stock Exchange General Index, the FIBV Returns Index and the IBEX-35 Index which is a capitalization weighted index of the 35 most traded shares on the continuous market. See the stock exchanges of **Bilbao, Madrid** and **Valencia.**

Barings

A distinguished English merchant bank, the history of which illustrates the difference between illiquidity and insolvency and between systemic and non-systemic dangers. In 1890 Barings suffered difficulties with South American Loans. The Bank of England rescued the firm, having determined that Barings was suffering a temporary liquidity problem but was otherwise solvent. Barings' failure would have threatened the banking system. The rescue was effected by the forceful Governor of the Bank of England, William Lidderdale, without help from the Chancellor of the Exchequer. Lidderdale borrowed from Russia and, through Rothschilds, from France and simultaneously organized a guarantee fund between 5pm on Friday and noon on Saturday. One reluctant bank was threatened that its account with the Bank of England would be closed and the fact announced in the evening newspapers.

In 1995 Barings discovered that a single trader in Singapore had accumulated losses greater than the bank's capital. The firm was therefore insolvent. Its difficulties were particular to itself and did not endanger the banking system. The bank was bought for £1 by a Dutch concern and continues to operate as ING Barings.

Barrier option

A form of path-dependent option. When the strike is set, another barrier price is set. If the underlying reaches or exceeds that barrier price, the option is cancelled (in the case of a knock-out option), or (in the case of a knock-in option), the option exists only once the underlying has reached the barrier price.

Barrier price

The price which causes a barrier option to be triggered.

Basis

(1) The spot or cash price minus the forward or futures price, or

(2) The changing relationship between prices or rates in two markets, or

(3) The number of days used in calculating the actual interest payable on a loan or security.

Basis point

0.01 percent in yield.

Basis risk

The possibility that prices in two related but not identical markets or instruments may vary. For example, a trader might choose to hedge an interest rate swap in which he paid a fixed rate and received LIBOR, by buying a government bond of equivalent maturity or duration. This purchase would provide an approximate hedge against an absolute change in interest rates but the trader would still be at risk on any change in the relationship between swap rates and government bond yields. See **risk**.

Basis swap

An interest rate swap where the legs are at different variable rates. For example, one leg might be based on six-month LIBOR and the other on a commercial-paper-related average rate.

Basis trading

Generally the execution of transactions which try to profit from expected changes in the relative prices of two instruments or of a derivative and its underlying.

In the futures market, it has a specific meaning, which is the simultaneous exchange of a cash bond, together with an appropriate offsetting number of futures contracts. The gross basis is defined as:

Gross basis = clean cash bond price − (actual futures price x price factor)

There are execution risks associated with a basis trade: these are met on LIFFE by a Basis Trading Facility (BTF), which allows both legs of the futures part of a basis trade to be executed simultaneously. As of October 1996, LIFFE's BTF was available in Bund, BTP and Long Gilt futures.

Example of a basis trade

Assume that the CTD (cheapest to deliver) bond is the UK gilt 9% 12 July 2011. Today is 8 July. A trader sees that the CTD bond's basis is at 29 ticks (in 32nds). The trader decides to sell the basis. In doing this he undertakes to sell the underlying bond and to buy an appropriate number of futures contracts.

The cash bond is as follows:

Maturity	12 July 2011
Coupon	9%
Nominal amount	£5,000,000

Price	106–30	
The repo rate	5.75%	

The future is as follows:

Price	106–03
Price factor	0.9994350

The futures hedge ratio is calculated as the nominal value of the cash bond × the price factor of the cash bond divided by the nominal value of the futures contract, which in this case is:

(£5,000,000 × 0.9994350)/£50,000

which equals 100 futures contracts to the nearest whole number.

The trader therefore sells £5,000,000 nominal of the gilt and buys 100 futures. Then on 12 July the trader closes his position. The gilt price is 107–27 and the future is at 107–04. How do we calculate the result?

His two gilt trades were as follows:

Date	8 July	12 July
Price	106–30	107–27
Accrued interest	–0.098630	0.000000
Total price	106.838870	107.843750
Total cash price	£5,341,943	£5,392,188
Difference on cash price		(45,313)
Difference in accrued interest		(4,932)

His two futures trades were:

Date	8 July	12 July
Price	106–03	107–04
Total price	106.09375	107.12500
Cash sum	5,304,687	5,356,250
Difference	51,563	

The gain on the basis is therefore £6,250 (51,563 – 45,313).

The cost of carry must also be calculated. We saw above that the coupon cost was £4,932. Taking the repo rate of 5.75%, we can calculate the cost of financing the position for four days as:

$$106.84 \times £5,000,000/100 \times 5.75\% \times 4/365$$

$$= £3,366.$$

The trader's net cost of carry was therefore £1,566.

The trader therefore made a total profit of £4,684 on the trade (£6,250 – £1,566).

(Source: LIFFE)

Basket

Usually used to mean a set of related instruments, such as the equities of companies in a particular industry, which are specially chosen as a reference for a derivative transaction or a sub-index. In foreign exchange, the value of a single currency is sometimes expressed in terms of a basket of other currencies, chosen and weighted for example to reflect that country's trade.

Bavarian Stock Exchange

German stock exchange founded in 1830, now a part of the German Stock Exchange, Deutsche Börse AG, with the other seven German exchanges.

Bear

Someone who believes prices will fall.

Bear floater

A floating-rate note (FRN) designed to pay more when interest rates fall. This is achieved by setting the periodic variable interest rate as a fixed rate less LIBOR. The lower LIBOR is, the more the interest paid will be. The position of the investor is like that of a counterparty to an interest rate swap who has agreed to receive a fixed rate and pay LIBOR. Simple versions of this structure can be valued by reference to the interest rate swap market. The bear floater structure can be geared by setting the coupon as a fixed rate less n – LIBOR, where n might be 2 or 3 for example.

Bear market

A falling market.

Bear spread

An option spread position which increases in value as the value of the underlying falls up to a certain point. (See Figure B2.)

To sell the bear spread, a trader would buy a call at Y, and sell a call at X. Both positions would have the same expiry date. The strike price of the short position would be lower than that of the long position. The trader believes that the price of the underlying will fall or he is happy to earn premium while capping his downside risk.

Both potential profit and potential loss are limited. The maximum profit will be if, at expiry, the underlying is trading at or below X. The trader's profit will be the net premium income received on establishing the position. The maximum loss will be if, at expiry, the underlying is trading at or above Y. The trader's loss will be $(Y - X)$ less the net gain on establishing the position. Breakeven is when the underlying is trading at a price equivalent to Y less the net gain on establishing the position. See **bull spread** and **butterfly spread**.

Figure B2

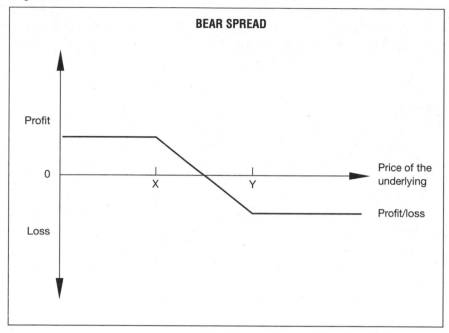

BEAR SPREAD

Profit

0

X   Y

Price of the underlying

Profit/loss

Loss

Bearer bond

A bond, the ownership of which is not recorded in a register, but is evidenced by possession. For an investor, theft is a greater risk, which is balanced against the benefits of anonymity.

Bearer depository receipt

A depository receipt issued in bearer form.

Bearer participation certificate (BPC)

A share-like non-voting security which is issued in bearer form, and incorporates the right to participate in net profits, dividends and liquidation proceeds, and to subscribe to new shares. See **bearer bond**; *cf.* common stock, share or **equity, participation certificate, preference share** and preferred stock.

Beijing Commodity Exchange

Formed in 1993, the exchange trades futures on corn, soya beans, rapeseed oil, soya bean meal, peanuts, wheat, rice, green beans, red beans, copper, aluminum, sodium carbonate, plywood, and polypropylene.

Belgian Futures and Options Exchange (BELFOX)

Established in 1991 in Brussels. Trading is automated with an order-book-matching mechanism and an auction mechanism for block trades. BELFOX is the counterparty to all transactions. Futures contracts are traded on a notional Belgian government bond, on three-month BIBOR, and the BEL 20 Index. There are options and long-term options on individual shares, and options on the BEL 20 Index, Belgian government bonds and the USD/BEF exchange rate.

Belgrade Stock Exchange

Beogradska Berza was re-established in 1989, in the Federal Republic of Yugoslavia. The exchange trades shares, short-term commercial paper and government securities. Securities are traded either in order at a single price per session or continuously. Official trading takes place on Tuesdays and Thursdays.

Bellwether bond

American slang name for a benchmark government bond.

Below par

A price below the nominal, or par, value of a security.

Benchmark bond

A large, liquid, issue the price of which is considered to be a good indicator for similar securities of a similar maturity or sometimes for the market as a whole.

Berlin Stock Exchange

Founded in 1685 and now part of the German Stock Exchange, *Deutsche Börse AG*. The exchange trades shares, bonds, options and warrants.

Bermuda option

An option which may be exercised only on certain specified dates over its life. See **American option** and **European option**.

Best efforts basis

In contrast to underwriting, dealers undertake to sell a new issue, but not to take up unsold securities themselves.

Best execution

The obligation on intermediaries to obtain the best price for their clients.

Beta

The measure of the price performance of a single security or of a portfolio when compared to the market as a whole. A beta of 1 implies that the security or portfolio exactly follows the market while a beta of 2 implies that the security moves up or down twice as much as the market as a whole.

Bhubaneswar Stock Exchange

Indian stock exchange founded in 1989. The exchange trades shares, debentures and mutual fund units. Trading is by open outcry. Settlement is through the exchange's clearing house. See **National Stock Exchange of India**.

BIBOR

Brussels interbank offered rate.

Bid–asked spread

The difference betwen the offer price and the bid price which is the dealers' spread.

Bid price

The price a trader will offer to pay for a financial instrument, commodity or currency as opposed to the higher offer price at which the trader will offer to sell.

Bid to cover ratio

The ratio between the value of bids at an auction and the value of those bids which were accepted. A high figure would indicate strong demand and competition.

Big Board

Slang term for the New York Stock Exchange.

Bilan de commerce, bilan commerciale

French phrases for the balance of trade.

Bilateral facility

A loan made by a bank which is not part of a syndicated loan.

Bilateral margining agreement

Agreement which requires either party to post collateral if the mark-to-market value of a transaction or group of transactions between them changes by more than a specified amount.

Bilateral netting

The netting of obligations between two counterparties, so as to reduce the risk each runs on the other. See **multilateral letting**.

Bilbao Stock Exchange

Spanish exchange established in 1890 which trades equities and debt securities. See the stock exchanges of **Madrid, Barcelona** and **Valencia**.

Bill

A short-term, interest-bearing or discounted instrument which can be traded. Bills are usually issued at a discount.

Bill for collection

A bill of exchange which is given to a bank to be presented to the accepting or paying bank for collection.

Bill of exchange

A short-term instrument for financing trade. The purchaser of goods undertakes to pay on a certain future date and signs a promise to pay – the bill of exchange.

Under English law, a bill of exchange is defined as an unconditional order in writing, addressed by one person to another, signed by the person giving it, requiring the person to whom it is addressed to pay on demand or at a fixed or determinable future time, a sum certain in money to, or to the order of, a specified person or bearer.

A bill may be accepted, that is guaranteed, by a bank. The bill may then be sold at a discount to its face value by the seller of the underlying goods who thus receives payment (less interest charges) before the buyer of the goods has paid for them. A bill of exchange which has been accepted by a bank is called a **bank bill** in the UK and a **bankers' acceptance** in the USA.

Billet de trésorerie

French phrase for **commercial paper**.

Binomial model

A model used in option pricing to assign probabilities to future prices of the underlying. Such a model assumes a finite number of time periods with two (or sometimes three – "trinomial") possible price movements in each period. These models tend to approach the normal distribution as a limit and are therefore not very reliable when dealing with an underlying distribution which is not normal or lognormal.

A simple way of looking at this is to imagine a binomial tree representing all the possible results of tossing a coin 40 times. The chance of achieving 40 heads or 40 tails represent the extremes of the tree. The chance of achieving 20 heads and 20 tails is much higher and there are many routes through the branches of the tree to this outcome. A four-stage binomial tree is shown in Figure B3.

Figure B3

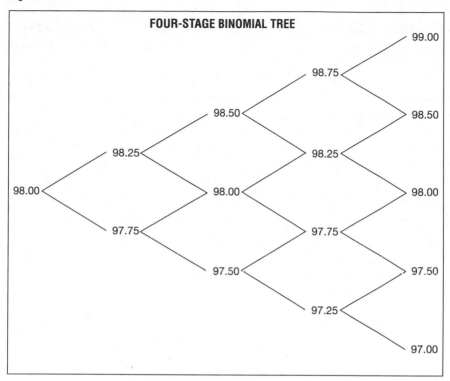

FOUR-STAGE BINOMIAL TREE

The binomial model is useful because it allows adjustments for cash flows or early exercise. It also permits the valuation of path-dependent options where not only the final outcome, but also the route taken to get there is important.

Birr

The national currency of Ethiopia.

Black Monday

19 October 1987. The date of a large fall in stockmarket prices.

Black–Scholes Model

An option-pricing equation, which is consistent with the capital-asset-pricing model but which makes certain restrictive assumptions.

In 1973 Fischer Black and Myron Scholes published a theoretical valuation formula for stock options. It was based on the idea of the cost of a riskless hedge. A "riskless hedge" was closely defined and certain assumptions were made. The definition was that for small price changes close to the current price of the underlying, it is possible to construct a hedge position in the underlying, which will change in value exactly with the option being hedged. This is what we now call "delta hedging."

The assumptions made included: (1) that the proportion of the underlying to the option can be continuously adjusted at no cost, and (2) that fractions of the underlying can be traded if necessary.

Because in theory the hedge is riskless, the fair value of an option is that price at which the hedged position earns a return equivalent to the risk-free short-term interest rate.

The formula aims to calculate the fair value of a European call option on a non-dividend-paying stock. The formula is:

$$C = SN(d_1) - Xe^{-rt} N(d_2)$$

where:

C	=	call option price
S	=	current stock price
X	=	exercise price
r	=	short-term risk-free interest rate
e	=	2.718
ln	=	natural logarithm
t	=	time remaining to expiry expressed as a fraction of a year
s	=	standard deviation of the stock price
$N(\ )$	=	the cumulative normal probability

$$d_1 = \frac{\ln(S/X) + (r + 0.5s^2)t}{s\sqrt{t}}$$

$$d_2 = d_1 - s\sqrt{t}$$

This formula makes important assumptions which should be reviewed:

Interest rates
It is assumed that the short-term interest rate is a known constant. Clearly interest rates are not constant and may change over the life of an option.

Price of the underlying
It is assumed that stock prices follow a random continuous walk, and that at the end of a period, the distribution of possible prices is lognormal. However market movements are not random and the returns are not always lognormally distributed. Prices do not always move continuously but can jump.

Volatility
Volatility is assumed to be constant. In practice, the volatility of the underlying will change over the life of the option. It is also the case that the volatility used to price an option differs according to whether the option is in-, at- or out-of-the-money. Volatility does not remain constant.

Exercise

The formula values only European options exerciseable at maturity.

Dividends or income

Income generated by the underlying (e.g., interest or dividends) is not accounted for. In practice the payment of unequal quarterly dividends on a stock may materially change the value of an option on the underlying stock. For many stock options, it may be sufficient to subtract the present value of expected dividends from the stock price. However, problems remain with large dividend payments, or with options that are short-term, and at- or in-the-money.

The picture may be further complicated by the question of whether a call-option holder should exercise early in order to capture a particular dividend payment. As has been noted above, the Black–Scholes formula is based on European exercise at expiry.

Commissions

It is assumed that there are no transaction costs in buying or selling either options or the underlying.

Each of these assumptions are more or less important depending on the type of the underlying. Many practitioners live with the defects, being content to increase their volatility assumptions when in doubt.

Blind broker

A form of interdealer broking where neither principal knows the other's identity.

Blue sky bids

In the UK, the name given to bids by individual dealers in government securities, known as gilt-edged market makers or GEMMs, to buy gilts from the Bank of England after the initial tender for a tap issue.

Blue sky laws

In the USA, colloquial name for laws which generally require securities to be registered and which prevent worthless securities being sold to gullible investors.

Board of Trade Clearing Corporation (BOTCC)

The clearing house for the Chicago Board of Trade.

Bogotá Stock Exchange

The Bolsa de Bogotá was founded in 1928 and is the chief exchange in Colombia. Shares, bonds, bankers' acceptances and certificates of deposit are traded on the Exchange. The main indices are IBB (*Indice de la Bolsa de*

Bogotá), the IRBB (*Indicator de Rentabilidad de la Bolsa de Bogotá*) and a Bond Price Index.

Bolivar

The national currency of Bolivia.

Bolivian Stock Exchange

The Bolsa Boliviana de Valores began trading in 1989. The exchange trades debt securities by **open outcry** on the floor of the exchange. Settlement is by 17.00 on the transaction date.

Bolsa

The Spanish word for exchange.

Bombay Stock Exchange

Established in 1875, the exchange trades shares and debentures. Trading is mostly by the BSE Online Trading (BOLT) system. Settlement is through the exchange clearing house. Settlement periods are 14 days for liquid, specified shares, and seven days for the less liquid, unspecified shares. Certificates for trades in unspecified shares, are not delivered through the clearing house, but directly from broker to broker. The chief indices are the Bombay Stock Exchange Sensitive Index of 30 shares, the 200-share Index and the National Index of 100 leading shares quoted on Indian exchanges.

A single unified electronic stock exchange for India is now in existence. See **National Stock Exchange of India.**

Bond

Negotiable debt security, generally long-term. Fixed rate bonds with maturities up to 100 years have been issued. Perpetual floating rate debt has also been issued. The variety of bonds issued is great. Some chief types may be summarized as follows:

Zero-coupon bond

The buyer of a zero-coupon bond buys the security at a discount to its nominal value, and earns a return to the extent that the market value of the bond moves towards its nominal value with the approach of the maturity date. Figure B4 shows how a non-interest-bearing bond of any maturity may be represented in diagramatic form.

Fixed-rate bond

The buyer of a fixed-rate bond receives equal, known interest payments at regular intervals (usually annual or semi-annual) over the life of the bond. Figure B5 shows how a fixed-interest-bearing bond may be represented in diagramatic form.

Other variations can be gathered into three groups: variations in purchase, variations in interest and variations in redemption.

Figure B4

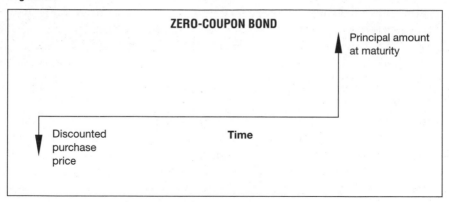

ZERO-COUPON BOND

Principal amount at maturity

Discounted purchase price

Time

Figure B5

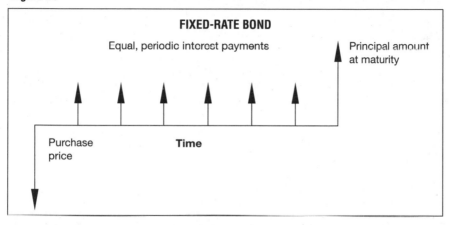

FIXED-RATE BOND

Equal, periodic interest payments

Principal amount at maturity

Purchase price

Time

Partly paid bonds

At issue, the investor is not required to pay all the consideration at once, but in two or more stages over a specified period of time. Figure B6 shows a pos-

Figure B6

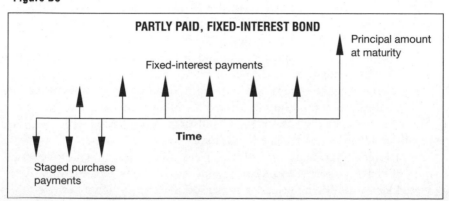

PARTLY PAID, FIXED-INTEREST BOND

Principal amount at maturity

Fixed-interest payments

Time

Staged purchase payments

sible diagramatic representation of a fixed-rate partly paid bond with one interest payment due before the final purchase payment. Interest is paid only on that part of the total price which has been actually paid. For the investor, a partly paid bond is a more leveraged bond in its partly paid state than a conventional bond. There may be also an advantage in having secured a known return on funds to be invested on certain specified future dates.

Variable-rate bonds

In the case of variable-rate bonds, the absolute rate of interest is not known. It is set for each interest period in relation to inter-bank rates or to the yield on certain short-dated instruments such as treasury bills. A possible diagramatic representation of a variable-rate bond is shown in Figure B7. Variable-rate bonds carry relatively little market risk for the investor in normal market conditions. Other things being equal, the bond should trade close to par at least on each interest reset date when the coupon is set at or near current market levels.

Figure B7

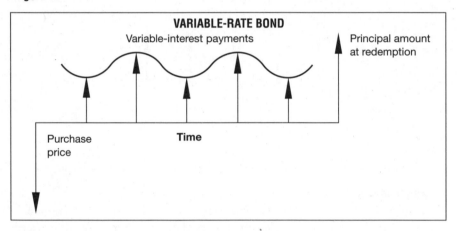

Index-linked bonds

Index-linked bonds may have payments of interest, principal or both tied to an index. Usually this is an index of inflation and the bonds carry an interest rate set at a margin above the index.

In diagramatic form, an index-linked bond in a period of continuing steady inflation might be as shown in Figure B8. An investor will accept a lower coupon related to his real yield requirement rather than, as in the case of a fixed-rate bond, a coupon related to his nominal yield requirement. There may, too, be institutions such as insurance companies with long-term liabilities which can be matched with index-linked securities.

A possible disadvantage arises if the index used, often a retail price index, does not have a direct relevance to the investor's needs. In the UK the Retail Price Index includes the prices of some 600 items including muesli, aerobics

Figure B8

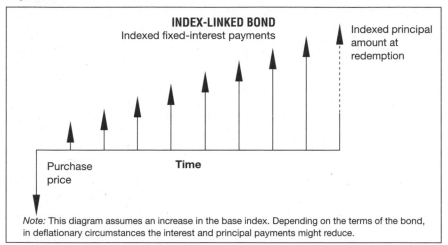

INDEX-LINKED BOND
Indexed fixed-interest payments
Indexed principal amount at redemption
Purchase price
Time

Note: This diagram assumes an increase in the base index. Depending on the terms of the bond, in deflationary circumstances the interest and principal payments might reduce.

classes and funerals. This index is the basis for the UK's index-linked government bonds.

Puttable and callable bonds

A puttable bond carries an option which gives the investor the right but not the obligation to require the issuer to redeem a security at a specified price at specified times prior to its specified maturity date.

A callable bond, which is the opposite of a puttable bond, carries an option which gives the issuer of the security the right but not the obligation to redeem the security prior to its specified maturity date.

In diagramatic form, a bond with a put option could be described as shown in Figure B9. The value of both puttable and callable bonds lies in the option embedded in the bonds. In the case of a puttable bond the issuer grants an option to the buyer, who "pays" for this by accepting a lower yield than for a straight bond with a similar final maturity date. In the case of a callable bond, the investors grant an option to the issuer and are "paid" for so doing by a higher yield than would otherwise be paid. The value attached to the option in either case by investors does not always match the "real" value which gives rise to arbitrage possibilities.

Perpetual bonds

Some bonds are issued with no redemption date, though they may have call provisions. These are almost equivalent to annuities, and therefore trade well below their nominal value. Figure B10 gives a possible diagramatic representation of a perpetual bond.

Banks have issued perpetual debt which is classified as part of the bank's capital base. In some cases, perpetual debt is issued with an escalating interest rate, so that after a set number of years the debt becomes very expensive.

33

Figure B9

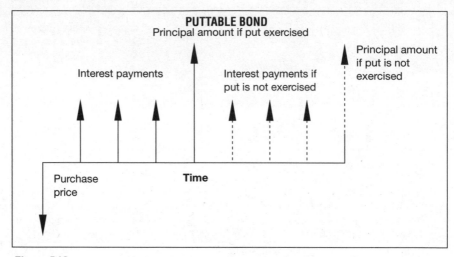

PUTTABLE BOND
Principal amount if put exercised

Interest payments

Interest payments if
put is not exercised

Principal amount
if put is not
exercised

Purchase
price

Time

Figure B10

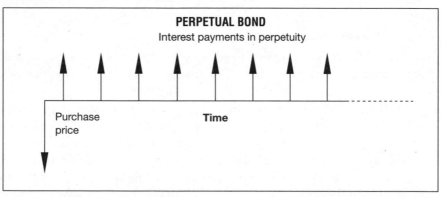

PERPETUAL BOND
Interest payments in perpetuity

Purchase
price

Time

This is intended to give investors comfort that the call provision will be exercised. Some perpetual issues are very old, and carry coupons which are low so that, while in theory they may be redeemed, such a prospect is unlikely. For example, the United Kingdom undated gilts (government bonds) known as Consols 2.5 percent trade at about 30 percent of their nominal value.

One form of bond which has not been issued is a zero-coupon perpetual bond!

Bond basis

Method used to calculate interest on bonds. It assumes a year of 360 days divided into 12 months of 30 days each. The days elapsed are calculated on this basis and divided by 360.

Bond equivalent yield

Method used in US to calculate the semi-annual bond equivalent yield on a non-interest-bearing short-term security sold at a discount. The formula for calculating the equivalent of a discount yield in bond yield terms on a treasury bill of three or six months maturity is as follows:

> Bond equivalent yield is face value minus purchase price, divided by the purchase price; multiplied by the number of days in the year following the issue date, divided by the number of days to maturity.

Bond option

Option where the underlying securities are bonds. The underlying bond may be a specific bond or a notional bond. In either case, exercise of the option may result in a cash payment or in delivery of the underlying. In the case of delivery, this may be of a specific bond or of one bond (the cheapest to deliver) chosen from a list of deliverable bonds published by an exchange.

Bond rating

Bonds are rated by many different rating agencies including Standard & Poors, Moody's Investor Services, Duff & Phelps, Fitch Investor's Service and IBCA.

Two leading agencies categorize borrowers as shown in Figure B11.

Figure B11

CATEGORIES OF BORROWERS		
Explanation	*Moody's*	*Standard & Poors*
Highest quality	Aaa	AAA
High quality	Aa	AA
Upper medium grade	A	A
Medium grade	Baa	BBB
Quite speculative	Ba	BB
Speculative, low grade	B	B
Poor quality	Caa	CCC
Highly speculative	Ca	CC
Lowest quality	C	C
In default, in arrears, etc.		DDD – D

In the case of Moody's ratings, the ratings from "Aa" to "B" are modified numerically, so that, for instance, within the category "Baa" the ratings are, in fact, "Baa1," "Baa2" and "Baa3." Ratings of "Baa1" and above are considered to be "Investment Grade." Ratings of "Baa3" and below are termed "Speculative Grade."

Ratings which are not yet final are often termed "Provisional," sometimes signalled with a "P" after the rating. Existing ratings subject to review are

Figure B12

MOODY'S RATINGS
Aaa   The best quality. The smallest degree of investment risk. Interest payments are protected by a large or by an exceptionally stable margin, and the principal is secure.
Aa   High quality by all standards. Margins of protection may not be as large as with Aaa bonds or may fluctuate.
A   Many favorable investment attributes. Upper-medium-grade obligations. Factors giving security to principal and interest are considered adequate.
Baa   Medium-grade obligations, neither highly protected nor poorly secured. Interest payments and principal security appear adequate for the present, but certain protective elements may be lacking or unreliable over time.
Ba   Bonds with speculative elements, without a well-assured future. Protection of interest and principal may be very moderate.
B   Bonds lack the characteristics of a desirable investment. Assurance of performance over time may be small.
Caa   Bonds of poor standing which may be in default.
Ca   Speculative to a high degree and often in default.
C   Lowest-rated class of bonds. Extremely poor prospects of ever attaining any real investment standing.

"Watchlisted," and the direction of the possible change is signalled.

Figure B12 shows summaries of definitions given by Moody's in order to explain what the ratings mean.

Although rating agencies act on behalf of investors, they are also paid by borrowers. There is, therefore, a potential conflict of interest. Most ratings are "solicited." That is to say the borrower approaches the rating agency expecting that an explicit rating will improve that borrower's access to the financial markets. Some ratings are "unsolicited." That is to say that the rating agency assigns a rating to a borrower's debt, where the agency sees investor need for such a rating, without having the detailed discussions with financial management which would be part of a typical solicited rating process.

The policies of the rating agencies differ. Standard & Poor's gives unsolicited ratings in the US for SEC-registered companies but does not do so for issuers outside the US. Moody's and IBCA, for instance, will provide unsolicited ratings.

Many institutional investors operate under policy guidelines which prevent them from investing in unrated debt or allow them to invest only in debt of a certain minimum rating. For such investors, the existence or variation in a rating may lead them to buy or sell securities. A downgrading in particular may lead to substantial change in the price of a security as investors become forced sellers.

In the retail-focused markets, credit judgement is more subjective, with well-known but lowly rated companies having a relative advantage over highly rated habitual deficit financing issuers. See **rating agencies**.

Bond washing

The practice of selling securities just before an interest payment date so as to convert interest income into a more lightly taxed or untaxed capital gain. Legislation in many countries has tended to remove the fiscal advantage in recent years by levying income tax on the interest which accrues during the period in which the bond is held by an investor whether or not a coupon payment has been made.

Bonos de consolidación (Bocon)

Argentinian government securities, denominated in both pesos and US dollars, issued to pay government debts.

Bonos de la República

Fixed-rate US-dollar-denominated bearer bonds issued by the Republic of Argentina and listed on the Luxembourg Stock Exchange.

Bonos del estado

Spanish government bonds paying interest annually with maturities of three and five years.

Bonos del Tesoro (Bote)

US-dollar-denominated registered bonds issued by the Republic of Argentina and listed on the Buenos Aires Stock Exchange.

Bonos Externos (BONEX)

Variable-rate US-dollar-denominated bearer bonds issued by the Central Bank of Argentina, guaranteed by the Republic of Argentina and listed on the Buenos Aires Stock Exchange.

Bons du Trésor à taux annuel et intérêt annuel (BTANs)

Fixed-rate French franc and ECU treasury notes issued by the French government with maturities of two and five years. At 30 November 1996 a total of FFr749.3 billion of FFr BTANs were outstanding with a further ECU8.1 billion of ECU BTANs. The average maturity was 2 years and 114 days.

Bons du Trésor à taux fixe et intérêt précompté (BTFs)

Discount fixed-rate French franc treasury notes issued by the French government with maturities from four to 52 weeks. At 30 November 1996 a total of FFr297.7 billion was outstanding with an average maturity of 87 days.

Book-entry

An ownership registration system under which securities do not have a physical existence. Ownership rights are represented by entries in a computerized register.

Bookrunner

The firm having responsibility for the pricing, documentation, syndication, and distribution of a new issue of securities. The key role in an issue and therefore much desired by securities firms. Carries far more prestige than roles such as joint-lead or co-lead manager as well as more opportunities for profit.

Borsa valori

The Italian phrase for stock exchange.

Börsenhandel

Swiss word for the official stock exchange trading market.

Börsenumsatzsteuer

German stock exchange turnover tax.

Börsenvorstand

German stock exchange management committee.

Boston Option

A break-forward or cancellable option

Boston Stock Exchange

Founded in 1834, the third-oldest stock exchange in the US, and now linked by the Intermarket Trading System with six other US exchanges and by an electronic link to the Montreal Exchange. Shares, bonds, warrants and units are traded on the exchange. Trading by the Beacon system is settled through the Boston Stock Exchange Clearing Corporation (BSECC).

Botswana Stock Exchange

The market began trading in 1989 though it did not become a formal stock exchange until 1995. Shares and debt instruments are traded, and 12 shares are listed. Stockbrokers Botswana Ltd act as agent between buyers and sellers. The Botswana Stock Exchange All-Share Index comprises the 12 shares traded on the exchange.

Bourse

The French word for stock exchange.

Box Spread

Offsetting synthetic long and short positions.

Brady Bonds

US-dollar-denominated bonds issued by certain troubled countries to convert international bank loans into long-term bond debt. The repayments of principal are collateralized by 30-year zero-coupon US Treasury bonds. Brady bonds are therefore the most liquid securitized bank debt. The bonds of many countries have been volatile securities. Over US$140 billion of bank debt has been securitized by 14 Latin American and other developing countries since 1990. By 1996, some countries were able to retire their Brady bonds, and refinance with conventional, uncollateralized debt.

Brady Plan

Announced on 10 March 1989 by the US Treasury Secretary, Nicholas Brady, as a solution to the problem of less-developed countries (LDC) debt. Gave rise to Brady bonds.

Bratislava Options Exchange

Bratislavská Opčná burza, as (BOB), began trading in 1993. Trading is by telephone, and the exchange trades forward contracts on the shares of 84 companies, and options on the shares of nine companies. Trading on the floor of the exchange ended in 1995.

Bratislava Stock Exchange

Wertpapierbörse Bratislava AG is the stock exchange of Slovakia which began trading bonds and shares in 1993. Trading is by the Electronic Stock Exchange Trading System (ESETS). Settlement is on T+3 and delivery-versus-payment is achieved through the exchange's settlement system. Securities are partly dematerialized (see **dematerialize**). The Slovak Stock Index (SAX) is made up of the most frequently traded securities. The exchange has been licensed to trade derivatives.

Brazilian Futures Exchange

The Bolsa Brasileira de Futuros in Rio de Janeiro began trading in 1984. It is a partly owned subsidiary of the Rio de Janeiro Stock Exchange. Trading is by open outcry and by automated system. The exchange trades gold spot, and futures contracts on gold, the US dollar, the CDI Interest Rate Index, the Sao Paulo Stock Exchange Index (IBOVESPA), the ISENN Stock Index and the DI Interest Rate Index. There are options on gold, the ISENN Stock Index and the DI Interest Rate Index.

Break forward contract

Conventional forward foreign-exchange contract, with one special feature which allows the counterparty to cancel, or break, the contract at a specified exchange rate, called the break rate.

Break rate

Rate at which a break forward contract can be cancelled.

Break-even analysis

Method of analyzing possible transactions or investments to determine under what circumstances the returns of different courses of action would be equal.

Break-even exchange rate

The future exchange rate at which the returns from two possible transactions in different markets would be equal.

Break-even point

The future price of the underlying at which the buyer of an option will make a sufficient profit to recover the premium paid for the option. In the case of a call option, this will be the exercise price plus the premium paid and costs. In the case of a put option, this will be the exercise price minus the premium and costs.

Break-even time

The time it would take for the premium over conversion value to be erased by a convertible's yield advantage – i.e., the conversion premium divided by the yield advantage. This is not a completely satisfactory way to value convertibles.

Breakout level

The price of a security at which it is considered to have deviated from its previous trading pattern and to be beginning a new phase.

Breakpoint

The price at which a new issue trades which is equal to the fees and commissions, i.e., the point below which the syndicate will face a loss.

Bremen Stock Exchange

German stock exchange which trades shares, bonds and warrants. It is now a part of the German Stock Exchange, the Deutsche Börse AG.

Bretton Woods

1944 international conference at Bretton Woods in the US to design an international monetary system which created the International Monetary Fund and World Bank. The Bretton Woods system was based on fixed exchange rates, and broke down in 1971, though not officially until 1973.

Bridge agreement

The agreement in March 1992 between Cedel and Euroclear, the two clearing houses for the Euromarkets, intended to link more effectively their differing settlement procedures. It provided for five exchanges of delivery information to take place each day.

Bridge financing

Interim or short-term loan intended as temporary financing until other transactions have been arranged to replace it. These loans carry a large element of market risk since they are dependent on other transactions for repayment. Typically, these other transactions are issues of new equity or long-term debt securities, or the disposal of assets.

Briefkurs

German world for the official price, used on German and Swiss stock exchanges.

British Bankers' Association (BBA)

An association of banks active in London, not just British banks. The BBA is active in representing common interests of banks on technical matters to the regulatory authorities and in setting market standards.

British Bankers' Association Interest Rate Swap (BBAIRS)

Standard terms and conditions for interest rate swaps of less than two years maturity in specified currencies, published in London by the BBA.

British Merchant Bank and Security House Association (BMBA)

Formed in 1988 from the Accepting Houses Committee and Issuing Houses Committee.

Broken dates

Transactions undertaken for value dates that are not standard periods.

Broken period interest

Interest accrued in a period which is not a normal one for that type of transaction. For example, on the assignment of an already-existing swap, the new counterparty might pay or receive variable rate interest for a period other than the three or six months' periods which would be normal.

Broker

An intermediary who introduces the two parties in a transaction to each other. Brokers do not in general take positions, but inter-dealer brokers (IDBs) and other matched-book brokers act as principals to preserve the anonymity of their clients. In foreign exchange particularly, new automated order matching systems are replacing traditional brokers. See **EBS**.

Brokerage

The commission charged by brokers.

Brownian motion

One of the earliest studies of irregular movement was by an English botanist studying pollen suspended in water. The random process which Robert Brown observed in 1828 is called Brownian motion. A mathematical model which takes a starting price and a random variable can be used as the basis of an option-pricing model. Such a model is sometimes referred to as a stochastic process. The particular random variable generating process is chosen so as to match the empirically observed pattern of the underlying as closely as possible.

Brussels Stock Exchange

Société de la Bourse de valeurs mobilières de Bruxelles/Effectenbeursvennootschap van Brussel is the chief stock exchange of Belgium. The exchange trades shares and bonds. Trading is both cash and forward with the latter institutional market being the largest part of trading volume. Trading is divided between three sectors; the bond market, the rings market and the floor market. The rings market is for the more liquid securities with several prices in each trading session. Trading in the floor market is for less liquid securities at one price per session. Continuous trading is on the CATS system. Settlement is through the clearing system, the Caisse Interprofessionnelle de Dépôts et de Virements de Titres (CIK). The chief indices are the BEL 20 Index, and the Domestic Shares Forward Market Index.

BTAN

See *Bons du Trésor à taux annuel et interêt annuel (BTANs)*.

BTB

Belgian Treasury Bills, multi-currency short-term debt instruments of the Belgian Government similar to Euro-commercial paper (ECP).

BTF

See *Bons du Trésor à taux fixe et interêt precompté (BTFs)*.

Bucketing

When a series of future cash flows is analyzed, perhaps for risk measurement purposes, it is often easier to gather the flows into a number of time periods of "buckets" to make the analysis more simple. Typically the time period for a single bucket will be much shorter for near-term cash flows than for more distant flows. Thus the net flows on each day in the near future will be calculated, but cash flows five years out might be gathered into buckets covering a week or month. The danger in this approach to risk measurement is that it may ignore the sources of the different flows and underestimate the **basis risk** between the markets.

Budapest Commodity Exchange (BCE)

Established in 1989 as an agricultural futures market, the BCE is the largest futures exchange in Eastern Europe. The exchange is regulated by the 1994 Commodity Exchange Act. The initial corn and feed wheat contracts have been expanded to include milling wheat, black seed, feed barley, BL-55 wheat flour, live hogs, a three-month HUF interest rate future and currency futures (DEM, USD, JPY and XEU). Trading is by open outcry. The BCE combined with the BSE and the National Bank of Hungary in 1994 to form a joint clearing house and depository, the KELER.

Budapest Stock Exchange

The exchange was refounded in 1990. The exchange trades shares, government bonds, treasury bills, corporate bonds, investment funds and compensation notes. Most trading is in the first three of these. Futures are traded on the BUX index, three-month Treasury bills and DEM/HUF, USD/HUF and XEU/HUF currency futures. Trading is by both electronic order matching and **open outcry**. Automated trading began in 1994.

Buenos Aires Cereal Exchange

The Bolsa de Cereales de Buenos Aires was founded in 1854. Trading is divided between spot and futures. Trading is by **open outcry**. Futures on corn, sunflower seed, soya beans, and wheat are traded.

Buenos Aires Futures Market

The Mercado a Término de Buenos Aires was founded in 1907. Trading is by

43

open outcry. Futures and options are traded in US dollars in wheat, corn, sunflower seed, and soya bean.

Buenos Aires Stock Exchange

Established in 1854, the Bolsa de Comercio de Buenos Aires trades shares, debt instruments, forwards on shares and bonds, and options on shares, indices and bonds. Trading is split between open outcry and continuous trading by SINAC, a computer trading system. Cash transactions are settled between T+0 and T+3, while forward transactions may be settled up to T+120. The Caja de Valores is the central depository for all share certificates.

Building society

Now an endangered species in the UK, building societies are mutual organizations which take in retail savings in order to finance residential mortgages. In the UK, building societies operate under more demanding capital requirements than do banks, which tends to offset their cost advantage in being mutual entities which do not pay dividends. Several of the largest societies have either incorporated themselves or have been bought by banks.

Bulgarian Stock Exchange

See **First Bulgarian Stock Exchange**.

Bulge bracket

Term for the leading US securities houses which dominate the issuance of securities in the US domestic market, as well as being very active in international markets. Goldman Sachs, J P Morgan, Lehman Brothers, Morgan Stanley, Merrill Lynch and Salomon Brothers are examples of such firms.

Bull

Someone who believes a price will rise.

Bull spread

An option spread position which increases in value as the value of the underlying rises up to a certain point. (See Figure B13.)

To buy a bull spread, a trader would buy a call at X and sell a call at Y. Both positions would have the same expiry date. The strike price of the short position would be higher than that of the long position. This is also called a *vertical spread*. The trader believes that the price of the underlying will rise, but wants to limit his risk or is only moderately bullish about the underlying. By giving away some of the upside potential of owning a call, the trader reduces the cost of the position.

Both potential profit and potential loss are limited. The maximum loss will

Figure B13

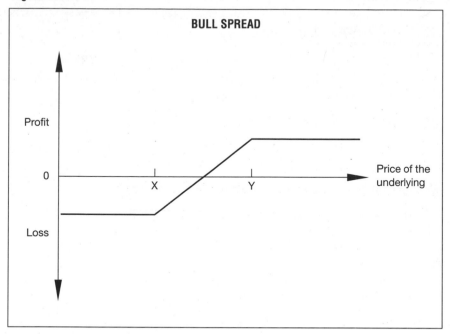

BULL SPREAD

Profit

0

X   Y

Price of the
underlying

Loss

be if, at expiry, the underlying is trading at or below X. The loss will be the net cost of the position (i.e., the cost of the long call position at a strike price of X, less the premium earned by selling the call at Y). The maximum profit will be if, at expiry, the underlying is trading at or above Y. The profit will be (Y – X) less the net cost of the position. Breakeven is when the underlying is trading at a price equivalent to X plus the net cost of the position.

See **bear spread** and **butterfly spread**.

Bulldog bond

A sterling-denominated bond issued in the UK by a foreign borrower.

Bullet maturity

A bond or loan where the principal amount is repaid on the final maturity date and not over the life of the bond or loan.

Bulletin de la Côte Officielle

Daily official list published by the French Stock Exchanges' Association (Société des Bourses Françaises – SBF), giving opening and closing prices as well as the day's highest and lowest price for each security.

Bundesanleihen (Bunds)

German government income securities. The majority of bunds are issued with a maturity of 10 years though some have been as long as 30 years. A 10-year bund is accepted as the 10-year benchmark in the D-mark bond market. See **German Government Bonds**.

Bundesbankliquiditäts unverzinsliche schatzanwiesungen (Bulis)

German discounted treasury certificates with maturities from one to two years. See **German Government Bonds**.

Bundesobligationen (Bobls)

German fixed-rate bonds with annual coupons, a five-year bullet maturity and no puts or calls. See **German Government Bonds**.

Bundesschatzanweisungen (Schätze)

German federal treasury notes. Fixed-rate bonds with annual coupons and a four-year maturity. See **German Government Bonds**.

Bundesschatzbriefe

Savings notes of the German Federal Government with maturities of six or seven years. See **German Government Bonds**.

Bunny bond

A coupon-paying bond which gives the investor the right to receive interest either in cash or in the form of more bonds of the same issue at par. Such a bond offers the investor reinvestment protection if interest rates fall. The structure was originally devised in the USA, where they were known as "variable duration bonds." It was introduced to the Euromarkets in the early 1980s, when not too many people knew what duration was. It was easier to think of them and sell them as bonds, which produced more bonds which produced more bonds, hence the name. Such bonds are notably **convex**.

Buoni del Tesoro in Ecu (BTE)

Italian treasury bills denominated in ECU. Short-term instruments having maturities of about 12 months

Buoni del Tesoro poliennali (BTP)

Italian fixed-rate treasury bonds with maturities ranging from three to 30 years. From 1 January 1997, BTP are no longer subject to a 12.5 percent withholding tax *after* their first coupon payment in 1997.

Buoni ordinari del Tesoro (BOT)

Italian treasury bills with maturities of three, six or 12 months.

Business day

In most markets, any day excluding Saturdays, Sundays and legal or statutory holidays on which business can be conducted.

Business risk

The danger that the value of an investment will be affected by factors specific to an individual company, such as poor sales, reduced earnings and so forth. See **risk**.

Butterfly spread

A butterfly spread combines a vertical bull spread and a vertical bear spread with the same expiry dates for all the options and the same strike price for all short options. A "perfect" butterfly spread would require no net premium payment. The premium received on the options sold would equal the premium paid for the options bought. Butterfly spreads are rarely profitable.

To buy a long butterfly spread, a trader would buy calls at strike prices of A and C and sell two calls at B. Assume A and C are equidistant from B. The trader expects the underlying to move significantly, but is not willing to take a view on the direction of that move.

The maximum loss is the cost of the spread, whether the underlying moves up or down. The maximum profit will be earned if the underlying is trading below A or above C at expiry. The maximum loss will occur if the underlying closes at B. There are two breakeven points: prices equivalent to either A plus the cost of the spread, or C less the cost of the spread.

To sell a short butterfly spread, the trader would sell calls at A and C and buy two calls at B. In this case the trader has the opposite view, and expects the underlying to stay close to B, but wants to be protected should the underlying rise or fall substantially.

Figure B14

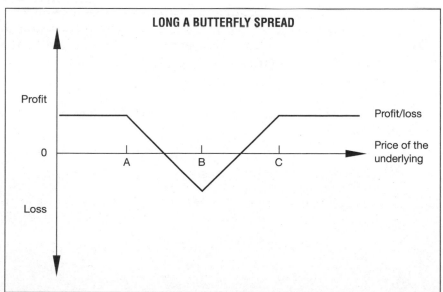

Figure B15

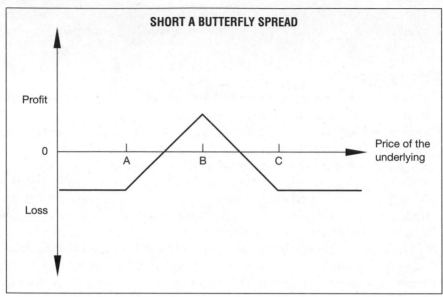

SHORT A BUTTERFLY SPREAD

Profit

0

Loss

Price of the underlying

A   B   C

The maximum profit is the net premium received on establishing the spread. The maximum profit occurs when the underlying closes at B. The maximum loss will be earned if the underlying is trading below A or above C at expiry. There are two breakeven points: prices equivalent to either A plus the initial credit, or C less the initial credit.

Buy-in

In new issues of securities, where traders have large short positions, or where the available float is small, a lead-manager may issue buy-in notices forcing those who have sold short to cover their positions, often at very high prices with securities bought from the lead-manager.

Buy–write

Simultaneous purchase of the underlying and sale of a call to create a covered call position.

C

Cable

A word used in the London foreign exchange market for the US dollar/pound sterling rate

CAC-40 Index

The index of the 40 leading shares on the Paris Stock Exchange.

Cairo Stock Exchange

The capital market law of 1992 allowed for a more active stock exchange. The exchange is now linked to the Alexandria Stock Exchange and both operate as a single market, trading by a continuous and automated system. Trading is in bonds and shares. Settlement is on T+3. A central depository and delivery against payment system were expected to be introduced in late 1996.

Caisse d'épargne

French savings and mortgage association.

Caja de ahorro

Spanish savings and mortgage bank.

Calculation agent

In a swap or loan agreement, the agent who calculates the amount of interest to be paid on the variable rate part of the transaction.

Calcutta Stock Exchange

Indian stock exchange, linked to the other major stock exchanges of Bombay, Delhi, Ahmedabad and Madras by the PTI Stockscan service. See **National Stock Exchange of India**.

Calendar roll

Procedure whereby a futures or options position on an exchange is closed in one contract month and re-opened in a further contract month.

Calendar spread

A position where the option sold expires before the option bought. The amounts bought and sold are the same, and the options have the same strike price. The intention of a calendar spread is to exploit differences in time decay between options with different expiry dates.

Call

The right, but not an obligation, of an issuer to redeem a bond before its specified maturity date.

Callable bond

A bond which may be redeemed at the option of the issuer before its specified maturity date. See **puttable bond**.

Call-adjusted yield

The yield of a callable bond calculated to the date of the first call, and incorporating the price at which the call may be exercised rather than the par value.

Call date

The date on which, at the option of the issuer, a bond may be redeemed before its specified maturity date.

Call loan rate

The rate at which short-term loans secured on securities are made to brokers in the US. Generally these loans are repayable on demand, hence the name.

Call money

Deposits which can be withdrawn at 24 hours' notice.

Call option

An option which gives the holder a right, but not an obligation, to buy a financial instrument, commodity or currency at a specified price on or before a specified date. See Figure C1.

Figure C1

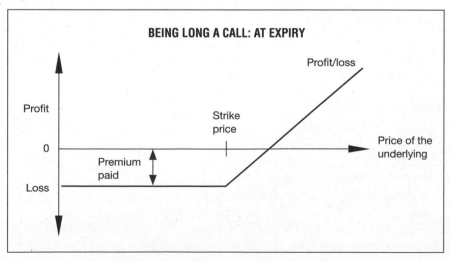

Call premium

The amount above par which a borrower must pay in order to redeem a bond before its specified maturity. The call provisions of a bond issue often provide for a high-call premium in the early years of a bond's life, reducing gradually thereafter.

Call price

The price at which a bond may be redeemed early at the wish of the borrower.

Call protection

Assurance that a bond will not be called before a certain date.

Call risk

The risk that a callable bond will be called. If a bond is trading above par and may be called at any time at par, the investor risks a loss. The borrower might take advantage of lower interest rates to refinance the issue at a lower cost. In the UK gilt market, for example, callable gilts which are trading above par have their yield calculated to the first call date while callable gilts which are trading below par are not expected to be called and therefore their yield is calculated to the final maturity date. A call is an embedded option granted by the investor to the borrower. Callable bonds should therefore trade at a lower price than non-callable bonds of equivalent quality and the same final maturity date. See **risk**.

Call spread

An option position in different calls on the same underlying.

Called away

The process which causes a securities position to be exchanged for cash by the exercise of a call option.

Cambiste

French word for a foreign-exchange dealer.

CAMEL rating

CAMEL stands for capital, assets, management, earnings and liquidity. A CAMEL rating is a measure of the relative soundness of a bank and is used by bank regulators to assess the quality of banks on a scale of 1 (high quality) to 5 (low).

Canada Deposit Insurance Corporation (CDIC)

Institution which offers protection to bank depositors in a manner similar to

51

Figure C2

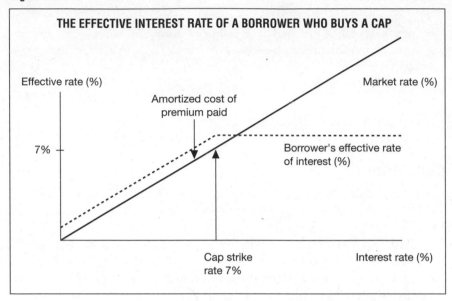

THE EFFECTIVE INTEREST RATE OF A BORROWER WHO BUYS A CAP

Effective rate (%)

Market rate (%)

Amortized cost of premium paid

7%

Borrower's effective rate of interest (%)

Cap strike rate 7%

Interest rate (%)

the US Federal Deposit Insurance Corporation (FDIC).

Canadian Mortgage and Housing Corporation (CMHC)

Provides insurance for pooled mortgages and guarantees timely payment to investors in mortgage-backed securities.

Candlestick chart

Japanese charting technique similar to bar charts.

Cap

An agreement which gives the buyer a limit on the upward movement of an interest rate. If the reference rate exceeds the strike rate on an interest reset date, then the seller of the cap makes a payment equivalent to that excess. If on the other hand, rates fall, the buyer of the cap enjoys the lower rate. Caps can be thought of as a series of short-dated interest rate options. (See Figure C2.)

In order to agree a premium and conclude a cap contract, the buyer and seller must set the following parameters.

The cap strike	Usually a single rate (e.g., 7.00 percent) but sometimes variable
Term	E.g., three years
Reference rate	E.g., six-month LIBOR, but many rates are possible
Principal amount	Not only the amount but also whether it remains constant or amortizes

Reset frequency	E.g., three months or six months
Reset date	Often two business days before the start of each period
Start date	Often one interest period after the trade date

See **floor** and **collar**.

Capital adequacy

The maintenance of a legally required ratio of capital to assets by a bank. Capital is fairly easy to define. The asset part of the equation is harder. Assets are usually weighted according to their nature to calculate "risk-adjusted assets." Trading positions and risk from off-balance sheet transactions and derivatives are harder to evaluate. Measures of capital adequacy include:

(1) risk-adjusted capital ratio, which is calculated as Tier 1 capital (ordinary share capital plus certain types of preferred shares) divided by total risk-adjusted assets;

(2) total capital to total assets ratio, which is calculated as Tier 1 and 2 capital (ordinary share capital, preferred share capital, subordinated debt and loan loss reserves) divided by total average assets;

(3) leverage ratio, which is calculated as Tier 1 capital divided by total average tangible assets;

(4) total risk-adjusted capital ratio, which is calculated as total risk-based capital divided by risk-adjusted assets.

See **value at risk (VAR)**.

Capital Adequacy Directive (CAD)

European Union directive which determines the minimum level of capital required by financial institutions.

Capital asset pricing model (CAPM)

A theoretical framework for structuring investment portfolios. The risk and reward characteristics of a portfolio are not equivalent to the aggregate of the individual components.. Risk may be divided into systematic (or beta) and unsystematic (**alpha**) risk. The former depends on factors common to all investments, while the latter is security-specific and may be reduced by diversification. The expected return on a specific asset equals the risk-free return plus a risk premium. The formula is expressed as:

$$E(R) = R_f + ß(R_m - R_f)$$

where

$E(R)$ = expected return

R_f = risk-free return
R_m = return on the market
ß = beta, the measure of the sensitivity of
    the asset to the market.

See the **Arbitrage Pricing Theory (APT)**.

Capital gain

A profit realized from buying a security at one price, and subsequently selling it at a higher price.

Capital markets

The market for medium- and long-term financial instruments such as bonds, loans and equities. The linkages between these instruments and the derivatives based on them provide many of the trading opportunities available to financial institutions.

Capital risk

The risk of a total loss on an investment. This may arise for reasons specific to a company or security, or it may happen for reasons which affect an industry, financial market or country. See **risk**.

Capitalization

A corporation's outstanding debt and equity, including retained earnings and share premium accounts. Capitalization can also be used to mean the total market value of a company's equity.

Capitalization issue

Transaction in which a part of a company's reserves is converted into issued capital, which is then distributed to shareholders in proportion to their original holdings. Also known as a bonus or **scrip issue**. Such transactions do not change the value of the firm.

Capped floating-rate note (capped FRN)

A **floating-rate note (FRN)** with an upper limit on the **coupon** payable. The borrower would typically sell a **cap** at the same **strike rate**, and use the **premium** received to reduce its all-in cost of funds to a level lower than would otherwise be obtainable in the FRN market. The investor for his part typically receives a higher variable rate than otherwise would be available so long as the cap does not operate.

Capped heaven and hell bond

A **heaven and hell bond** with a cap on the redemption proceeds.

Capped swap

Swap in which the floating rate is subject to a cap.

Caption

Option to buy a cap – an example of an option on an option.

Caracas Stock Exchange

The Bolsa de Valores de Caracas is the chief exchange in Venezuela. Shares, bonds and warrants are traded. The main indices are the Indice Bursatil Caracas, a general index of 17 shares, and the Indice de Capitalizacion Bursatil (IBVC), introduced in 1995 as a capitalization weighted index of 19 shares. Trading is by an electronic system, the SATB. Cash trades are settled from T to T+3, regular trades are settled on T+5 and forward trades are settled between T+6 and T+60. Settlement is through a multilateral netting system among transfer agents for shares and a bilateral netting system for fixed-income securities.

Carried interest

Free shares or options on shares held by a fund manager as part of the fund manager's reward package.

Carry

The net cost of holding a position in securities or derivatives: it is the income from the position held, less the interest payable on the funds borrowed to take the position. When the income earned is greater than the cost of funds this is called "positive carry;" when the cost of funds is greater than the interest earned it is referred to as "negative carry."

Carter bonds

United States treasury notes issued to investors outside the USA.

Casablanca Stock Exchange

Originally founded in 1929 and recently reformed in 1993. Plans for a central depository and an electronic trading system with French assistance were expected in 1996 to replace **open outcry** trading. Off-market trading has represented more than three-quarters of all trading activity. The IGB Index includes all the shares listed on the exchange while the CFG 25 Index is formed from the 25 most actively traded stocks.

Cash and carry

A combination of a long position in the underlying, and a short position in a futures contract such that the net position is equivalent to a short-term money-market security.

Cash collateral account

A credit enhancement technique, whereby a cash reserve is held by a trustee for the benefit of investors in a security, typically an asset-backed security. The funds are available to cover shortfalls in the income stream from the assets on which the securities depend.

Cash deficiency agreement

An undertaking by one party (typically a parent company) to ensure that a second party (typically a subsidiary) has sufficient cash available to meet its obligations as they fall due. The strength of this assurance will depend on the wording of the agreement, but in general it falls short of an unconditional guarantee.

Cash delivery

Same day settlement.

Cash flow

(1) In basic credit analysis, the key fact to establish is the cash flow of the business, preferably the net operating cash flow. This is a better indicator of the health of a concern than reported net income. Profitable businesses can be bankrupted because of insufficient cash flow.
(2) In risk analysis the different instruments in a trading book can be broken down into their constituent cash flows. These cash flows may be netted or *bucketed* (see **bucketing**) together to facilitate analysis of risk.

Cash index participation (CIP)

Contract on the Philadelphia Stock Exchange based on a basket or index of equities and settled in cash.

Cash management

The practice of effectively monitoring the cash balances of an organization so as to reduce borrowing to a minimum and to manage foreign exchange exposure most effectively.

Cash management bill

A US treasury bill used for short-term financing.

Cash market

The market in an actual financial instrument, commodity or currency on which derivatives may be based.

Cash price

A price quoted in a cash market.

Cash settlement

Settlement of a derivative contract not by delivery of the underlying but by a cash payment, calculated as the difference between the strike or exercise price and the settlement or spot price of the underlying.

Cassa di Compensazione e Garanzia

Italian company founded in 1993 to guarantee settlement of trades in equities, futures and options.

CBOT

See The **Chicago Board of Trade.**

CEDCOM

Electronic data transfer system for CEDEL (see *Centrale de Livraison de Valeurs Mobilières*).

Cedola di interesse

Italian phrase for a coupon.

Cedulas hipotecarias

Spanish phrase for mortgage bonds.

Central bank swap

A method by which central banks use FX currency swaps to inject or withdraw liquidity in their domestic money markets.

Central de Anotaciones

Spanish name for the centralized book-entry settlement office in Spain.

Central Gilts Office (CGO)

A department of the Bank of England which operates the book-entry transfer system between CGO members by which ownership of gilts is registered.

Central limit order book (CLOB)

An automated trading system on the Singapore first- and second-tier stock markets.

Central Money Markets Office

Bank of England book-entry system which clears sterling money market instruments.

Centrale de Livraison de Valeurs Mobilières (CEDEL)

A book-entry clearing facility (in Luxembourg) originally for Euro-securities through which transactions in domestic securities may also be cleared. With Euroclear, one of the two main clearing houses for the Euromarkets.

Certificate-for-automobile receivables (CARs)

A form of asset-backed security based on car purchase loans issued by Salomon Brothers for Chrysler Corporation.

Certificate of accrual on treasury securities (CATs)

Certificate representing coupon-stripped US Treasury bonds. Trade name devised by Salomon Brothers. Now supplanted to a large extent by the official stripping facility.

Certificate of deposit (CD)

A negotiable certificate, issued by a bank, representing a deposit of fixed maturity with that bank. Typical maturities run up to five years in the UK and up to 10 years in the US.

Certificati del Tesoro a sconto (CTS)

Italian treasury discount certificates. These are issues with partly a zero-coupon and partly a floating-rate in an indexed coupon. None has been issued since June 1987.

Certificati del Tesoro con opzione (CTO)

Italian treasury certificates with a maturity of six years and a put option for the investor after three years at par. Not issued after May 1992.

Certificati del Tesoro in Ecu (CTE)

Italian treasury five-year certificates denominated in ECU.

Certificati del Tesoro zero-coupon (CTZ)

Italian government two-year zero-coupon bonds.

Certificati di credito del Tesoro (a cedola variabile) (CCT)

Italian floating-rate treasury certificates.

Certificati di credito del Tesoro (CCT)

Italian treasury floating-rate certificates with maturities of between five and 10 years.

Certificati di deposito (CD)

Italian for certificate of deposit.

Certificats de Dépots Negotiables (CDN)

French negotiable certificates of deposit.

CFA Franc Zone

France introduced the CFA Franc in its former territories in Africa as part of a close continuing relationship with those countries. CFA stands for Communauté Financière Africaine (in west Africa) or Coopération Financière en Afrique (in central Africa). The African countries involved are Benin, Burkina Faso, Cameroon, Central African Republic, Chad, Congo, Equitorial Guinea, Gabon, Ivory Coast, Mali, Niger, Senegal and Togo.

CFP Franc Zone

Comptoirs Frrançais du Pacifique includes New Caledonia, French Polynesia and the Wallis and Futuna islands and forms another group with a currency linked to the French franc.

CFTC

The Commodity Futures Trading Commission, created by the US Congress in 1974 to oversee the trading of futures contracts on US futures exchanges. Its responsibilities include:

1 regulating exchange trading of futures, leverage contracts, options on futures contracts, and options on physical commodities trading on commodities markets;

2 approving all futures exchanges' rules and reviewing exchange policies and procedures;

3 approving new contracts to be traded on futures exchanges;

4 registering those who deal with public customers and enforcing the rules protecting customers' funds.

Chain rule

A method of calculating cross-rates in foreign exchange.

Chambre de Compensation des Instruments Financiers de Paris (CCIFP)

French financial futures and options clearing system.

CHAPS

Clearing House Automated Payments System, the UK same-day interbank clearing system for sterling payments, a part of the APACS system.

Chapter 11

Under the US Bankruptcy Reform Acts of 1978 and 1984 the Bankruptcy

Code has provisions for a troubled company to seek temporary respite from its creditors while it reorganizes itself and tries to work out a repayment schedule acceptable to a committee of creditors. During this process, usually the existing management will continue to control the business. If a repayment plan is confirmed against the wishes of some dissenting creditors this is known as "cramdown." For this to happen, at least one class of creditors who have been adversely affected must agree, and there must not be discrimination.

Chariots

Proprietary name given to an asset-backed financing, based on Italian car loans. Possibly sold to investors who have not driven in Italy.

Chart gap

A gap in the price history of a security when the market price opens above the previous session's traded high or below the traded low.

Charting

The use of graphs of price histories to analyse market trends and to predict prices. Popular and therefore to some extent self-fulfilling. Reflects, too, the 'herd' mentality of traders.

Chartist

A technical analyst. When chartists were a political movement in the UK in the 19th century one of their leaders took to signing his letters "Fergus Rex." Similar delusions aflict some modern chartists.

Cheapest to deliver (CTD)

Bond futures are usually priced on the basis of a notional bond, while delivery requires actual bonds. Futures contract specifications include a range of actual bonds which can be used for settlement and a price factor which is applied to each bond. Futures sellers will try to find the cheapest to deliver. See **basis trading**.

Cherry picking

Choosing carefully. In the context of bankruptcy or default, it means insisting on the performance of only those contracts where it is advantageous to do so. Thus if a bank has a series of contracts with a defaulting counterparty, the bank might cancel those contracts which could be replaced to the bank's advantage while making a claim as a creditor in respect of the others. Swap documentation is designed to prevent this happening by establishing a right of offset for both parties.

Chicago Board of Trade

The world's largest and oldest futures exchange was founded in 1848. Trading is by **open outcry** and by an after-hours computer system called Project A. All contracts are cleared through the Board of Trade Clearing Corporation.

Futures and options are traded in corn, wheat, rough rice, oats, soya bean, soya bean meal, and soya bean oil. Futures are traded on diammonium phosphate, and anhydrous ammonia. Corn yield insurance futures and options are traded for the US as well as for each of Iowa, Nebraska, Illinois, Indiana, and Ohio.

Futures and options are traded in US Treasury bonds, 10-year, 5-year and 2-year Treasury notes. Futures and options are also traded in yield curve spreads.

Other futures and options are on a Long Term Municipal Bond Index, 30-day Federal Funds (futures only), 10-year Canadian Government Bonds, silver and gold (futures only). There are also options on Property Claim Services (PCS) Catastrophe Insurance.

Chicago Board Options Exchange (CBOE)

The CBOE began trading in 1973 and is now the largest options exchange in the world with 1995 trading volume exceeding 178 million contracts. The CBOE lists options on more than 700 stocks as well as indices and sector indices. The indices include the S&P 100 Index (OEX), the S&P 500 Index (SPX), the NASDAQ-100 Index (NDX), the Russell 2000 Index (RUT), and the Nikkei 300 Index. S&P sector indices on which options are traded include Banks, Chemical, Health Care, Insurance, Retail, Transportation, Environmental, and Telecommunications. CBOE indices on which options are traded include Global Telecommunications, REIT, Gaming, Technology, and Computer Software. Options are also traded on the CBOE Israel, Mexico and Latin 15 Indices. The exchange also trades interest-rate options, long-term options (LEAPS) on single stocks and FLEX options. Trading is by **open outcry**.

Chicago Mercantile Exchange

Formed originally as the Butter and Egg Board, the CME consists of four divisions, the CME, IMM, IOM and, from 1995, the GEM (Growth & Emerging Markets). Members of each division may trade all the contracts listed in that division and those of any division ranked after it. CME members may therefore trade all contracts while GEM members may trade only GEM contracts. There are 625 CME members, 812 IMM members, 1,287 IOM members and 50 GEM members. Trading is by auction, open-outcry pit trading and by the GLOBEX system. Clearing, settlement and delivery is through the CME clearing house.

The exchange trades a wide range of currency futures and options on its IMM division including A$, GBP, C$, DEM, FFR, MXN, BRL, SFR as well as DEM/JPY cross rate futures and rolling spot and forward futures on A$, GBP, DEM, JPY C$, SFR and FFR.

Interest-rate futures and options are traded on the IMM division on three-month US Treasury bills, one-year Treasury bills, one-month LIBOR, Federal funds rate, three-month eurodollars, and three-month euromarks.

Agricultural futures and options are traded on the CME division on live cattle, feeder cattle, live hogs, lean hogs, frozen pork bellies, fluid milk, and broiler chickens.

Futures and options on the Goldman Sachs Commodity Index and on random length lumber are traded on the GEM and CME divisions respectively.

Index futures and options traded on the IOM or GEM divisions include the S&P 500, S&P 500/Barra Growth Index, S&P 500/Barra Value Index, S&P Midcap 400, Major Market, Nikkei, Russell 2000, and the FT-SE 100.

Chicago School

The University of Chicago is noted for a long line of economists who have been Nobel laureates. The wide range of talent has included a number of free-market economists.

Chicago Stock Exchange

The exchange began trading in 1882. In 1949 the exchange merged with those of St Louis, Cleveland, Minneapolis-St Paul and (in 1959) New Orleans. Common shares are by far the largest class of security traded. Amounts of preferred stock, warrants and others are relatively small. Orders in stocks traded by CHX specialists are routed and executed by SuperMax, which automates limit orders. The CHX Chicago Match order crossing system allows large institutional investors to trade directly with each other. It covers all ASE and NYSE stocks and 100 NASDAQ stocks.

China Commodity Futures Exchange

The CCFE was formed in 1993 in Haikou, Hainan. It is regulated by the China Securities Regulation Committee. The exchange has some 430 members throughout China who deal through a computerized trading system. Futures contracts are traded on natural rubber, palm olein, coffee, cocoa and malting barly.

China International Trust and Investment Corporation (CITIC)

Chinese State-owned overseas investment agency.

China Zhengzhou Commodity Exchange

Originally founded as a wholesale grain market in 1990, the exchange began trading futures in 1993. The exchange trades futures in wheat, corn, soya beans, green beans, round rice, peanut kernels, soya bean meal, red beans, aluminium, and cotton yarn. There are also futures on Treasury notes.

Chinese wall

The precautions taken to prevent market-sensitive information reaching traders from other parts of a financial institution which may have confidential contacts with client companies.

CHIPS

Clearing House Interbank Payment System, US system for US dollar payments between banks in New York.

Choice

UK traders' term for quoting a single price at which the counterparty may buy or sell. For example, a trader might quote "98.50 choice." If someone makes you a choice price, it is very bad manners not to deal on it.

Chooser option

An option which allows the purchaser to choose at expiration whether the option is a put or a call. In either case, the exercise price is the same.

Chuki kokusai

Japanese phrase for medium-term Japanese government bonds.

Chummy trading

The illegal practice of artificially trading between market participants at agreed prices in order to create the illusion of a liquid market. Also called "wash trading."

Churning

The unnecessarily frequent buying and selling of securities in a discretionary client portfolio by a broker in order to generate commission income.

CIBOR

Copenhagen interbank offered rate.

Cincinnati Stock Exchange

Now based in Chicago, the exchange trades equities though its fully automated execution system NSTS, which is linked via the Intermarket Trading System with the other major US exchanges. Trades are cleared and settled through the NSCC.

Circle

To gather investors prepared to purchase a planned new issue of securities at a certain price or yield. Underwriters of a new issue will try to circle investors to reduce their own risk before an issue is finally launched. The investors typically will buy the securities at the price they indicated, or have first refusal if the issue comes on different terms.

Circuit breakers

Many regulators and others fear the effects which derivatives traders, arbitrageurs, hedge funds and program traders can have on the cash markets in the underlying securities or commodities. In many markets, daily price change limits have been set, so that in volatile market conditions trading can be halted in the hope of calming the markets. These limits and the rules governing the suspension of trading are called "circuit breakers."

On the New York Stock Exchange, for example, there are three circuit breakers. Trading halts are called for one hour if the Dow Jones Industrial Average falls 250 points from the previous day's close, and for two hours if the Dow Jones Industrial Average falls 400 points.

Second, when the primary S&P 500® futures contract falls 12 points, equivalent to about 100 points on the Dow Jones Industrial Average, from the previous day's close all program-trading market orders entered in the system for S&P 500 stocks are diverted into a separate blind file for five minutes. After this sidecar period, orders are paired off and are executed. If this is not possible, trading in the relevant stocks is halted, the fact is publicized and new stop and stop-limit orders are banned for the rest of the day. The five minute sidecar rule does not apply in the last 35 minutes of trading.

The third circuit breaker is known as Rule 80A. When the Dow Jones Industrial Index moves 50 points from the previous day's close, index arbitrage orders in component stocks of the index are subject to a tick test. In down-markets, sell orders may be executed only on a plus or zero-plus tick; in up-markets, buy orders may be executed only on a minus or a zero-minus tick. The rule applies for the remainder of the day or until the index moves back within 25 points of the previous day's close.

City Code on Takeovers and Mergers

The UK code governing takeovers and mergers which is published and administered by the Panel on Takeovers and Mergers. The Panel is primarily concerned that the treatment of shareholders involved in a takeover should be equitable. Questions of the public interest are not its responsibility.

Class of options

The options of one type, puts or calls, on the same underlying.

Classic repo

The word "repo" is an abbreviation of repurchase, and is used to denote a sale and repurchase agreement. A repo is a sale of securities for cash with a simultaneous commitment to repurchase them on a specified future date. The repo market is simply a collateralized money market in which borrowers of cash lend liquid marketable securities as collateral against the loan.

In a repo, the seller usually delivers securities on a delivery-versus-payment basis and receives cash from the buyer. This money is lent for the period of the transaction at an agreed rate, the "repo rate." which is usually fixed for the term of the deal.

A repo is simply two simultaneous deals to sell and buy back the same security. An outright sale of a security is accompanied by an outright repurchase of the same security for value a more distant date.

The sale invoice price will include accrued coupon interest to the sale date and the buy-back price will include accrued coupon interest to the buy-back date. The clean price of the buy-back (that is excluding interest accrued) will be set at such a level as to represent an interest cost. The cost of borrowing cash by the sale and buy-back transaction lies in this price adjustment.

A classic repo is merely a more sophisticated sale and buy-back governed by a written agreement rather than merely being evidenced by deal confirmations. The written agreement will normally govern all such transactions between the counterparties. The agreement will typically include the right to mark transactions to market and to ask for variation margin as well as the rights to terminate transactions in the event of a default and to set-off one against another so as to net the exposure of the non-defaulting counterparty. A further difference of a practical nature is that the return to the supplier of cash is quoted separately. See **repo**.

Clawback

The ability of an agent in a loan agreement to recover funds from a participating bank.

Clean price

The price of a security without accrued interest.

Clearing

The process of matching, registering and guaranteeing trades, often performed by a clearing house.

Clearing bank

(1) Any US commercial bank through which securities transactions may be settled.

(2) One of the large UK cheque clearing banks that dominate the sterling and the UK retail banking markets.

Clearing corporation

US equivalent of a **Clearing house**.

Clearing house

Also known as a "clearing corporation." Company which registers, monitors, matches, settles and often guarantees trades on a futures or options exchange. Clearing houses are not all of equal credit standing. The factors which differentiate clearing houses may be summarized as follows:
- the adequacy of margining requirements
- the reliability of trade processing systems
- the procedures and resources to deal with a member default or multiple defaults
- membership requirements and the quality of surveillance
- the regulating environment and the degree of government support.

Clearing House Automated Payment System (CHAPS)

A UK electronic system for payments between banks.

Clearing house funds

Payments made through the New York Clearing House's computerized **Clearing House Interbank Payments System (CHIPS)**.

Clearing House Interbank Payments System (CHIPS)

US clearing system linking banks in New York, through which most Eurodollar transactions are cleared. Participants' net positions are settled through the Federal Reserve's funds transfer system.

Clearing member

A member firm of a futures clearing house. Each clearing member must also be a member of an exchange, but not all members of an exchange are also members of a clearing house. The trades of a non-clearing member are settled through a clearing member.

Clearing system

A depository or transaction settlement system. Three international security clearing systems are Cedel, Euroclear and First Chicago Clearing Centre,

Client money rules

A surprising number of people seem to forget the difference between their own and other people's money. Hence the need for these rules issued by the UK's Securities and Investments Board (SIB) requiring investment businesses to hold customers' funds in segregated accounts.

Cliquet option

French term applied to a **ratchet option** and/or knock-out option (see **barrier option**).

Close out

A transaction which leaves the trader with a net nil position.

Closed mortgage-backed security

Mortgages on which no prepayments are allowed, and which therefore offer investors certainty of cash flows. Normal mortgage-backed securities carry considerable uncertainty as to the timing of cash flows which depend on numerous individual decisions about refinancing individual mortgages.

Closed-end fund

(1) A mutual fund with a fixed number of shares.

(2) A pension fund where no new members are added.

Closing

The procedures necessary to the completion of a new issue on the closing date. At the closing, all the steps are considered to take place simultaneously and the closing is not completed until all the steps have been completed. In the case of a Eurobond issue, for example, the steps would be as follows:

(1) payment instructions given by lead manager paying the net proceeds of the issue to the borrower;
(2) receipt given by the common depositary for the temporary global note, and confirmation that it has paid the net subscription proceeds to the borrower in accordance with the lead manager's instructions;
(3) standard form letters of undertaking from Euroclear and Cedel;
(4) cross receipt signed on behalf of the lead manager and the borrower.

Despite its name, there are still things to be done after the closing of an issue. Again, taking as an example a Eurobond listed in Luxembourg, these final matters would be as follows:

(1) All-sold telexes and confirmation of the completion of the distribution of the notes to be sent by the lead manager to the borrower, the clearing houses, the trustee (if any), the principal paying agent and the managers.
(2) After the closing, the listing agent in Luxembourg would require from

the lead manager: Agency Agreement (three conformed copies), and specimen definitive notes (three),

(3) Publication of a "tombstone." The names under which securities firms conduct their business are not always those of a single legal entity, so care is needed.

Closing date

The date on which an issuer receives the proceeds of a new issue in return for issuing the securities, in temporary or definitive form.

Closing prices

The bid and offer prices being quoted by market-makers at the end of a day's trading. These are not necessarily prices at which transactions have been done.

Club loan

A syndicated loan with a small number of banks in the syndicate. Often the syndicate members are the house banks of the borrower and are involved as part of their overall relationship. A borrower could hope to organize such a loan facility quickly and in some privacy. By contrast the members of many large syndicates are hardly known to the borrower (and sometimes vice versa).

CME

See **Chicago Mercantile Exchange**, one of the largest futures and options exchanges in the world.

CMO

See **Collaterialized mortgage obligations (CMOs)**.

Cochin Stock Exchange

Exchange in Kerala, India, founded in 1878. Shares and debt securities are traded on the exchange. Trading is on an auction basis with dual capacity brokers. Indices are those of the Bombay Stock Exchange. A unified electronic exchange for the whole of India has been established. See **National Stock Exchange of India**.

Cock dates

See **broken dates**.

Code of Standard Wording, Assumptions and Provisions for Swaps

First attempt by ISDA (the International Swap Dealers Association, as it was then known) to codify the basic terms in swap transactions. Before it was introduced, each term of a swap transaction was negotiated each time a deal was done. For example, LIBOR might be determined as the average of quotations from named banks who would be contacted by a calculation agent. The identities of all these parties was subject to negotiation. Even calculation bases were argued about.

COFACE

The French export credit and insurance agency operated by the French government. The initials stand for Compagnie Française pour l'Assurance du Commerce Extérieur.

Coffee, Sugar & Cocoa Exchange, New York

Founded in 1882, the CSCE now has 527 full members and 250 associate members. Trading is by **open outcry**. Clearing is through the Commodity Futures Clearing Corporation. A merger with NYMEX has been proposed. The exchange trades contracts in coffees, sugars, cocoa, cheddar cheese, milk and non-fat dry milk.

Coimbatore Stock Exchange

Indian exchange which began trading in 1993. The exchange trades equities and debentures, and 166 companies are listed. See **National Stock Exchange of India**.

Co-lead manager

A member of the underwriting group in a new issue who usually has no real role in leading the transaction, but who is given a larger underwriting share and a more prominent place in any publicity. Co-lead managers rank below lead or joint-lead managers, but above co-managers.

Collar

Most usually the combination of an interest rate cap and a floor (see Figure C3). The cap is bought, and the floor is sold in order to give a borrower a collar. The reverse transactions are executed to give an investor a collar. It is possible in both cases to construct a zero-cost collar by setting the strike rates of cap and floor so that the net premium paid is zero. The buyer of a collar limits the maximum rate he will pay and sets a minimum rate which he will pay. His cost of funds is thereby confined to a range.

The premium paid for the cap component is partly or wholly offset by the premium earned on the floor component. The net premium, if any exists, can always be reduced by setting a higher cap strike (buying a cheaper cap) or by setting a higher floor rate (selling a more expensive floor).

Figure C3

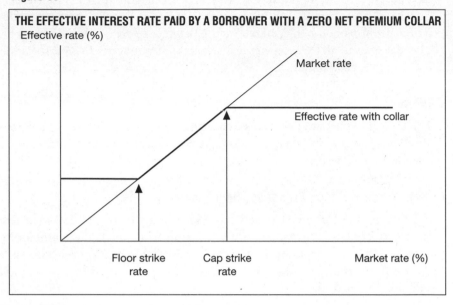

THE EFFECTIVE INTEREST RATE PAID BY A BORROWER WITH A ZERO NET PREMIUM COLLAR

Collar swap

An interest rate swap in which the floating-rate payments are subject to a maximum and minimum rate.

Collared floating-rate note (collared FRN)

A **Floating-rate note** with a collar which sets a maximum and a minimum on the coupon paid.

Collateral

Assets pledged as security in order to facilitate a transaction.

Collateral risk

In any structured transaction, the risk that the security involved will either not produce the cash flows required on time, or will not be valuable enough to achieve its purpose. See **risk**.

Collateral security margin

The difference between the value of collateral pledged and the lesser amount of the transaction it supports.

Collateralized bond obligation (CBO)

Repackaged low quality bonds.

Collateralized lease equipment obligations (CLEOs)

Securities backed by computer leases.

Collateralized mortgage obligations (CMOs)

Securities backed by a pool of mortgages owned by the issuer and guaranteed by a federal agency such as the Federal National Mortgage Association. The securities based on the pool are usually ranked in three or more tranches, with the last receiving no payments until the senior tranches are redeemed. See **companion bonds**.

Collection account

A separate account established to make and receive payments relating to a particular transaction or issue of securities.

Colombo Stock Exchange

The Sri Lankan exchange has 15 member firms. The exchange trades equities and debentures. Settlement and clearing is through the CDS automated system. A fully automated trading system was expected to replace open-outcry trading in 1996. Delivery versus payment settlement was expected to replace the old two-tier settlement system.

Colon

The national currency of El Salvador and Costa Rica.

Co-manager

An underwriter of a new issue who has a smaller share of the underwriting than a co-lead manager. Usually the most numerous group in a syndicate.

Combination

Any position involving put and call options which is not a **straddle**.

Combination matching

A portfolio strategy which combines dedication or cash-flow matching with immunization or duration-matching. Typically, the former will relate to known short-term liabilities while the latter will relate to longer-term liabilities which are known with less precision.

COMESA

Common Market for East and Southern Africa. Established in 1993 with the aim of achieving a common market by 2000. Based in Lusaka, Zambia.

Comfort letter

A document, without the force of a guarantee, which expresses intentions intended to give comfort to a prospective lender.

Comisión Nacional del Mercado de Valores (CNMV)

Government agency which regulates the Spanish securities markets.

Comité de la Réglementation Bancaire (CRB)

The French banking regulations committee is chaired by the Minister of the Economy. It formulates general banking rules, accounting rules, prudential and risk ratios, market rules and particularly rules governing the interbank market and markets in negotiable debt securities.

Comité des Établissements de Credit (CEC)

The French lending institutions committee is chaired by the Governor of the Banque de France. It licenses lending institutions (other than those supervised by the Commission Bancaire) and money brokers (*agents des marchés interbancaires*) under the Banking Act, and under regulations laid down by the Comité de la Réglementation Bancaire.

Commercial banks

Now difficult to define but generally taken to be those banks which are active through a retail branch network, for whom deposits and loans are a large part of the firm's business or which attempt to provide a wide range of services to a large number of corporate customers.

Commercial paper (CP)

Short-term debt securities issued in the US domestic market with maturities up to 270 days, though the most issued maturities are up to 90 days.

Commission

Fee charged by financial institution for a service.

Commission bancaire

French banking commission. Under the Act of 24 January 1984 the Commission is responsible for ensuring compliance by lending institutions operating in France with all legislation and regulations. The Commission has wide powers to obtain information, to impose measures and to punish erring institutions.

Commission broker

Member of an exchange who executes orders for others.

Commission des Opérations de Bourse (COB)

French stock exchange commission. The commission is responsible for investor protection. It supervises investor information, operation of the securities market, listed financial products and traded futures. It approves prospectuses, and licenses mutual funds (SICAVs) and investment trusts.

Commissione Nazionale per la Società e la Borsa (CONSOB)

Italian stock exchange commission.

Commitment fee

Fee payable in return for a commitment from a bank to lend money. Once money is borrowed, the fee is usually no longer payable on the amount of the facility drawn.

Committed facility

A loan facility which is not repayable on demand, but after a stated period of time, though usually the commitment is subject to certain covenants.

Committee on Banking Regulations and Supervisory Practices

A sub-committee of the Bank for International Settlements committee, also known as the Basle or Cooke committee, formed in December 1987. It produced "Proposals for the International Convergence of Capital Measurement and Capital Standards" which set out a method, based on the riskiness of different asset classes, for measuring the capital adequacy of banks.

Commodities Exchange Commission (CEC)

US body made up of representatives of the Commodity Exchange, the New York Mercantile Exchange, the Coffee, Sugar and Cocoa Exchange, the New York Cotton Exchange and the New York Futures Exchange.

Compagnie des Agents de Change (CAC)

Former name of the French stockbrokers' association, now the Société des Bourses Françaises (SBF).

Compagnie des Commissionaires Agréés (CCA)

The French commodity brokers' association.

Companion bonds

Collateralized Mortgage Obligation (CMO) securities face a problem of prepayment of the underlying mortgages. A typical structure to deal with this is to have different classes of security. Companion bonds absorb this prepayment risk ahead of other tranches such as Planned Amortization Class (PAC) or Targeted Amortization Class (TAC) securities.

Compensation fund

The fund maintained by an exchange to repay investors, should a member firm fail to meet its obligations.

Compensatory and contingency financing facility (CCFF)

An International Monetary Fund facility providing short-term loans to countries experiencing temporary shortages in foreign currency receipts.

Completion

Formal end of the construction of a project and the beginning of the operating phase.

Completion guarantee

A guarantee of performance by a construction company to complete a project.

Compliance officer

The official in an investment firm responsible for compliance with regulatory requirements. There was a time when this was a low-paid, much ridiculed job. Now compliance officers are highly-paid corporate bodyguards.

Compliance Review Committee

A committee of the New York Mercantile Exchange.

Compound interest

Interest accrued on interest not paid.

Compound option

An option on an option.

Comptroller of the Currency

The chief regulator in the US of nationally chartered banks to whom each nationally chartered bank must report at least four times per year. National banks used to issue their own notes until 1935. The Comptroller of the Currency is also one of the three directors of the Federal Deposit Insurance Corporation.

Concert party

A group of investors, acting together or under the control of one person, which buys the shares of a company with each holding at a level below the 5 percent mandatory disclosure level set out the UK 1985 Companies Act . This way of building a large holding by stealth is illegal.

Concession

A discount.

Conditional bargain

A transaction which is contingent on the outcome of a particular event.

Conditionality

The IMF principle of imposing conditions on lending to finance temporary economic problems. These conditions are usually implementation of certain economic policies designed to correct the economic problems.

Condor

A **butterfly spread** where the two short options have different strikes. Picturesque in name, but expensive in transaction costs.

Conduct of business rules

Under the UK regulatory system, the rules issued by a self-regulatory organisation governing the way in which its members carry out their investment business.

Conduit

A single-purpose company, formed as part of a financial transaction, through which payments are routed.

Conference Board

The US body which publishes a *Confidence Index*, a guide to US business conditions and consumer confidence.

Confidence level

The probability of the price of a given security (or the value of a portfolio) staying within a specified range during a specified period of time, usually expressed as a percentage. Used with value at risk methodologies to estimate potential losses based on analysis of historical price data.

Conseil des Bourses de Valeurs (CBV)

Formerly the French Stockmarket Supervisory Council. The CBV draws up and enforces stockmarket regulations. Now merged with the *Conseil du Marché à Terme* to form the *Conseil des Marches Financièrs (CMF)*.

Conseil des Marches Financièrs (CMF)

French securities regulator formed in the autumn of 1996 on the merger of the *Conseil des Bourses de Valeurs* and the *Conseil du Marché à Terme* which supervised the stock exchange and the futures and derivatives markets respectively.

The CMF is responsible for formulating conduct of business rules for investment firms, for authorising firms and for the takeover rules. Fund management companies are licensed and supervised by the *Commission des Opérations des Bourses (COB)*.

Conseil du Marché à Terme

Formerly the French body which supervises the MATIF under the Chambre de Compensation des Instruments Financiers de Paris (CCIFP). Now merged with the *Conseil des Bourses de Valeurs (CBV)* to form the *Conseil des Marches Financièrs (CMF)*.

Consols

Consolidated annuities. An English irredeemable gilt-edged government security issued during the Napoleonic wars and still traded.

Constant maturity treasury (CMT)

The interpolated average of yields on US Treasury instruments of specified maturity expressed as the yield of a theoretical treasury of constant maturity.

Consumer Price Index (CPI)

A US price index based on the price of a basket of consumer goods. There are in fact two indices, CPI-U (the most widely used consumer price index for all urban consumers) and CPI-W (a consumer price index for urban wage earners and clerical workers).

Contango

The amount by which the price for future delivery exceeds the price for spot delivery. Normally it will reflect the cost of holding a commodity between the two dates, but the activities of traders may distort or remove this effect.

Contingent immunization

Investment technique intended to make certain a minimum return on a portfolio, while leaving some opportunity for active management in pursuit of outperformance.

Contingent order

An order to sell one security and buy another simultaneously. Also known as a "net order" or a "not held order."

Contingent premium option

An option where the buyer pays a premium only if the option has value at expiry. The premium payable may well exceed the value of the option at expiry. See Figure C4.

Continuous trading

Unceasing trading during an official trading session on an exchange.

Continuously Offered Long-Term Securities (COLTS)

A World Bank borrowing program in the US medium-term note market.

Figure C4

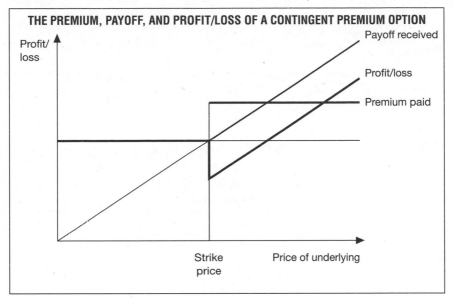

THE PREMIUM, PAYOFF, AND PROFIT/LOSS OF A CONTINGENT PREMIUM OPTION

Continuously Offered Payment Rights (COPS)

A World Bank short-term borrowing program in Swiss francs.

Contract

Standard specification of the terms of futures or options traded on an exchange.

Contract expiration date

The last date on which an exchange traded future or option contract may be traded.

Contract month

In a futures or options market, a future calendar month for which contracts may be traded. Also known as a "delivery month."

Conventional gilts

UK government bonds with a fixed coupon and maturity date. Called conventional in contrast to, for example, index-linked, undated or callable gilts.

Conventional mortgages

Term used in the US to denote mortgage loans which are not **Federal Housing Administration** (FHA) -insured or **Veterans' Administration** (VA) -guaranteed.

Conventional option

Term used in the US to denote an over-the-counter (OTC) stock option.

Convergence

The process whereby the prices of the underlying and derivatives converge towards one price as delivery approaches.

Conversion

(1) The purchase of the underlying and a put option together with the sale of a call. The whole is a low-risk strategy designed to lock in a profit.

(2) In the context of convertible securities, the exercise of the right to acquire a new security in exchange for an older security on previously specified terms.

Convertible

A bond which, at the option of the holder, can be exchanged for another bond with different terms.

Convertible adjustable preferred stock (CAPS)

Floating-rate preferred stock which is convertible, usually at each dividend resetting.

Convertible bond with put

A convertible bond which gives the investor the added benefit of a put option. In practice, this gives the investor an early exit from his investment if the issuer's share price does not rise as hoped. For the borrower, the put option is likely to be exercised at a time when the company is in difficulties. What began as quasi-equity, may becomes a call on the company's cash at a time of strain.

Convertible currency

A currency that can be freely exchanged for another currency.

Convertible exchangeable preferred stock (CEPs)

A type of stock convertible at the option of the investor into ordinary shares of the issuer and exchangeable at the issuer's option for the issuer's convertible debt.

Convertible floating-rate note (CFRN)

FRN convertible into another security, not necessarily equity.

Convertible gilt

UK government bond which is convertible into another, usually longer gilt, at the option of the holder.

Convertible money market preferred stock (CMMPS)

A US term for a security where the interest rate is reset periodically by auction and which is convertible into equity.

Convertible money market units (CMM)

Interest-bearing instrument which is economically similar to a covered call.

Convertible mortgage

Property-financing technique where a secured loan carries the right to convert into a certain percentage ownership of the property if not repaid.

Convertible option contract

Currency option with a trigger price at which the option converts into a forward foreign-exchange contract.

Convertible preference share

Preference share which may be converted into equity.

Convexity

With fixed-rate securities convexity is a measure of the sensitivity of duration to (large) changes in yield. If duration decreases as yield rises and increases as yield falls then the price of the bond in question will follow a curved path when plotted on a yield/price graph which is attractive to an investor. By contrast, mortgage-backed securities have negative convexity, because when interest rates fall far enough, the borrowers of the underlying mortgages tend to refinance themselves, paying off their old mortgages and taking on new, cheaper loans. These prepayments shorten the duration of the mortgage-backed securities.

Convexity (CX) can be approximated, using the following formula:

$$CX = 10^6 \times (P_1 + P_2 - 2P)/P$$

where

P = gross price of the bond at the current yield
P_1 = gross price of the bond if the yield were to increase by 0.1%
P_2 = gross price of the bond if the yield were to decrease by 0.1%

Example
Take the case of a 10-year 10% annual coupon bond trading at par. In this case:

P_1 = 99.388174, a yield of 10.1%
P_2 = 100.617105, a yield of 9.9%

therefore we can calculate convexity to be

$CX = 10^6 \times (99.388174 + 100.617105 - 200)/100$
$= 10^4 \times 0.005279$
$= 53$

In this case, we can see that the bond loses in price less than it gains in price for a change of the same size in yield in either direction. A rise in yields of 0.1 percent causes a 0.611826 fall in price while a fall in yields of 0.1 percent causes a 0.617105 gain in price.

In the case of options, convexity is the measure of the way in which the value of a position changes with a change in the volatility or price of the underlying.

Copenhagen Stock Exchange

The only Danish stock exchange was first subject to legislation in 1808. In 1993, liberalizing measures to conform to EU rules were enacted. Some 243 domestic shares are listed. The exchange trades ordinary and preference shares. Some 2,300 bond isues are also listed. Trading is by the ELECTRA electronic trading system. There is an automatic match trading system and a semi-automatic system for less liquid securities called the "accept system." For the most liquid bonds, there is the EBS system which is restricted to authorized market makers. Settlement is on T+3 through the Danish Securities Centre. The main indices are the Total Share Index, which is a weighted index of all the shares traded on the exchange, and the KFX Index, which is based on the 20 most liquid shares.

Córdoba Stock Exchange

Argentinian stock exchange where 156 companies are listed. Trading in government bonds, shares, corporate bonds and other instruments is by auction on the floor of the exchange. See the stock exchanges of **Buenos Aires, Mendoza, La Planta** and **Rosario.**

Corpus treasury receipt (corpus TR)

A zero-coupon certificate issued in respect of the principal payment of a US treasury security.

Correlation

The change in one variable following a change in another variable

Correlation coefficient

A measure of the relationship between two variables. Important in value-at-risk analysis and in replicating indices. A correlation coefficient of 1.0 indicates a perfect match, a coefficient of 0.0 indicates no observable relationship and a coefficient of –1.0 indicates a perfect offsetting relationship.

Correspondant en Valeurs du Trésor (CVT)

French term for a reporting dealer in French government securities. The designation is one rank below that of primary dealer, *Spécialiste en Valeurs du Trésor (SVT)*. At 1 March 1996 there were two CVTs, *Compagnie Financière BZW* and *ABN Amro Finance*. Their applications for SVT status were expected to be reviewed in early 1997.

Correspondent

A bank or financial organization which acts on behalf of another in a particular place.

Corruption

Defined as the misuse of public power for private benefit, international corruption is hard to measure. National prejudices are strong. For example, Italy in Europe and Nigeria in Africa suffer from a popular reputation for corruption. It is hard to prove either absolute or relative levels of corruption. It should be remembered, too, that while certain emerging countries have reputations for corrupt practices, bribes are often paid by companies from rich industrial countries which pride themselves on freedom from corruption. An international organization, Transparancy International, published in 1996 a poll of polls which ranked countries according to the perceptions of (largely western) business people (see Figure C5).

Corso secco

Italian phrase meaning a clean price.

Corso tel quel

Italian phrase meaning a gross price.

Cost of Funds Index (COFI)

A US interest rate benchmark index used in relation to adjustable rate mortgage-backed securities. It is based on the cost of funds of certain savings and loan associations.

Cost of funds index swap (COFI swap)

Interest rate swap in which one leg is based on the Cost of Funds Index (COFI).

Côte Officielle

The official list of the French securities market.

Figure C5

INTERNATIONAL PERCEPTIONS OF CORRUPTION

Rank	Country	Score*	Rank	Country	Score*
1	New Zealand	9.43	28	Greece	5.01
2	Denmark	9.33	29	Taiwan	4.98
3	Sweden	9.08	30	Jordan	4.89
4	Finland	9.05	31	Hungary	4.86
5	Canada	8.96	32	Spain	4.31
6	Norway	8.87	33	Turkey	3.54
7	Singapore	8.80	34	Italy	3.42
8	Switzerland	8.76	35	Argentina	3.41
9	Netherlands	8.71	36	Bolivia	3.40
10	Australia	8.60	37	Thailand	3.33
11	Ireland	8.45	38	Mexico	3.30
12	United Kingdom	8.44	39	Ecuador	3.19
13	Germany	8.27	40	Brazil	2.96
14	Israel	7.71	41	Egypt	2.84
15	United States	7.66	42	Colombia	2.73
16	Austria	7.59	43	Uganda	2.71
17	Japan	7.09	44	Philippines	2.69
18	Hong Kong	7.01	45	Indonesia	2.65
19	France	6.96	46	India	2.63
20	Belgium	6.84	47	Russia	2.58
21	Chile	6.80	48	Venezuela	2.50
22	Portugal	6.53	49	Cameroon	2.46
23	South Africa	5.68	50	China	2.43
24	Poland	5.57	51	Bangladesh	2.29
25	Czech Republic	5.37	52	Kenya	2.21
26	Malaysia	5.32	53	Pakistan	1.00
27	South Korea	5.02	54	Nigeria	0.69

*A score of 10 would represent a corruption-free country.

(Source: Transparancy International Corruption Perception Index 1996 by courtesy of Transparency International, Berlin and Dr. Johann Lambsdorf, Goettingen University)

Council of Europe Social Development Fund (CSDF)

Formerly called the Council of Europe Resettlement Fund, it is based in Paris and is the development bank of the Council of Europe. Legally separate, it borrows in the capital markets and lends to assist with social or economic problems.

Counter currency

A currency exchanged for the underlying or nominated currency in a foreign exchange transaction.

Counterparty

A party to an agreement or contract.

Countervalue

The value received in a transaction in exchange for the nominated quantity.

Country fund

A mutual fund invested in a single country.

Country limit

The overall maximum a financial institution puts on its exposure to a single country.

Country risk

That part of a risk which relates to the country of the obligor. It includes macro-economic and political risks. Also called "sovereign risk." The risk which arises from investing in a particular country. With the worldwide movement towards free capital flows, this risk is now less a question of possible legal or policy changes and more a question of government deficits. Most problem sovereign risks have chronic government deficits. See **risk**.

Coupon

(1) The nominal rate of interest payable on a security.

(2) The certificate attached to a security which entitles the holder to a particular interest payment when detached and presented to the paying agent.

Coupon date

The date when a coupon is to be paid.

Coupon stripping

The manufacture of a zero-coupon security from a conventional bond by taking away the coupons and selling them separately. This is done in a number of government bond markets including the US, French, and (from 1997) the UK markets.

Coupon treasury receipt (coupon TR)

A zero-coupon certificate issued in respect of an interest payment of a US treasury security.

Coupon washing

Sale of a security before an interest payment date with a repurchase after the interest payment date intended to avoid tax. Does not work in many countries.

Courtage

French word for brokerage fees.

Covariance

The degree of correlation between two variables.

Covenant

A clause in an agreement which places an obligation on one or both parties to do, or to refrain from doing, certain things, which, if not observed, causes acceleration or other changes to the contract. Typical covenants in a borrowing agreement are cross default, **pari passu** and negative pledge covenants. In a bank loan agreement, financial covenants are seen, such as minimum net worth, interest cover, or current ratio covenants. See **cross default clause, material adverse change** and **negative pledge**.

Cover

(1) Closing a transaction with an equal and opposite transaction.

(2) In auctions of securities the number of bids submitted compared with the number actually awarded.

(3) The cash, currency, security or commodity required to perform under a contract.

Covered call

Sale of a call option while being long the underlying.

Covered straddle

Sale of a **straddle** while being long the underlying.

Covered warrant

A warrant issued on a share where the issuer has covered his risk, either by owning an equivalent number of shares or by owning suitable derivatives based on that share.

Covered writing

Selling call options against an existing long position in the underlying.

Crack spread

Price difference between specified grades of oil. So called because the different grades of oil are made by a catalytic converter known as a "cat cracker."

For example, on the New York Mercantile Exchange, there are options traded on the crude oil/heating oil spread and on the crude oil/gasoline spread.

Cramdown

The confirmation of a debt repayment plan in a corporate bankruptcy or **Chapter 11** proceedings against the wishes of some creditors.

Creador de mercado

Spanish term for a market maker.

Credit card receivables

Credit card debts repackaged into asset-backed securities.

Credit card trust

A trust in which credit card receivables are held for the benefit of investors in asset-backed securities based on them.

Credit derivative

Derivative linked to the credit quality of a specified entity.

Credit enhancement

General term for all the things which can be done to improve a credit. These include posting collateral, obtaining a guarantee, purchasing insurance, or netting liabilities.

Credit equivalent amount

A way of expressing risk in an off-balance sheet instrument as if it were a loan. A US$10 million interest rate swap does not carry the same risk as a US$10 million loan. Therefore the risk of a derivative is expressed as a percentage of a loan of equivalent nominal amount. The appeal of this approach is that it can be fitted easily into the system which banks use to measure their total credit exposure to a single counterparty.

Banks generally do not mark-to-market their loan books, but they do usually mark-to-market their derivatives contracts. The risk of a derivatives contract changes constantly. A single market value measures the risk at a point but not what it will be in the future. A bank may choose between applying a standard percentage to each transaction from the start, or a hybrid approach, taking a mark-to-market value, plus an add-on to reflect how the risk might increase over the remaining life of the contract. Neither is very precise or satisfactory.

A further complication which is not easily reconciled with the credit equivalent method is the question of whether positive and negative contract values may be netted to give a smaller net exposure. Primarily this is a question of documentation and law. Where there is appropriate contract documentation to allow netting, a system of credit equivalents will tend to overstate the real exposure to a counterparty.

Credit for export (CFX)

Securitized export credit receivables.

Credit rating

See **rating**.

Credit risk

The risk that a counterparty to a financial transaction will fail to perform.

Credit risk insurance

Insurance taken out as protection against default by a counterparty.

Credit Watch

A credit rating agency will announce that it is putting a borrower on Credit Watch when it expects to change the credit rating of the borrower. This change may be up or down and the likely direction is usually signalled.

Creditors' committee

Group which represents creditors in dealings with an administrator or trustee in bankruptcy.

CREST

Paperless settlement system introduced in 1996–97 on the London Stock Exchange. The dematerialization of holdings is intended to facilitate the move to T+3 settlement of all equity transactions.

Cross-currency interest rate swap

A swap which involves two different currencies and two different interest rate bases.

Cross-currency cap

Cap on the difference between floating rates in two different currencies.

Cross-currency settlement risk

Because different currencies settle in different time zones, it is possible to have paid away, say, D-marks, and not to know whether you have received US dollars until much later in the day. This risk is sometimes known as "Herstatt risk," after the bank of that name which defaulted on foreign exchange contracts about midday European time, having received payment in European currencies, but not having paid US dollars against them.

Cross-default clause

Covenant which provides that a default by the borrower on any of its obligations will be equivalent to a default under the agreement which contains the clause. A lender with such a clause has the benefit of all the protective clauses in all the borrower's debt agreements. Borrowers try to limit the scope of such clauses to exclude at the least small amounts and disputed trade debts. Some succeed in limiting it to, not just borrowed money, but to just public securities issued by the subsidiary in question. In this case, the borrowing group could default on all its bank or private placement debt and other group companies could default on their public debt as well, without the clause taking effect.

Crossed market

Market where one bid is higher than another offer.

Cross-hedge

Hedging in something which is not a hedge, but which a trader thinks might be a hedge. The historical correlation between the underlying and the hedge might well break down when you need it most.

Crossing

Purchase and sale of securities by a broker for two clients.

Cross-rate

Exchange rate which does not involve the base or home currency of the dealer. Thus, for a US-dollar-based bank, a French franc/D-mark rate would be a cross-rate.

Cum

Latin word meaning "with," used in contrast to **ex** meaning "without."

Cumulative

Signifies a right to payment which if not satisfied in one period is carried forward into one or more future periods until payment is made. For example, see **cumulative preference share** below.

Cumulative auction market preferred stock (CAMPS)

A floating-rate preferred stock.

Cumulative preference share

A cumulative preference share is entitled to dividends which, if not paid, remain payable, and until such time as they are paid, it is usually the case that no dividend may be paid on any lower-ranking security or equity.

Curb market

(1) Trading after the end of official trading on some commodity markets. The word is said to come from the practice of trading on the pavement outside the exchange building.

(2) *And hence* any unofficial, unregulated market.

Currency future

An exchange-traded contract to buy or sell a standard amount of a foreign currency on a future date. Trading in these and in currency options declined in 1995–96, reflecting changes in the foreign exchange markets where the number of banks and proprietary traders also declined.

Currency-linked bond

A bond where the payments of interest and principal are calculated by reference to one currency although made in another currency.

Currency option

The right, but not the obligation, to buy or sell a currency against another currency at a fixed price during or after a specified period.

Currency option bond

Security where the principal and interest are denominated in one currency, but where the issuer has the option to redeem the security in another currency at maturity, The exchange rate implied by the two possible redemption amounts is fixed at the outset.

Currency overlay

Currency exposures deliberately acquired separately from the acquisition of assets as part of an asset management strategy.

Currency risk

Currency volatility is often higher than the volatility of individual securities. The decision whether or not to assume currency risk is therefore of crucial importance in investment decisions.

For example, the table in Figure C6 compares bond market and currency volatility for seven countries in the period 1990–94. Generally, currency volatility has tended to reduce in recent years.

For corporations, foreign currency risk is often divided into three types: transaction risk related to specific transactions; translation risk relating to the balance sheet; and economic or strategic risk relating to long-term trends and their effect on competitiveness. See **risk**.

Figure C6

```
BOND MARKET AND CURRENCY VOLATILITY 1990–94
```

Country	Volatility of bond yields	Volatility of exchange rates
United States	0.23	1.5
Japan	0.38	2.4
Germany	0.22	0.9
France	0.31	0.7
Italy	0.46	1.9
United Kingdom	0.36	2.0
Canada	0.31	1.1

Volatility is measured as the standard deviation of monthly changes in percent.

(*Source: OECD, Economics Department Working Papers, No 154, 1995*)

Currency swap

A contract which commits two counterparties to exchange interest payments denominated in different currencies and, at the end of the agreed period, the principal amounts. The final exchange is at an exchange rate set at the outset of the swap at or close to the spot rate, not at the forward rate for the final maturity date. This is so, because the interest differential between the two currencies is paid over the life of the swap. See **swap**.

Currency warrant

A negotiable currency option which is often issued in connection with another security.

Current asset ratio

Liquidity measure expressed as current assets divided by current liabilities.

Current coupon

(1) In the case of a fixed-rate security, a coupon close to current yields implying a price close to par.

(2) In the case of a floating-rate security, the rate of interest for the current period.

Current yield

The interest rate of a security expressed as a percentage of the security's market price; also called "flat yield," "income yield," "interest yield," or "running yield." See **yield**.

CUSIP number system

A US alphanumeric system used for the identification of security issues. A nine-digit code is assigned to each issue and is printed on the face of the security. The first six digits identify the issuer in alphabetic sequence, the next two characters (alphabetic or numeric) identify the particular issue, and the ninth digit is a check digit. CUSIP stands for Committee on Uniform Securities Identification Procedures.

Customer repurchase agreement

A sale and repurchase agreement arranged by the US Federal Reserve for foreign central banks.

Cylinder option

The combination of buying one option and writing another option of the opposite type at a different strike price. The general intention is to reduce the cost of insurance against an unfavorable movement in the underlying by giving up some of the possible gain from a favorable movement in the underlying.

D

Daily Official List

The daily publication of the price of all securities listed on the London Stock Exchange.

Daily price limit

The maximum price change permitted by the rules of an exchange for a futures contract. See **circuit breakers**.

Daimyo bond

Yen-denominated securities issued in the Japanese market by supranational agencies. They settle through Cedel and Euroclear, are usually listed in Luxembourg and may be bought by non-residents of Japan.

Daisy chain

In finance, it is used to mean artificial trading between dealers, intended to give the appearance of a rising market and thus draw in investors.

Data Encryption Standard

A US standard, published by the National Institute of Standards and Technology, for the protection of sensitive financial information.

Dawn raid

Phrase used in UK to describe the sudden acquisition of a large block of shares, often as the first step in a takeover bid. So called because often done at the start of trading.

Day count bases

Conventions employed to calculate interest. In each case, the numerator shows the number of days between the dates and the denominator indicates how many days are assumed to be in a year, e.g. 365/360.

Daylight exposure

The risk of counterpart default during the day on which a transaction is to be settled after funds or securities have been delivered, but before the corresponding funds or securities have been received. See **Herstatt risk**.

Daylight overdraft

Intraday exposure which arises in payments systems as a result of timing or structural features of the clearing systems. These are usually limited in some way. The US Federal Reserve, for example, limits the maximum permitted daylight overdraft to certain multiples of capital.

Dealer

(1) A person or firm which acts as a principal in buying and selling securities, derivatives, commodities or foreign exchange in contrast to a broker who acts as an agent for others.

(2) A financial institution dealing in or placing a borrower's debt under a debt issuance program, particularly used in relation to Eurocommercial paper programs.

Dealer loan

Overnight, collateralized loan to a securities dealer.

Dealer spread

The difference between a dealer's bid and asked prices.

Debenture

(1) UK term for a corporate debt security which is usually secured.

(2) In the US, the term signifies an unsecured debt.

Debit cylinder

Cylinder option transaction where the net premium is negative, in contrast to a credit cylinder where the net premium is positive.

Debt convertible

Security which can be converted at the option of the investor into another security with a different interest rate or maturity. "Convertible" without qualification usually means a security convertible into equity.

Debt–equity swap

Method by which the foreign-currency obligations of a highly indebted country may be changed into an equity investment in the country.

Debt leverage

The increase in the profit or loss earned when an investment is made with borrowed money.

Debt ratio

The proportion of a company's long-term debt to its capital. There are many ways of looking at the relationship of a company's liabilities to its capital. Care is needed to avoid confusion between them.

Debt register claim

The evidencing of a debt by entry in a register rather than by creation of a physical security.

Debt rescheduling

Changing the terms of the debt of a troubled borrower. Almost always a process which involves economic loss to the lenders.

Debt service

The obligation to make payments of principal and interest on outstanding debt. For some heavily indebted states, the debt service burden represents substantially all of the country's budget deficit.

Debt warrant

A warrant which entitles the holder to buy a specific security at a fixed price during or at the end of a given period of time.

Declaration date

Exercise or expiry date.

Declining call schedule

The list of prices at which a borrower may call a debt issue for redemption prior to its final maturity date. These prices will begin at a premium to par and decline towards par over the life of the issue.

Dedication

The structuring of a portfolio so that its cash flow matches specific future liabilities. See **immunization**.

Deep discount bond

See **original issue discount (OID) bonds**.

Deep discount stepped interest loan stock

Debt security sold below its par value, with a low initial coupon which increases in stages. The investor's return in the early years is a mixture of the low coupon and amortization of the discount.

Default

Failure to observe the terms of an agreement or the failure to perform under a contract.

Default interest

The interest paid on a overdue debt, typically set at a higher rate than that charged before the default.

Defaulted receivable

A receivable which is written off as uncollectable

Defeasance

The use of a portfolio of riskless (usually government) bonds to provide for the service and repayment of other debt. In legal defeasance, the bond issuer puts the riskless bonds into an irrevocable trust for the benefit of the bondholders. The trust then becomes the primary obligor to the bondholders. The original borrower may then be able to remove the liability from its balance sheet.

Deferred premium option

An option where the premium is paid at expiration

Deferred start option

An option which may be bought and sold before all of its terms are fixed.

Deferred swap

A swap whose terms and conditions are fixed, but which begins at an agreed date in the future.

Deficit financing

The habit of borrowing by governments to pay for high spending or low taxation. The argument that a transfer of resources within an economy, from investors to government, did not necessarily burden future generations of taxpayers may have been of some comfort when governments borrowed at home. Liberalized capital markets have greatly increased the amount borrowed from foreign investors by profligate governments. The repayment of this debt, if it should ever happen, would involve transfers out of national economies which would indeed be a burden on future generations.

Definitive securities

The permanent certificates which replace a temporary bond (temporary global note in the Euromarkets) shortly after a new issue has been made. Definitive securities may be registered or bearer securities, and may be contrasted with book-entry securities.

Delayed capped floating-rate note

A floating-rate note where the rate paid is capped after an initial period for the remainder of the life of the transaction.

Delayed convertible

A convertible security where conversion is permitted only after a specified date.

Delhi Stock Exchange

A major Indian stock exchange with more than 3,000 listed companies. Computerized dealing on the DOTS system began in November 1995. Settlement varies according to whether a share is specified or non-specified. Specified share transactions are settled every two weeks. Trades in non-specified shares settle at the end of each week. See **National Stock Exchange of India.**

Delinquent receivable

A receivable which has not been paid when due, but which is not yet classified as a defaulted receivable.

Deliverable

In derivatives markets, a financial instrument which meets the contract specifications and which may therefore be delivered against it.

Deliver-out repo

A repo where collateral is physically delivered to the supplier of cash. One of various methods for ensuring that collateral exists and is not pledged to anyone else.

Delivery

Settlement of a contract by tender of a financial instrument or cash.

Delivery date

The day, or days, during which delivery against a futures contract can be made.

Delivery factor

With futures contracts which have a number of deliverable securities, the delivery price of each is adjusted by a factor to determine the delivery amount of each security. Also known as the "conversion factor."

Delivery mechanism

The procedure followed to meet futures contract obligations at delivery date.

Delivery month

See **contract month.**

Delivery notice

A seller's notice of intention to make delivery against a short futures position on a specified day.

Delivery points

Locations designated by an exchange at which delivery may be made under the terms of a derivative contract.

Delivery price

The price, set by a clearing house, at which deliveries under a futures contract are invoiced.

Delivery risk

See **settlement risk.**

Delivery versus payment (DVP)

The objective of most settlement systems. Payment mechanisms are so designed that a seller knows that a sold security will not be released until payment is assured and, on the other hand, a buyer knows that his cash will not be paid away until delivery of the bought security is assured.

Delta

The ratio of the movement of the price of an option to the movement in the price of the underlying. This is a key ratio for hedging. See **gamma, kappa** and **theta.**

Delta hedge

A hedge where an option position is offset by a position in the underlying which will neutralize, within a narrow range of price movements, the price change of the option position.

Delta neutral

The result of being delta-hedged, that is not being exposed to a change in the price of the underlying, only to a change in delta or to implied volatility. Dealers often aim to be delta-neutral.

Demand loan

A loan which is repayable at any time.

Dematerialize

Replace physical securities with electronic book-entry systems.

Demerger

The process of dividing a company into smaller parts. For example, a conglomerate with many different businesses might try to demerge a part where a separately quoted share might hope to trade on a higher P/E multiple than the group as a whole. The shareholders would hope that the combined value of their shareholdings after the demerger was greater than before.

Not all demerger announcements are welcomed by the equity markets (e.g., that of the UK company Hanson in 1996). It is also the case that the credit rating agencies may downgrade the debt of the group as a result, thus affecting investors in the group's debt securities.

Denomination

The face value of a security. Securities intended to be sold only to institutional investors will be printed in large denominations, as is compulsory under some jurisdictions. Securities intended for retail distribution will be printed in much smaller denominations, which adds a little to the printing and paying agency costs of the issue.

Depo rate

The rate paid on deposits in the interbank market.

Déport

French word for **backwardation**.

Deposit note

Unsecured obligation of a bank. In the US deposit notes rank below deposits but are backed by federal deposit insurance up to a total of US$100,000 in principal and interest. In the US, deposit notes are issued for maturities of two to five years and are SEC exempt.

Depository Trust Co

A subsidiary of the Chicago Mercantile Exchange, formed under Illinois law, which was expected to become operational in the spring of 1997 as a depository for swap collateral. The DTC was intended to act as custodian, but not to guarantee or clear swap contracts. Similar plans have been formed by the CBOT and, in Luxembourg, by CEDEL.

Depository Trust Corporation (DTC)

US corporation chosen by the Public Securities Association to manage a computer settlement system. It is owned by US brokerage firms and provides a computerized securities settlement system.

Dépôt

French word for "deposit."

Depreciation

(1) Accountancy term for regular reductions in the book value of a fixed asset.

(2) Loss of value of one currency against others.

Depth of market

Phrase relating to the capacity of a market to absorb large transactions without delay or price change.

Deregulation

Relaxation of rules governing markets and financial institutions. The process is competitive as the authorities of different countries try to enhance their attractiveness as places for international institutions to conduct business. Inevitably there is a tension between this international competition and the statutory duty to protect investors, particularly the widows and orphans of legend. Oddly, too, in many countries, the authorities have freed their banks to trade as much as they like in new markets while still being bound to rescue them when they loose catastrophic amounts of money as some inevitably have done and will continue to do. Taxpayers will have to pay for deregulation in the end, unless the new deregulated activities are segregated from the old banking activities of national importance. Indeed, the latter have cost taxpayers in France and Japan quite enough on their own.

Derivative instruments

Derivatives are leveraged contracts over securities, commodities, interest rates or foreign exchange rates. Many variations and combinations are possible. Futures, which are obligations to buy or sell a quantity of the underlying at a date in the future, are traded on margin. Options, which carry the right, but not the obligation, to buy or sell a quantity of the underlying at or before a date in the future, may be bought by the payment of a single premium. Derivatives may be traded over-the-counter on privately negotiated terms, or as is more usual, may be traded on exchanges on standardized terms and conditions. The crucial benefit of the latter is that exchange-traded derivative positions can always be valued and probably closed out. This is not so of private, structured OTC transactions.

What traders in derivatives do is to take views on the future price of the underlying and/or on the volatility of the price of the underlying. Types of option positions they take according to their view of these two variables are illustrated in Figure D1.

Derivative product company

Company set up specifically to deal in derivatives, often a subsidiary of a

Figure D1

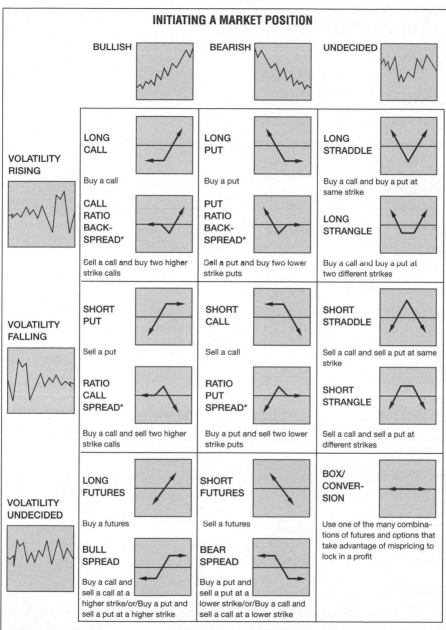

INITIATING A MARKET POSITION

	BULLISH	BEARISH	UNDECIDED
VOLATILITY RISING	**LONG CALL** Buy a call **CALL RATIO BACK-SPREAD*** Sell a call and buy two higher strike calls	**LONG PUT** Buy a put **PUT RATIO BACK-SPREAD*** Sell a put and buy two lower strike puts	**LONG STRADDLE** Buy a call and buy a put at same strike **LONG STRANGLE** Buy a call and buy a put at two different strikes
VOLATILITY FALLING	**SHORT PUT** Sell a put **RATIO CALL SPREAD*** Buy a call and sell two higher strike calls	**SHORT CALL** Sell a call **RATIO PUT SPREAD*** Buy a put and sell two lower strike puts	**SHORT STRADDLE** Sell a call and sell a put at same strike **SHORT STRANGLE** Sell a call and sell a put at different strikes
VOLATILITY UNDECIDED	**LONG FUTURES** Buy a futures **BULL SPREAD** Buy a call and sell a call at a higher strike/or/Buy a put and sell a put at a higher strike	**SHORT FUTURES** Sell a futures **BEAR SPREAD** Buy a put and sell a put at a lower strike/or/Buy a call and sell a call at a lower strike	**BOX/ CONVER-SION** Use one of the many combinations of futures and options that take advantage of mispricing to lock in a profit

* All ratio spreads and ratio backspreads need more analysis. These strategies do not fit neatly into any of the nine market scenarios. Define your market expectation more closely and work out examples with different market scenarios before choosing these strategies. Also, ratio strategies are sometimes done at ratios other than one by two.

Source: CME

bank. Credit enhancement techniques are often employed to improve the credit rating of the subsidiary, sometimes to the extent that it exceeds that of the parent holding company.

Designated-broker scheme

Term used at LIFFE in London. Designated brokers undertake to support and trade a new contract.

Designated primary market-maker (DPMM)

A specialized floor member of the Chicago Board Options Exchange (CBOE).

Detachable warrant

A warrant which is attached to a security, and which may be traded either with the security or independently. Often the market for a warrant will be among different investors from those who might buy the host security. Independent trading is more usual.

Deutsche Börse AG – DTB Deutsche Terminbörse

DTB, which merged with the central stock exchange in 1994, is the German derivatives market and the clearing house counterparty for all trades. Members of the DTB may have a market-making function or not. Clearing members may be general clearing members, direct clearing members or non-clearing members. Trading is by a country-wide electronic network.

The exchange trades futures on a notional Bund, a notional Bobl, three-month DM LIBOR, one month euromarks and the DAX stock index. Options are traded on shares, the DAX stock index, the DAX future, the Bund future and the Bobl future.

Deutschemark

The national currency of Germany, abbreviated to DM, DEM, D-mark.

Deutscher Aktienindex (DAX)

The most referred to German stock index, made up of 30 stocks actively traded on the Frankfurt Stock Exchange.

Devaluation

A fall in the value of one currency when the value of that currency has been fixed against others, e.g., within the EMS.

Development capital

Theoretically, the capital required after an initial start-up phase to finance the expansion of a growing business. The phrase is sometimes used to cover all forms of capital financing for small or growing firms.

Devisen

German word for currency.

Devisenkassamarkt

German word for the cash or spot foreign-exchange market.

Devisenterminmarkt

German word for the forward foreign-exchange market.

Devises

French word for currency.

Diagonal spread

The combination of a purchase of a longer-term option with a sale of a shorter option, with the longer option having a higher strike price.

DIBOR

Dublin interbank offered rate.

Diff swap

See **quanto**.

Digital option

An option where the holder is paid a fixed amount if the underlying reaches or exceeds the exercise or strike price.

Dilution

The reduction in earnings per share and net assets per share following an issue of new shares or options.

Dilution factor

The amount by which the total number of shares outstanding in a company would be diluted in the event of conversion by the holders of warrants, options or convertible securities.

Dingo

Zero-coupon Australian-dollar security, created by stripping an Australian government bond.

Direct bid facility

Feature of a debt issuance program under which tender panel members may make unsolicited bids to the borrower.

Direct placement

Selling securities directly to an end-investor, without the help of a securities firm or other intermediary.

Dirty float

When an exchange rate is allowed to float, subject to intervention by the monetary authorities. Prudent authorities generally try only to smooth the path of a currency, rather than trying to sustain a particular value against the market.

Dirty price

The price of a security which includes accrued interest.

Disagio

The discount on a bond from **par**.

Discontinuity risk

The risk that the price of a particular security, currency or commodity will not trade continuously, but will jump up or down suddenly, an event known as "gapping." This risk is particularly serious for investors who leave stop-loss orders or have other complex strategies, and for traders who delta-hedge their positions. See **risk**.

Discount

The difference between the **par** value and the price of a security, when such price is lower than par.

Discount basis

A method for quoting the annualized return on non-coupon securities.

Discount broker

Brokerage firm which offers a cheap dealing service.

Discount house

Firm which underwrites and trades in UK treasury bills It is authorized by the Bank of England, with whom it has a direct dealing relationship. Becoming less significant with the growth of the gilt repo market.

Discount rate

Rate at which a central bank is prepared to discount bills for financial institutions, so as to regulate the liquidity of the money market. In the US, this is the rate charged by Federal Reserve Banks for loans made through the Federal Reserve's **discount window**.

Discount securities

Money market instruments which do not pay interest, but which are issued at a discount and redeemed at maturity at face value.

Discount swap

Swap in which certain payments are below the market rate with a compensating payment at maturity. Clearly, the internal rate of return will not be at a discount.

Discount window

Facility made available by a central bank to chosen banks which permits them to manage their liquidity at preferential rates.

Discounted cash flow

The present value of a future cash flow, calculated by applying a discount rate to the future flow. See **yield**.

Discretionary account

Money placed with an institution to be managed or placed at the discretion of that institution.

Discretionary orders

An order where the broker has discretion as to when he executes the order. The intention is that the client should get the best price.

Disintermediation

The process by which financial transactions which would have been executed through a bank are concluded without the intermediation of a bank. Depositors who might once have placed money with a bank now buy short-term money market instruments issued by borrowers who would once have borrowed only from a bank. The process is thought to be good for everyone except banks.

Distributable reserves

That part of retained profits and reserves of a company which may be distributed to shareholders in the form of dividends.

Distribution

(1) Payment of a dividend.

(2) The ability of a securities firm to place securities with end-investors. Of all the things investment bankers say, statements about distribution require the greatest skepticism.

Diversification

Holding a range of different securities to reduce risk.

Dividend

That part of a company's earnings which is distributed to shareholders. Dividends ought to be a seen as a sign of failure: effectively the management is saying, "we can't do anything sufficiently profitable with this money." In fact, dividend yield is one of the principal reasons investors, particularly private investors, buy shares.

Dividend arbitrage

An option-trading strategy in which the trader buys a share which is close to paying a dividend, and at the same time buys an **at-the-money** put on the share. If the time value of the put is less than the impending dividend, the trader will make a profit.

Dividend cover

Calculated as earnings per share divided by gross dividend per share. It is a measure of the security of the income of a share.

Documentary credit

The most frequent commercial letter of credit. The exporter will be paid on production of the stipulated documents which give evidence that the goods have been shipped to the buyer.

Documented discount note

Short-term note supported by back-up bank credit facilities and a bank letter of credit guaranteeing that the note will be repaid at maturity.

Dog

Slang word for a spectacularly unsuccessful new issue.

Dollar roll

In the US mortgage-backed market, a simultaneous sale of a security combined with a purchase of the same security at a forward date. The price difference between the sale and repurchase and the interest earned on the cash in the period between them are combined to calculate the return on the operation. See **repo**.

Domestic bond issue

An issue by a borrower which is denominated in their own domestic currency and settled in their own country. This may include government issues which may also be settled through one or more of the international clearing houses as well.

Domestic rates

The interest rates applicable to domestic deposits rates may vary from Euro-rates, owing to taxation and other differences.

Double-dated

A security which, besides having a final date of redemption also has a date or period during which it may be redeemed early. The term is most used of UK government gilts.

Double option

An option to buy or sell, but not to do both.

Double taxation agreement

An agreement between two countries intended to avoid the double taxation of income.

Double taxation relief (DTR)

The relief which prevents a single source of income being taxed twice either under the terms of a double taxation agreement or through action by an investor's own domestic tax authorities.

Double witching hour

The simultaneous expiry of futures and/or options in two related instruments. Considered to make trading in the underlying more volatile.

Dow Jones averages

The Dow Jones averages are compiled from NYSE closing prices. There are four averages.

- The Dow Jones Industrial Average is based on the average price of 30 industrial stocks. It is the most widely referred to of the Dow Jones averages.
- The Transportation Average is made up of 20 transportation stocks.
- The Utility Average is made up of 15 utility stocks.
- The Composite Average is made up of the 65 stocks in the Industrial, Transportation and Utility Averages.

Down-and-in call

Option contract where the option becomes a standard call if the underlying falls to a predetermined (the **instrike**) price.

Down-and-out call

A **call option** which expires if the underlying falls to a predetermined (the **outstrike**) price.

Downgrade

The lowering of credit rating.

Drawdown

The act of borrowing of money under the terms of a facility.

Drawdown period

The period of time during which a credit facility is available to be drawn on, a shorter period than the life of the facility. A revolving facility would have a drawdown period co-terminous with the life of the facility.

Drawing

A random process by which a certain number of bonds are chosen for early redemption under the terms of an issue.

Drop-lock floating-rate note

FRN which automatically converts into a fixed-rate bond if short term interest rates fall below a trigger rate.

Dropout option

Type of **barrier option** which expires early if the price of the underlying reaches a specified level (the dropout level).

Dual capacity

Term used in connection with the London Stock Exchange referring to the ability to act as both agent and principal.

Dual-currency option

An option which confers the right to buy or sell one of two currencies against another currency at one of two pre-selected strike prices.

Due date

The date on which a payment is due and payable.

Duration **D**

Due diligence

(1) The obligation on a securities firm contemplating a new issue of securities to explain the new issue to prospective investors.

(2) In mergers and acquisitions, the process of reviewing the condition of a company in detail.

Due from balance

US term for "nostro account."

Due to balance

US term for "vostro account."

Dun & Bradstreet

US company which supplies corporate credit rating and analysis services and financial information and which owns Moody's Investor Services.

Duration

Duration is calculated as the average time to maturity of the cash flows of a security, the time to maturity being weighted by the present value of each cashflow. For all except zero-coupon securities, duration is less than the nominal maturity. Duration changes with substantial changes in yield.

For a bond with a fixed coupon g, payable h times per annum, with a normal first coupon payment, which is redeemable on one coupon date, duration (D) can be calculated as

$$f1/h + (g \times v^{f1})/(P \times h^2) \times \{v + 2v^2 + (n-1)v^{(n-1)}\} + C/(P \times h) \times (n-1)v^{(n+f1-1)}$$

where

g = annual coupon rate %
h = number of coupon payments per year
n = number of coupon payments to redemption
P = gross price of bond (including accrued interest)
C = redemption price
$f1$ = fraction of period from value date to first coupon date
v = discounting factor: for example, if the yield compounded h times per annum is y, then $v = 1/(1+y/h)$

The formula set out above can be modified, so as to calculate the duration of a perpetual security. The formula reduces to:

$$D = f1/h + 1/y$$

where the terms are as given above.

Duration was first expressed by Frederick Macaulay in 1938, and is sometimes called "Macaulay Duration" to distinguish it from "Modified Duration." Modified Duration is expressed as: Macaulay Duration divided by the periodic yield, and provides a measure of percentage price volatility. The larger the modified duration, the greater the price volatility for a specified yield change.

The formula for modified duration (*MD*) is

$$MD = dP/dy \times 1/P$$

where

P = gross price of bond (including accrued interest)
dP = small change in price
dy = small change in yield compounded with the frequency of the coupon payment

The relationship between duration (*D*) and modified duration (*MD*) can be expressed as:

$$MD = D \times v$$

where

v = discounting factor. For example, if the yield compounded h times per annum is y, then $v = 1/(1+y/h)$
h = number of coupon payments per year

Of the two forms of duration, the former tends to be used for immunization, the latter for measuring volatility.

Düsseldorf Stock Exchange

Founded in 1935 on the merger of the Cologne, Düsseldorf and Essen exchanges. Now a part of the *Deutsche Börse AG*.

E

EAC

East Africa Co-operation, agency formed in 1996 by Kenya, Uganda and Tanzania to promote free trade and regional cooperation. Based in Arusha, Tanzania.

EADB

East African Development Bank, founded in 1967 to encourage development in Kenya, Uganda and Tanzania. Based in Kampala, Uganda.

Early exercise

Exercise of an option (American or Bermudan) before its expiry date.

Earnings before interest and taxation (EBIT)

Popular measure of earnings defined as operating income, plus any other recurring income, plus consistent equity income received in cash less any non-recurring expenses.

Earnings per share (EPS)

The net income of a company attributable to each ordinary or common share after the payment of taxes and any preferred share dividends.

EASDAQ

A screen-based European stock market which began operations on 30 September 1996 backed by a private group of about 80 European and US bankers, brokers and venture capitalists. It is modelled on the **NASDAQ** market in the US and aims to attract rapidly growing technology companies. The first two private companies to be floated on EASDAQ were a software company and a biotechnology company.

EBS

(1) See *Elektronische Börse Schweiz*.

(2) EBS Partnership is an electronic order-driven currency broking system founded by a group of banks to compete with the Reuters 2000 system. In 1996, EBS had 14 members. It is now thought to have between 30 percent and 40 percent of total spot broking activity in London and Asia.

(3) The Educational Building Society, an Irish financial institution.

Écart

French word for spread. Also used in Switzerland to mean the difference in price between a bearer share and a registered share in the same company.

Echéance

French word for maturity.

Econometrics

The use of statistical and mathematical methods to develop economic theories.

Economic exposure

See **currency risk**.

Economic risk

The risk a company faces that changes in exchange rates or local regulations might hamper the company and favor a competitor. See **risk**.

ECU

European Currency Unit. Figure E1 shows the composition of the ECU, fixed by Council Regulation No. 3320/94 of the European Union on 22 December 1994.

Figure E1

COMPOSITION OF THE ECU AT 22 DECEMBER 1994			
0.6242	D-mark	0.130	Luxembourg franc
0.08784	Pound sterling	0.1976	Danish krone
1.332	French francs	0.008552	Irish pound
151.8	Italian lire	1.440	Greek drachmas
0.2198	Dutch guilder	6.885	Spanish pesetas
3.301	Belgian francs	1.393	Portugese escudos

ECU Banking Association (EBA)

An association of banks which runs an ECU payments netting system and which plans to offer a Euro payment system which may partly compete with **TARGET**.

Edge Act corporation

Bank or non-bank corporations in the US, formed for the purpose of financing international transactions, owned by nationally or state-chartered banks, which are allowed to have interstate branches, to invest in foreign companies and to accept deposits outside the US.

Effective date

The date on which a contract takes effect, in contrast to the date on which a contract is agreed, the trade date.

Effective exchange rate

Usually measured against a trade-weighted basket of the currencies expressed as an index. It is an indicator of a country's international competitiveness.

Effekten

German word for security.

Efficient market hypothesis

Theory developed by Fama and others, which states that the prices in financial markets reflect all publicly available information. One of the consequences is that, provided the conditions of an efficient market are met, individual investors will not achieve returns above the market average in the long run.

El Salvador Stock Exchange

Mercado de Valores de El Salvador, SA de CV began trading in 1992. The exchange trades shares, debt securities and foreign exchange. Seven companies have shares listed, and 20 companies have debt instruments listed. The exchange trades both on the floor and electronically. A central depository was expected to begin operations during 1996.

Electricity forward agreement (EFA)

Forward pricing agreement for electricity.

Electricity futures

Contract planned to be traded on the New York Mercantile Exchange. The contract unit is 736 megawatt hours (MWh) delivered over a monthly period. The delivery rate is 2 MW throughout every hour of the delivery period. The delivery period is 16 on-peak hours from 0600 to 2200 prevailing time. Trading in the delivery month ceases on the third business day prior to the first day of the delivery month. Prices are quoted in dollars and cents per MWh with a minimum price fluctuation of $0.01 per MWh. The maximum permitted price is $3.00 per MWh above or below the preceding day's settlement price. Buyer and seller must follow Western Systems Coordinating Council scheduling practices.

Elektronische Börse Schweiz

Swiss computerised dealing and settlement system which has brought together the three Swiss stock exchanges (Basel, Geneva and Zurich) and **Soffex**, the derivatives exchange. The improved price transparency achieved by EBS is not without limits. Trades of more than Sfr200,000 may be executed outside the market and reported afterwards.

Eligible bankers' acceptance

Acceptance eligible as collateral for loans at the US Federal Reserve discount window. To be so, it must arise from a commercial transaction, have a maturity not greater than 90 days, and have a member bank endorsement on its face.

Eligible bill

UK term for a bank bill accepted by an eligible bank. As such, it is eligible for purchase by the Bank of England in its money market operations.

Embedded option

An option which is part of another security and which cannot be separated from it.

Emerging Market Traders' Association (ETMA)

Association of traders, dealers and brokers in LDC debt. Not a regulatory body.

Emerging markets

Those countries where the development of securities markets has brought them to the borders of the investable universe, as seen from the large financial centres. In many cases, the high growth rate of the economy must be balanced against imperfections in information flows, legal systems or market structures. Returns from investment in emerging markets can vary widely. At the end of September 1996 single-country sub-indices in the ING Baring Securities Emerging Markets Index (expressed in US$ terms and based at 100 on 7 January 1992) included Peru at 1174.69 and China at 44.25.

What constitutes an emerging market is not easily determined. The ING Baring Securities Emerging Markets Index include the countries shown in Figure E2.

Emerging Markets Clearing Corporation

A clearing house formed as a result of an agreement between the Emerging Market Traders Association and the International Securities Clearing Corporation in 1996, the EMCC was expected to begin with **Brady bonds** and subsequently to include Euro- and domestic securities. The EMCC was expected to reduce settlement risk for traders in emerging market securities.

Figure E2

THE ING BARING SECURITIES EMERGING MARKETS INDEX	
	Number of stocks
Latin America	124
Argentina	22
Brazil	24
Chile	18
Colombia	13
Mexico	27
Peru	13
Venezuela	7
Europe	131
Czech Republic	13
Greece	19
Poland	25
Portugal	18
South Africa	30
Turkey	26
Asia	194
China	27
Indonesia	27
Korea	25
Malaysia	23
Pakistan	13
Philippines	20
Taiwan	31
Thailand	28
World	**449**
Source: ING Baring Securities	

Emission

French word for issue.

Employee Retirement Income Security Act (ERISA)

US law enacted in 1974 which set investment and conduct guidelines for pension and profit sharing plans and which established the Pension Benefits Guarantee Corporation.

Employee Stock Ownership Plan (ESOP)

US mechanism whereby employees buy shares in their company. These purchases may be through a leveraged ESOP (i.e., with borrowed money) which has certain tax advantages for the company.

113

Emprunt

French word for borrowing or loan.

Emprunt d'Etat

French government debt issue.

EMU

Under the Maastricht Treaty members of the European Union are planning to introduce a single European currency by 1999. This step requires that the economies of the different countries should converge. Convergence must be achieved in government deficits, national debts, inflation and interest rates. While there are considerable differences in deficits and unemployment, it seems that there is a political will prepared to ignore these difficulties.

The powerful arguments against monetary union tend to focus on two points. The first is the anti-democratic movement of considerable economic power to a European Central Bank. The second is the structural differences which exist between the different economies. Monetary union may force painful social upheavals on member countries.

On balance, it would seem that German love of order combined with French love of rational systems may triumph temporarily over economic reality. In the long term, EMU may damage the single market rather than be its completion. In the circumstances, it may seem odd that Poland, Hungary, Slovakia and the Czech Republic, having so recently emerged from the shadow of one totalitarian system, are so anxious to join another political system which is itself increasingly totalitarian.

Endfälligkeit

German word for maturity.

End-user

A participant in a financial transaction who is not an intermediary.

English auction

See auction.

Enhanced Structural Adjustment Facility (ESAF)

International Monetary Fund (IMF) loan facility to support long-term economic reform programs in less-developed countries (LDCs).

Enterprise value

The sum of a company's market capitalization and borrowings, enterprise value is a measure of the worth of a business irrespective of its capital structure. Enterprise value is not independent of capital structure. Increasing a company's debt does not have a simple linear effect on the company's market capitalization.

Entidad gestora

Spanish phrase for a registered dealer.

Entrepôt

In international trade, term for a place to which goods are sent for onward shipment.

EPFR

Etablissement Public de Financement et de Restructuration, the French entity formed by the Government in 1995 to administer the financial support provided by the State for the troubled Crédit Lyonnais banking group.

Equipment Trust Certificate (ETC)

Form of security issued in the US by transportation companies to finance new equipment. Title to the equipment is held by a trustee until the related financing has been repaid.

Equity

(1) A share in the ownership of an enterprise, generally with the right to participate in dividends, and to vote on important decisions affecting shareholders' interests. Referred to as "common stock" in the US and as an "ordinary share" in the UK.

(2) The value of the shareholders' interest in a company after all claims have been paid.

(3) Value of real property after deduction of any debt outstanding.

(4) Fairness in legal arguments in contrast to strict interpretation of statute.

Equity commitment note

A US term for an issue of capital notes for a bank where the bank is required to redeem the notes from the proceeds of a new issue of common stock. Typically such notes have a life of 12 years, and must be repaid in three equal parts after four, eight and twelve years. These notes count as debt, in that the interest paid on them is a tax-deductible expense for the issuer, but also count as capital for certain capital ration calculations.

Equity contract note

A US term for an issue of capital notes for a bank, which are convertible into common stock at a fixed price on a date in the future. If this conversion is mandatory, the notes qualify as **Tier 2** capital.

Equity convertible

Security which may be converted into the ordinary shares of the issuing entity.

Equity index-linked note

Interest-bearing note where the return to the investor is partly or entirely dependent on the performance of a particular equity index.

Equity kicker

Opportunity for a lender to share in the profits accruing to the owners of a particular company or project. Most often seen in real-estate loans. Twenty years ago, many banks had credit policies which prohibited such features, which were thought likely to cloud the judgement of the lending banker.

Equity swap

A swap where one of the legs is defined by reference to the return on an equity position.

Equity warrant

A warrant giving the right to buy an equity.

Equity-linked foreign exchange option

A quantity-adjusting option used to hedge the foreign-exchange element of an equity position.

Equity-linked notes (ELN)

Notes where the return to the investor depends on the performance of a specified equity, basket or index.

Equivalent bond yield

For a discounted security, it is defined as the **coupon** of a bond trading at **par**, which would give the same return assuming a re-investment rate equal to the coupon rate. Also called the "coupon equivalent yield."

Equivalent life

An expression of the life of an amortizing security or of a portfolio, defined as the weighted average maturity, using as weights the present values of the **redemption** payments.

Equivalent taxable yield

A US term for the yield on a taxable security which is equivalent to the after-tax return earned on a tax-exempt security.

Escompte

French word for discount.

Escrow account

Account subject to an escrow agreement, which provides for a bank or trust company to hold funds for a specific purpose on behalf of the parties to a contract.

Escudo

The national currency of Portugal.

Estimated total return (ETR)

The expected return on a security which is calculated using a re-investment rate other than the internal rate of return.

Euclid 90

Euroclear's data transfer system.

Euro

The proposed single European currency (see **EMU**). The timetable for the introduction of the Euro is shown in Figure E3.

Eurobond

Publicly issued, listed debt security in bearer form outside the home market of the currency of denomination. Issuers are sovereign and supranational entities, large corporations and banks. Eurobond documentation usually includes selling restrictions in the country of the currency and the US.

Eurobond warrant

A warrant entitling the holder to buy a **Eurobond** on set terms, on or before a fixed date. Often issued with a callable bond where the borrower plans to call the first bond as the second bond is brought into being, by exercise of the warrants. The Kingdom of Denmark once brought a transaction where the second bond was also callable. Clearly a warrant into a bond which is callable is not worth very much, as the market quickly decided.

Euro-certificate of deposit (Euro-CD)

A certificate of deposit issued in Euro-currencies, rather than in domestic currencies. Many Euro-CDs are issued in London.

117

Figure E3 PLANNED TIMETABLE FOR THE INTRODUCTION OF THE EURO

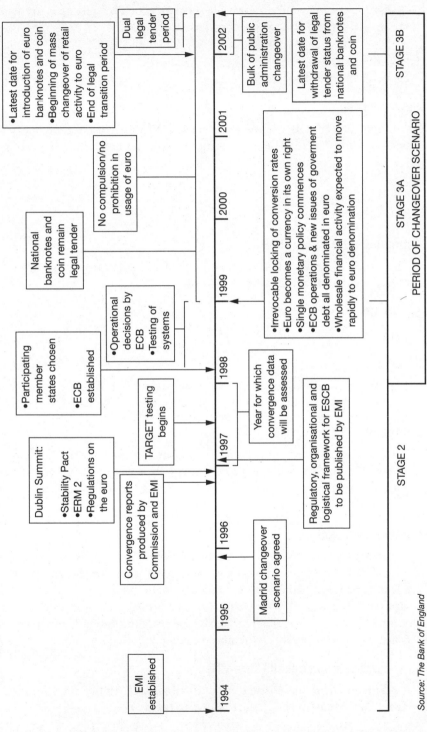

Source: The Bank of England

118

Euroclear

Clearing facility used to settle international securities transactions. Many domestic settlement systems have links to Euroclear and to its rival CEDEL.

Eurocommercial paper (ECP)

International issue of commercial paper in Eurocurrencies.

Eurocurrency

Any currency held and traded outside the country of that currency's origin.

Eurocurrency deposit

Bank deposit held outside the country of the currency in which the deposit is denominated, for example, a US dollar deposit in London.

Eurodollars

US dollars outside the US. In the years after 1945, an increasing amount of US dollars came to be held by non-Americans. At the same time, the US Federal Reserve's regulation of domestic deposit interest rates allowed banks outside the US to pay higher rates for deposits. Thus, there grew up a dollar deposit market in Europe.

Eurofima

European company jointly owned by national railway companies for the financing of railroad rolling stock. A frequent issuer of Eurosecurities.

Euromarket

A general term for the international capital markets.

Euronote

A short-term negotiable bearer note, usually issued at a discount.

Euronote facility

A facility to issue short-term discount notes, often with an undertaking by a group of banks to buy any notes which are not placed with investors.

Euro-rates

Interest rates quoted for Euro-currencies. These may differ from domestic rates for reasons to do with tax or reserve requirements.

Euro-treasury warrant

A warrant issued in the Euromarkets which carries the right to buy a US treasury bond.

Euro-equity placement

The techniques associated with the international distribution of new issues of shares. These began as a variation on the Eurobond syndicate structure, and allowed international securities firms with little or no track record in the placement of domestic equity in a country to tell a convincing story to would-be sellers and issuers. Certain early privatizations were partly distributed in this way in the mid-1980s. Gradually the story has become more sophisticated as the volume of cross-border equity investment has grown. Book-building is now a feature of international placement of equity and equity-linked securities. Syndicate members are asked to identify long-term holders of the equity, and are allocated securities in proportion to the demand they find. Not all securities firms realize how international the business has become. Syndicate officials remember with amusement the successful convertible issue for a Far Eastern borrower in 1996, where a leading oriental securities house asked for a large part of the issue, saying that it had an order from a named investment management firm in Hong Kong. It was only a matter of minutes before the American lead-manager established that the order was fictitious.

Euro-medium-term note (EMTN)

A wide range of securities may be described as EMTNs. They are as diverse as the ingenuity of bankers and the demands of investors can make them. Maturities may run from 30 days to 30 years. Numerous currencies and interest rate bases are available. EMTNs are issued under a program. The Prospectus will describe the borrower, announce a maximum total amount for the program and will otherwise be written to allow as much flexibility as possible. Each tranche of securities issued under it will be the subject of a pricing supplement giving details of the terms of the issue. A typical EMTN program would include the information shown in Figure E3.

Comparison with Eurobonds

EMTNs resemble bonds in that they are typically unsecured, fixed-rate, non-callable debt securities. They differ chiefly in having a different primary distribution process. An agent under a note program sells securities on a "best efforts" basis. The agent does not usually underwrite the issue, and a borrower is not therefore guaranteed funds.

A second difference is that EMTNs are often offered continuously, or at least at regular intervals, and in smaller amounts than traditional bond issues which are usually large, discrete transactions.

Neither the similarities nor the differences described above always apply. The flexibility of a program has been exploited to issue structured notes with interest or principal repayment linked to various reference rates, exchange rates or indices. Underwritten notes are sometimes issued in large transactions which are Eurobonds in all but name, being issued under a note pro-

Figure E4

TYPICAL EMTN PROGRAM	
Program amount	Can be set in any currency but with the provisions that issues can be up to its equivalent in any currency and that the amount may be increased or decreased.
Ratings	Usually the program will provide for all the debt issued under it to rank equally as to seniority, and therefore the program is rated and not each tranche.
Form	May be registered or bearer or both. Clauses dealing with US restrictions (e.g., 144a) are also often included.
Settlement	Through Euroclear and CEDEL.
Fungibility	Allowance is usually made for issuance of further tranches of the same security. Further issues will be fungible most quickly if they carry a full first coupon and are sold at a price plus accrued interest.
Issue price	Issues may be at a discount, at par or at a premium, with or without accrued interest.
Redemption	May be at par or at a price determined by a formula in the case of structured notes.
Interest rate	May be interest-bearing (fixed, floating or structured formula) or zero-coupon.
Denomination	Any, though printing many small denominations may add to marginal costs.
Early redemption	According to the specific provisions of the pricing supplement for that tranche.
Listing	May be listed (typically London or Luxembourg) or unlisted.

gram to simplify documentation. Increasingly, too, borrowers sell tranches of notes to intermediaries acting as principals for their own account, who subsequently resell the notes to investors.

Contrast with domestic US MTNs

The first EMTN program was set up in 1986, but growth was not very fast until the 1990s. Until 1988, EMTNs were denominated in US dollars. The Kingdom of Spain launched a multicurrency EMTN program in that year. Since then, the EMTN market has been active in many currencies.

121

In contrast to the US domestic market, EMTNs are not subject to national regulations such as registration requirements. EMTN programs have tended to have higher credit ratings than domestic US MTN programs. Another difference is that EMTN issuance has not involved long maturities (over 10 years) to the same extent as in the US market.

A difficulty as to classification remains in that it is sometimes difficult to distinguish a EMTN from a domestic MTN issued in, say, a European country.

Advantages

The theory is that issuing EMTNs allows an issuer to price more exactly and thus reduce its cost of funds. A public bond issue must be priced at such a rate as will sell the last bond to the marginal buyer. Smaller amounts of debt should be sold at lesser yields. The volume of EMTN issuance suggests that the illiquidity premium which might be required by investors in EMTNs is not large or an effective deterrent to issuers.

A second advantage of such programs is that they reduce the costs associated with issuing bonds by establishing one set of documents to cover many issues. This cost saving may be particularly significant if the issuer borrows regular small amounts.

A program may be so set up as to constitute a Global Program, combining a 415 shelf registration in the US with the possibility of issuing notes internationally in any currency.

A fourth advantage is the ability to sell relatively small amounts of debt at short notice to meet some particular requirement of investors. This flexibility has been used to create collateralized, asset-backed, subordinated or amortizing notes as well as notes of longer maturities than are common in the bond markets.

The dealers appointed for each program fulfill a two-way function: on the one hand, they bid for notes when required by the issuer, on the other, they may approach an issuer with suggestions based on known investor needs. Most programs provide that any securities firm may make a "reverse inquiry" to a borrower, and buy notes issued under the facility, if the proposal meets the issuer's requirements.

Issuance tends to follow fashions, so that, for instance, demand for complicated coupon or redemption formulae might be replaced by demand for Yen-denominated notes. A bullish period where fixed-rate notes were popular, might be followed by a bearish phase, when only floating-rate notes are in demand.

The type of EMTN issued is generally determined by investor demand. The issuer will simultaneously neutralize any option embedded in an issue, and will swap the liability thus created into the rate and currency bases required by its funding targets.

Structured transactions have been a feature of the EMTN market. These are notes with embedded option features generally issued to meet investor appetite for a particular exposure not otherwise easily obtained. The growth and collapse of this fashion repeatedly have taught investors the difference between credit quality and asset quality. Broadly, there are two sorts of variation: structures which vary the **coupon** and structures which vary the **redemption** amount. Securities incorporating the latter see the largest fluctuations in price, and may become valueless even though issued by a prime credit. The former sort will usually have a minimum value as a zero-coupon instrument if the coupon formula becomes worthless.

European Bank for Reconstruction and Development (EBRD)

The EBRD was formed to make loans to, and equity investments in, the countries of Central and Eastern Europe. It also provides merchant and development banking services to both private sector and state-owned enterprises.

European Currency Unit (ECU)

See ECU.

European depository receipt (EDR)

Depository receipt issued and traded in Europe.

European exercise

See European option.

European Federation of Financial Analyst Societies (EFFAS)

A body formed from national societies of investment analysts.

European Free Trade Association (EFTA)

Formed in 1960 by Austria, Finland, Iceland, Liechtenstein, Norway, Sweden and Switzerland as a duty-free zone.

European Investment Bank (EIB)

Institution formed by the European Union to provide long-term financing for regional development. The EIB is based in Luxembourg. It is an active borrower in the Euromarkets.

European Monetary Institute (EMI)

The intended forerunner of the European Central Bank, located in Frankfurt.

European Monetary System (EMS)

Mechanism established in 1979 in the hope of achieving stability of exchange rates in the European Union. It combines all the disadvantages of monetary union with none of the advantages.

European Monetary Union

See **EMU**.

European option

An option which may only be exercised on the expiry date. See **American option** and **Bermuda option**.

European Options Exchange

The EOE-Optiebeurs was established in Amsterdam in 1978. Options are traded on stocks, currencies, bonds, precious metals and share indices. Futures and options are traded on the Amsterdam EOE-index, the Dutch Top 5 Index, and the Eurotop 100 Index.

European Regional Development Fund (ERDF)

European Union fund which gives grants to member states for infrastructure projects.

Eurosecurity

Security issued in the international markets.

Eurotop 100 Index

A weighted index based on the shares of 100 leading European companies from the UK, Germany, France, Switzerland, Italy, the Netherlands, Spain, Sweden and Belgium. Country base weights are based on the country's market capitalization. The selection and weighting of stocks from a particular country are determined on the basis of share turnover over the last three calendar years. The index is reviewed annually.

The index is calculated by the EOE-Optieburs, the European Options Exchange, in Amsterdam where options on it are traded. These options are European style and cash-settled.

The Eurotop 100 Index is calculated continuously on the basis of the most recent transaction prices. The value of the shares is expressed in ECU. The settlement value is calculated on the last day of trading as the average of values calculated for the index at five-minute intervals between 12.30 and 13.00 Central European time.

US-dollar-denominated contracts on the Eurotop 100 Index are listed in New York, futures and options on COMEX, and options on AMEX. These contracts are currency-neutral, and are not directly fungible with the ECU-denominated contracts listed in Amsterdam.

Eurotrack 100 Index

Index developed by the London Stock Exchange and the *Financial Times* of 100 European shares. The shares of UK companies are excluded. Prices are derived from SEAQ International and are quoted in D-marks.

Eurotrack 200 Index

Index made up of the shares in the Eurotrack 100 Index and the FT-SE 100 Index. The index is quoted in *ECU*.

Euroyen

Yen held outside Japan.

Event of default

An event which gives one party to an agreement the right to accelerate or cancel the contract. Typically, an agreement governing a borrowing transaction will include events of default. These may cover such things as the discovery of factual inaccuracies in the warranties given by the borrower, the failure to observe conditions or financial ratios stipulated in the agreement, or the commission of certain acts which are prohibited in the agreement. Often an agreement will not be terminated, if an event of default is remedied within a specified period of days. See **covenants** and **cross-default**.

Event risk

The risk of an investor suffering a loss due to unforeseen events such as a merger, or takeover. This risk is distinct from credit risk, market risk or political risk. See **risk**.

Evergreen loan

A loan with a rolling period of time to maturity. For example, a company might have an overdraft facility where the lender would be required to give at least 12 months' notice of its cancellation. Such debt would not count as short-term debt in the company's balance sheet.

Ex

Without, the opposite of **cum** (with).

Exchange

A marketplace, either physical or electronic, where securities, derivatives or commodities may be traded. The evolution of exchanges from comfortable clubs protected by regulation into providers of settlement services in a competitive world has not been easy. Many exchanges are engaged in competitive deregulation as to their listing and membership requirements, while trying to improve the quality of their markets and settlement procedures.

The failure of the London Stock Exchange's Taurus system, and the uncertain performance of its successor CREST, bear witness to the trauma modern conditions inflict on venerable institutions.

Exchange control

The imposition of limits on flows of currency in and out of a country. The usual intention is to limit flows of cash out of a country and/or to limit the flow of goods into a country. The abolition of exchange controls removes one of the traditional controls a government may exercise on its own economy and financial markets. With free capital movements, a government can no longer control long-term interest rates, but must try to use short-term rates to smooth-out the currency movements over which also it has little control.

Exchange delivery settlement price (EDSP)

The price for physical delivery of the underlying or for cash settlement of an expiring contract set by a derivatives exchange.

Exchange for physical (EFP)

The exchange of futures for the underlying (or cash). If a would-be buyer and a would-be seller of the underlying have both hedged themselves with futures, the most efficient unwinding of their hedges is for them to exchange futures positions. Thus, a would-be buyer who is long futures will transfer his position to the would-be seller who is short futures. Such transactions are agreed between the parties, but must usually be reported to the exchange.

Exchange option

Option entitling the holder to exchange one asset for another.

Exchange rate

The price of a currency expressed in terms of another currency. Typically a foreign exchange rate is quoted as two rates (bid and offer) for value "spot," that is, for value $T+2$. Generally, but not always, a rate is expressed in terms of the lower unit value, e.g., the ¥/US$ rate might be 110.235 which is the number of yen per dollar. Usually it is the case against the US dollar that the rate is the quantity of the foreign currency which is worth one US dollar. The exceptions are the rates against sterling, the Irish punt and ECU which are quoted in terms of US dollars per unit. Many currencies are quoted to four decimal places, the exceptions being those currencies with a low unit value such as the Japanese yen, the South Korean won, the Italian lira, the Greek drachma, the Portugese escudo and the Spanish peseta.

Care is needed when two currencies are near parity. The £/IR£ rate might be quoted as 0.9750, which is the number of Irish punts per pound sterling.

Forward exchange rates are not predictions of future rates but are dependent on interest rate differentials. In other words, a forward rate is the rate which prevents profitable arbitrage by simultaneously borrowing in a low-coupon currency, selling the proceeds spot for a high-coupon currency, lending in that high-coupon currency and covering the exchange exposure with a forward FX contract.

Forward rates are quoted in points added to or subtracted from each side of the spot rate. This is because the forward rate points change with changes in the interest differential but change very little for a change in the spot rate. Since the latter is more volatile, it is easier to quote points relative to spot rather than an absolute forward rate. When you are quoted forward points, and you are uncertain whether to add or subtract the points, remember that the bid/offer spread will be wider for the forward price. So, for example, if adding the points narrows the spread, then you are wrong and should be subtracting the forward points from either side of the spot price.

Exchange rate agreement

Contract where payment is made according to the difference between two FX rates.

Exchange traded contract

Option or future traded on an exchange on standardized terms. The trade-off is between liquidity and flexible terms. By gathering together potential interest into certain strike prices or maturity dates, an exchange increases the liquidity of the contracts traded. OTC contracts lack this liquidity and the transparent price setting mechanism which it represents. OTC contracts, however, have almost infinite flexibility. In response to this, some exchanges have introduced flexible products where, provided there is a minimum level of interest, they undertake to list new contracts in a relatively quick procedure.

Exchangeable debt

Debt which gives the holder the right to exchange his securities for others, perhaps issued by an entirely different borrower.

Exchangeable money market preferred stock (EMMPS)

Money market preferred stock which is exchangeable at the option of the holder for some other type of security.

Exchangeable preference share

Preference share which is exchangeable at the option of the holder for some other, usually subordinated, type of security.

Excise tax

A tax or duty which is levied on the volume rather than the value of certain goods.

Ex-date

The first date on which a share is traded without the entitlement to the next dividend. The price at which a share trades on this day is likely to be lower than on the previous trading day by an amount roughly equal to the dividend.

Execute

To carry out a transaction.

Execution risk

Risk that a transaction will not be executed as expected. For example, in a fast-moving market, it may not be possible to execute a trade at a particular price because the price is gapping up or down or because trading has been suspended altogether.

Exempt security

Instrument exempt from the registration requirements of the Securities Act of 1933, or the margin requirements of the Securities and Exchange Act of 1934. Exempt securities include those issued by governments, certain agencies, municipal securities, **commercial paper**, and private placements.

Exercise

In the case of an **option,** the process whereby the holder of an option decides to exercise his right to buy (call) or sell (put) the **underlying**.

Exercise price

The price at which an **option** may be exercised, i.e., the price which the holder of an option will pay or receive in exchange for delivery of the **underlying**. It is not the same as the premium which is paid to buy an option.

Exit bond

Term used in sovereign debt rescheduling to describe a long-term bond issued as part of a rescheduling, with a coupon set well below market levels, which confers on the holder the right of exemption from participation in any further reschedulings. Exit bonds give a way-out to banks wanting to cease sovereign lending.

Exotic

Once a term used in a favorable sense to describe any transaction, particularly in options, with unusual features. Now probably pejorative.

Expectations theory

The belief that long-term interest rates reflect the markets consensus on the future level of short-term interest rates. Has its basis in the mathematical process of calculating implied forward interest rates which, in summary, is as follows:

The formula for the present value of a future payment is:

$$PV = FV/(1+i)^n$$

where:

FV is the future cash sum,
i is the periodic interest rate, and
n is the number of periods

The present value of a series of cash flows (CF_1, CF_2, CF_3, etc) each discounted at its own appropriate rate (i_1, i_2, i_3, etc) over a number of years (t_1, t_2, t_3, etc) can therefore be expressed as

$$PV = \frac{CF_1}{(1+i_1)^{t_1}} + \frac{CF_2}{(1+i_2)^{t_2}} + \frac{CF_3}{(1+i_3)^{t_3}} + \frac{CF_4}{(1+i_4)^{t_4}} + \frac{CF_n}{(1+i_n)^{t_n}}$$

Once we have calculated a pair of zero-coupon rates, say for the dates t_1 and t_2, we can also calculate the forward rate which would be offered now for a deposit starting on the first date (t_1) and ending on the second (t_2). To prevent **arbitrage**, this must be the forward rate ($_1f_2$) which satisfies the following equation:

$$(1+i_1) \times (1+\,_1f_2) = (1+i_2)^2$$

The significance of this rate is that this is the extra return available for extending an investment horizon from (t_1) to (t_2) but also it can be thought of as the rate which the market expects to be the market rate at the future date t_1.

Expected maturity

In the case of certain asset-backed securities, their maturity is not known, but depends on the rate at which the underlying financial assets are repaid. Thus the maturity date has to be projected on the basis of assumptions about interest rates and other factors. The maturity thus estimated is called the "expected maturity."

Expiry date

The last business day on which an option may be exercised.

129

Exploding option

A form of **barrier option** which is extinguished if the **underlying** breaches the trigger price.

Export Credit Guarantee Department (ECGD)

UK government agency which provides insurance for exporters.

Export Development Corporation

Canadian government agency which promotes foreign trade. Has also been an active borrower in the Euromarkets.

Ex-redemption

Where a bond issue is subject to redemption by a sinking fund, bonds traded after the drawing date but before the redemption date, which are not to be redeemed on the next drawing date are said to be "Ex redemption."

Ex-rights

A share trading without the entitlement to subscribe for a rights issue, that is an issue of new shares to existing shareholders.

Example

Suppose a company has a "one-for-five" rights issue. The share price before the rights issue is £1.00 and the new share price is set at £0.88. The ex-rights price is calculated as:

the pre-rights price of five shares	£5.00
plus the price of one new share	£0.88
six shares after the rights issue will be worth	£5.88
so the ex-rights price will be £5.88 ÷ 6 or	£0.98

Extel card

Financial information service, originally in card form, provided by a company under the requirements of the London Stock Exchange for shares or debt securities listed on the Exchange.

Extended financing facility (EFF)

Medium-term International Monetary Fund (IMF) facility granted to member countries in economic difficulties.

Extendible

(1) Security which gives the holder the right to postpone repayment on a first maturity date and to hold the security on unchanged terms until a subsequent previously agreed date.

(2) Sometimes the security may have a provision for a regular rate-resetting after which the holder may choose to hold the bond for another period or to have it redeemed.

Extortionate credit transaction

Credit transaction on grossly unfair terms which may be challenged by an administrator in the case of a bankruptcy.

Extrinsic time

In the case of an option, that part of its value which is not intrinsic, but which relates to time value. See **intrinsic value**.

Ex-warrants

Securities issued with warrants from which the warrants have been detached.

Face value

The nominal value of a security which, in the case of physical securities, is inscribed on the face of the certificate.

Facility

Any arrangement a bank makes available to a customer which involves the assumption of credit risk. Usually this will be a loan facility, but other types of business (e.g., foreign exchange) may be involved.

Facility fee

Fee charged by a bank for making available credit or another service.

Factor

Used as a verb, meaning to borrow money against the security of specific trade receivables. Variations in structure include whether or not the trade debtor is notified of the factoring and whether or not the lending institution has recourse to the borrowing company if a particular debtor delays payment or defaults entirely. In the US, non-recourse factoring is called "accounts receivable financing." The law concerning the perfecting of security varies from country to country.

Fail

A trade is said to fail, if at settlement, matching instructions from both parties have not been received by the clearing house, or if performance does not take place for any reason.

Fair value

The worth of an option determined by a mathematical model. Not the same as the price.

Fälligheit

German word for maturity.

Fannie Mae

The US Federal National Mortgage Association. Unlike securities issued by the Government National Mortgage Association, Fannie Maes are obligations of the agency alone and are not backed by the full faith and credit of the US.

Farm Credit System

US co-operative system which provides agriculture-related credit. There are three parts to the system: Banks for Co-operatives which lend, Farm Credit Banks which make loans secured on property, and the Federal Farm Credit Banks Funding Corp., through which the Farm Credit System issues debt.

Debt of the Farm Credit System, other than that issued by the Federal Agricultural Mortgage Corporation (Farmer Mac), is insured by the Farm Credit System Insurance Corporation. The Farm Credit Financial Assistance Corporation provides capital assistance and issues bonds guaranteed by the federal government.

Farmer Macs

Mortgage-backed securities based on rural housing and agricultural loans, guaranteed by the US Federal Agricultural Mortgage Corporation.

Fast market

A term used to denote hectic market conditions during which price information displayed on screens may not keep up with activity on a trading floor and must be treated as being only indicative.

Fat-tailed distribution

The distortion caused to a normal distribution by larger than predicted price changes. When plotted on a graph, a normal distribution takes the shape of a bell-like curve. The tails referred to are the ends of the bell curve. If a sample has a wider dispersion about the mean than would be expected with a normal distribution when the sample is plotted it will still resemble a bell curve but with fat tails. This phenomenon is also called "leptokurtosis."

FAZ Share Index

Index published by the *Frankfurter Allgemeine Zeitung*, based on the official fixing prices of 100 leading shares on the Frankfurt Stock Exchange. The index is a capitalization-weighted arithmetic index.

Federal Agricultural Mortgage Corporation

US government-sponsored, privately owned corporation created to develop a secondary market securitized agriculture-related debt

Federal Deposit Insurance Corporation (FDIC)

A US federal agency which manages the bank insurance fund and the savings association insurance fund which provide protection to depositors, in banks and in savings and loans associations respectively, up to US$100,000 per account. So long as there is no limit on the interest rate which can be paid on FDIC-insured deposits, this system will tend to encourage careless banking. Institutions which are perceived to be of low credit quality can still fund themselves by paying high rates for retail deposits from investors who consider that FDIC insurance is equivalent to US government risk. However the Federal Deposit Insurance Improvement Act of 1991, which recapitalized the Bank Insurance Fund, also expanded the ability of the bank regulators to act against undercapitalized or badly managed banks.

Federal Financing Bank

US federal institution which borrows from the US Treasury in order to lend to federal credit agencies which do not themselves borrow directly. Its obligations are direct obligations of the US Treasury.

Federal funds (Fed funds)

Funds on account with the US Federal Reserve to meet reserve requirements. Can be transferred to other banks in the Federal Reserve System over Fedwire at the Fed funds rate.

Federal Home Loan Bank Board (FHLBB)

US regulator of savings and loans institutions through a system of 12 regional federal Home Loan Banks which lend to mortgage institutions.

Federal Home Loan Bank System (FHLBS)

US System, established in 1932, of 12 regional Federal Home Loan Banks, whose main function is to provide credit to their members. The banks are regulated by the Federal Housing Finance Board.

Federal Home Loan Mortgage Corporation (FHLMC)

US body created in 1970 to increase the availability of mortgage credit. Known as Freddie Mac, the FHLMC raises funds by issuing securities based on pools of mortgages which are known as Freddie Macs. The corporation's participation certificates are collateralized by mortgage loans and are considered to be agency debt though not guaranteed by the US government.

Federal Housing Administration (FHA)

US government agency which offers mortgages to those who might not otherwise be able to buy their own homes.

Federal Housing Administration experience (FHA experience)

A US prepayment model for 30-year mortgages which is based on studies of FHA mortgages by the US Department of Housing and Urban Development.

Federal Housing Administration/Veterans Administration (FHA/VA)

The US Federal Housing Administration (FHA) insures home loans and the Veterans Administration (VA) guarantees loans to veterans of the US forces. Together with Farmers Home Administration loans, FHA/VA loans may be included in Government National Mortgage Association (GNMA) pools.

Federal National Mortgage Association (FNMA)

US government-sponsored privately owned corporation regulated by the Secretary of Housing and Urban Development. Known as Fannie Mae, it buys and sells residential mortgages insured by the Federal Housing Administration (FHA) or guaranteed by the Veterans Administration (VA), as well as other home mortgages. These mortgages are financed by the issue of securities known as "Fannie Maes."

Federal Reserve Bank

One of 12 regional banks in the Federal Reserve System. They are situated in Atlanta, Boston, Chicago, Cleveland, Dallas, Kansas City, Minneapolis, New York, Philadelphia, Richmond, St Louis, and San Francisco. Each bank provides services such as payment clearing and advances at the **discount window**, as well as acting as depositaries for member banks in their region. Each bank is owned by the commercial banks in its district which are member banks in the Federal Reserve System. Nationally chartered banks are required to be members, state-chartered banks have the option.

Federal Reserve Board

Seven-member board appointed by the President of the US for 14-year terms. The chairman is appointed for a four-year term. The Federal Reserve Board supervises the US banking system.

Federal Reserve Open Market Committee (FOMC)

A committee of the US Federal Reserve which sets monetary policy and open-market operations acting through the open-market desk of the Federal Reserve Bank of New York.

Federal Reserve open-market operations

Conducted through the Open-Market Desk at the Federal Reserve Bank of New York, these operations are intended to add or withdraw reserves from the banking system by buying or selling government securities either outright, to achieve long-term impact, or through the **repo** market, to have a short-term effect on bank reserves.

135

Federal Reserve System

The Fed is the central banking system of the US. Despite the existence of the 12 Federal Reserve Banks, most decision-making is effectively concentrated in the Federal Reserve Board of Governors in Washington.

Federal Savings and Loan Insurance Corporation (FSLIC)

Federal agency which used to provide deposit insurance for savings and loan banks. It became insolvent, and was replaced in 1989 by the Savings Association Insurance Fund which is operated by the FDIC.

Federation of European Stock Exchanges (FESE)

Association of the stock exchanges of the European Union, Norway and Switzerland.

Fedwire

Book-entry transfer system run by the US Federal Reserve transfer Fed funds and US Treasury securities between banks.

Feedstock

The supply of raw material to a processing plant.

FÉLINs

Fonds d'État Libres d'Intérêt Nominal, French fixed-rate zero-coupon bonds.

Festverzinslich

German word for fixed interest.

FIBOR

Frankfurt interbank offered rate.

Fiduciary

A person who has the duty of acting for the benefit of another.

Fiduciary deposit

A deposit placed in the name of one party, usually a bank, but for the account of another party, often a client of the bank, who accepts the risk of the transaction.

Fill or kill

Slang phrase for an order which must be executed or cancelled immediately.

Final dividend

Dividend paid by a company after the end of its financial year, where the company has also paid an interim dividend part way through the year.

Finance houses

UK non-bank institutions which fund consumer hire purchase agreements.

Finance lease

Financing transaction used where the user of an item of equipment is unable to make use of the tax allowances available to the purchaser of the equipment. A leasing company buys the equipment and benefits from the tax allowances while leasing the equipment to the user. The lease payments cover the full cost of the equipment plus interest. At the end of the lease, the user may either continue to use the equipment in return for a small payment to the leasing company or arrange for it to be sold. The user typically will keep most of the sales proceeds. Finance leases are different from operating leases.

Finance vehicle

A subsidiary company formed by a parent company with the sole purpose of borrowing, usually under the guarantee of the parent company, and on-lending the proceeds to other parts of the group. Such companies are usually incorporated in a favorable fiscal jurisdiction.

Financial Accounting Standards Board (FASB)

US institution whose seven board members set accounting rules for certified public accountants which are the basis for what are known in the US as "generally accepted accounting principles."

Financial engineering

Slang term for any specially designed financial transaction. The required mastery of financial, legal and fiscal matters provides an intellectual challenge missing from much of the capital markets. The activity is sometimes referred to dismissively as "bricolage" in French-speaking countries.

Financial futures contract

Futures contract based on a financial instrument.

Financial Futures Market, Amsterdam

The FTA began trading in 1987. The most liquid contract has been the future on the Amsterdam-EOE Index (FTI). Other index futures contracts are on the Euro TOP-100 Index (FET) and the Dutch TOP 5 Index (FT%). There are also futures on the US dollar/guilder (FUS) and on the Dutch government bond (FTO). Trading is by **open outcry** on the floor of the exchange, except for trading in the Dutch government bond future which is through the ATM screen trading system.

Financial guarantee insurance

Insurance which guarantees the timely payment of interest and principal in financial transactions.

Financial Institutions Recovery, Reform and Enforcement Act (FIRREA)

Important US legislation passed in 1989 to fund insolvent **savings and loan associations** and to impose new rules and regulatory procedures on the industry. The savings and loans were obliged to adopt new capital standards broadly equivalent to those imposed on national banks. A new federal agency, the Resolution Funding Corporation, was formed to finance the liquidation of insolvent institutions. A second new agency, the Resolution Trust Corporation, was formed to sell the assets of the failed institutions. The Federal Savings and Loan Insurance Corporation was abolished, to be replaced by the Savings Association Insurance Fund which is managed by the FDIC. The regulatory powers of the Federal Home Loan Bank Board were transferred to a new Office of Thrift Supervision within the US Treasury. Enforcement powers were enhanced and bank fraud was added to the list of crimes covered by the Racketeer Influenced and Corrupt Organizations Act.

Financial Instruments Exchange (FINEX®)

A division of the New York Cotton Exchange, formed in 1985. Contracts traded include currency futures and options, US Dollar Index® futures and options, ECU futures and options, and two-year and five-year US Treasury note futures.

Financial Reporting Council (FRC)

UK body which supervises the development of financial reporting standards. The Accounting Standards Board and the Financial Reporting Review Panel work with the FRC to issue and revise accounting policies and enforce accounting standards.

Financial Reporting Exposure Draft (FRED)

The name for a draft UK Financial Reporting Standard issued for general comment.

Financial Reporting Review Panel

UK body authorized to investigate company accounts. It is able to apply for a court order compelling a company to correct and republish its accounts.

Financial Reporting Standard (FRS)

Definitive UK accounting standard issued by the Accounting Standards Board.

Financial Services Act 1986

Important UK legislation which established the framework for the regulation of all investment business in the UK. Authorized the formation of the Securities and Investments Board, the SIB, which supervises the regulatory system.

Finanziaria

Italian word used to mean (1) a finance company, and (2) the legislation giving effect to the annual State budget.

Finanzierungs-schätze

German Treasury discounted financing bills with maturities from one to two years.

FINEX

The financial futures and options arm of the New York Cotton Exchange (NYCE). In early 1997, FINEX which then traded 10 currency futures contracts announced plans for a further 13 contracts. FINEX trades 16 hours each day through FINEX Europe in Dublin and through the NYCE's usual trading hours. A trading floor in Asia to give 24-hour trading is planned.

Finnish Options Exchange

Oy Suomen Optiopörssi Finlands Optionsbörs Ab, known as SOP, was founded in 1986. The larger part of trading is in currency-related futures and options. There are futures and options on the FIM vs USD, DEM, SEK and GBP. There are rolling spot futures and options on DEM/FIM, USD/FIM and USD/DEM. There are forwards and options on three-month HELIBOR. There are also forward contracts on Finnish government bonds and the Estonian kroon vs FIM. SOP, which is also a clearing house, has developed its own trading system, Sop Trade.

Finnish Options Market

Suomen Optiomeklarit, known as SOM, was founded in 1987. The exchange trades FOX Index futures, based on the 25 most-traded shares on the Helsinki Stock Exchange, and stock futures on 23 Finnish shares. Options are traded on the FOX Index and on nine Finnish shares. The exchange trades futures and options on GBP, SEK, DEM and USD. A Finnish government bond future is also traded. The exchange also has a stock lending contract (LEX) based on a large number of individual shares.

Trading is between about 20 brokers and four market-makers via the exchange's electronic system. SOM is a party to all contracts. Margin requirements are calculated using the exchange's Optiva system.

Fiona

The Frankfurt interbank overnight average rate. In 1996 a market in overnight money-market swaps developed, based on Fiona as part of a wider effort to strengthen the German money markets.

Firewall

Internal barriers within a group intended to give effect to the separation of banking and securities businesses under the US **Glass-Steagall Act**. Included in the term are the Federal Reserve System rules limiting the sharing of information between a bank and its securities affiliate, and the selling of securities to customers of the bank.

Firm

(1) A business.

(2) Definite, a price might be said to be firm in contrast to indicative.

(3) Strong or rising, a market might be described as firm.

First Bulgarian Stock Exchange

Founded in Sofia in 1991, FBSE trades government securities, shares and foreign exchange options. Trading is by **open outcry**. A computerized clearing and settlement system is in development. Information is available on Reuters pages FBSD-I.

First Chicago Clearing Centre

A book-entry clearing facility.

First mortgage bond

A debt instrument secured by a first mortgage.

First notice day

The first date on which notice of intention to deliver the **underlying** against a futures contract may be given.

Fiscal agency agreement

The agreement between a fiscal agent and a borrower, a frequently seen part of the documentation of a bond issue.

Fiscal agent

In the context of an issue of securities, a fiscal agent works for the borrower, unlike a trustee who represents the investors. The role of a fiscal agent includes that of principal paying agent and a number of other administrative functions. Clearly a fiscal agent has none of the fiduciary responsibilities of a trustee.

Fitch Investors Service

US credit rating agency.

Five Cs

Old saying of credit officers, the Five Cs are a qualitative way of judging a potential borrower's credit standing. They are Character, Capacity, Capital, Collateral and Conditions.

Fixed charge

A form of security granted over specific assets which is preferable to a **floating charge**.

Fixed exchange rates

Currencies which have set values against each other. An unnatural phenomenon which appeals to the bureaucrat or the wishful thinker, but not to the realist or the trader. No two countries grow at the same speed, have the same balance of payments or the same government borrowing need. A fixed exchange rate can be maintained only at a cost to one of the parties. The weaker government will have little or no control over its own interest rates, and, since it has a fixed exchange rate, little control over its own economy.

Fixed income

See **fixed interest**.

Fixed interest

Interest calculated as a constant specified percentage of the principal amount of a security and paid regularly.

Fixed price

Method of pricing an offering of securities long used in the US, but only since 1989 in the Euromarkets. The members of an underwriting syndicate in a fixed-price issue are obliged to offer securities at a fixed price until the lead manager breaks the syndicate and determines that the issue is free to trade. This price usually represents a spread to government bonds which has been discussed with the potential underwriters before the pricing is fixed. The technique is supposed to achieve an orderly distribution of securities, and improve the chance of a profitable outcome for syndicate members.

Fixed-fixed currency swap

Currency swap in which both parties pay a fixed rate of interest.

Fixed-rate bonds

Debt securities where the **coupon** is set at the date of issue as a fixed percentage of **par** value.

Fixed-rate payer

The party to an **interest rate swap** who pays a fixed rate of interest and receives a variable rate of interest.

Fixing

(1) Determination of a variable interest rate for an interest period usually two business days before the beginning of the interest period.

(2) The setting of a price by a known method at regular times. For example, in London there is a gold fixing each morning.

Flat

(1) A yield curve is said to be "flat" when there is little difference between short and long-term interest rates.

(2) Quotation of a price excluding accrued interest.

(3) A flat fee is payable once,

(4) A trader's book is said to be "flat" if he has no net position.

(5) A price or yield is said to be "flat" to another price or yield if it is the same as it.

(6) *But* a "flat" yield is the same as a current or running yield, i.e., the **coupon** divided by the price of the security.

Flexible exchange rate

A form of managed **float**. A case of the bureacratic mind meeting the real world, but not giving up.

Flight capital

Capital brought from one country to another, not always legally, because of fears about economic or political stability.

Float

(1) The amount of an issue in the hands of traders or other ready sellers. If the float of an issue is large, it implies that the securities were not well placed originally and the issue may therefore trade on a higher yield than would otherwise be the case. If the float is too small, an issue will be illiquid which may also distort the price and which will certainly widen the bid–offer spread quoted.

(2) The balance of cash in the hands of a bank which occurs in the course of making and receiving payments for customers. A traditional and lucrative source of bank income which partly offsets the cost of the payments system.

Floater

Floating-rate note.

Floating capital

Capital not invested in fixed assets.

Floating charge

Security granted to a creditor over the general assets of a company. The composition of these assets will change from time to time in the normal course of business. Sometimes offers less good protection than a fixed charge.

Floating strike option

Another name for an **average strike option**.

Floating–floating swap

A **basis swap** where the two parties exchange payments based on two different variable rate bases (e.g., **LIBOR** and an average CP rate).

Floating-rate certificate of deposit (FRCD)

A **certificate of deposit** paying variable interest. An alternative to FRNs for those perhaps not allowed to issue FRNs.

Floating-rate collateralized mortgage obligation (FRCMO)

Variable-rate bond classes of CMOs.

Floating-rate enhanced debt security (FRENDS)

Securitized mezzanine (i.e., unsecured) debt.

Floating-rate note (FRN)

FRNs are a form of variable-rate note with coupons typically set at a margin over **LIBOR** though many structures are possible. FRNs are an alternative to syndicated bank loans and to swapped fixed rate bond issues. FRNs are issued, therefore, only when they offer some advantage over these other methods of raising floating-rate debt.

The history of the FRN market has been eventful. Very large sovereign issues have been launched from time to time, but there have also been times when liquidity in the secondary market became very poor and prices fell reflecting investor disenchantment. Factors which influence the rate of issue include, as one would expect, the appetite of banks for lending, the relationship of swap rates to new issue bond yields, and the liquidity of the secondary market.

Volume of issues

As can be seen from the table in Figure F1, issue volume has fluctuated significantly both in absolute value and in percentage of total new issues.

Figure F1

FLOATING-RATE NOTES: ISSUE VOLUME 1981–95		
Year	Amount in US$ bn	% of total new issues
1981	7.09	26.59
1982	11.20	23.28
1983	14.65	31.42
1984	31.64	39.65
1985	54.72	41.08
1986	49.48	24.45
1987	15.72	11.01
1988	17.53	10.08
1989	20.24	9.68
1990	36.84	23.01
1991	15.83	6.90
1992	45.94	16.45
1993	72.25	17.91
1994	107.43	25.23
1995	86.10	19.12

Source: IFR Securities Data

In the period 1993–95, FRN (and VRN) new issues could be summarized as shown in Figure F2.

Looking at Eurobonds alone the pattern of issuance by country of FRNs and VRNs was as shown in Figure F3.

Characteristics

FRNs have smaller fees than fixed-rate issues. These are not standard but might be, say, 0.125% whatever the maturity.

The interest rate on an FRN is based on a reference rate. This might be **LIBOR, LIBID** or **LIMEAN**. Reference rates from other financial centres are also used. While rates are most often set semi-annually or quarterly in advance, various other mechanisms have been used, including lookback rate settings and average rate settings. The reference rate is usually determined by reference to a named multicontributor screen page or to named reference banks from whose quotations an arithmetic mean is derived.

The margin is a stipulated amount added to (occasionally subtracted from)

Figure F2

EUROBONDS AND INTERNATIONAL ISSUES 1993–95 (AMOUNTS IN US$ MILLIONS)						
Currency	No of issues 1995	US$ m 1995	No of issues 1994	US$ m 1994	No of issues 1993	US$ m 1993
US dollars	302	42,968	370	70,675	326	48,481
Pounds sterling	41	5,771	64	11,975	54	8,713
Japanese yen	196	10,306	207	18,756	61	7,831
D-marks	68	16,146	44	7,679	67	4,740
Hong Kong dollars	6	834	20	1,779	3	492
Italian lire	9	2,246	13	1,482	13	1,533
Canadian dollars	0	0	8	1,353	13	1,064
French francs	8	1,383	8	1,348	20	2,615
Swiss francs	9	265	25	1,286	16	924
Australian dollars	3	159	5	448	0	
Austrian schillings	0	0	2	412	0	
Portugese escudos	23	2,248	5	276	0	
Spannish pesetas	7	779	3	236	0	
Dutch guilders	2	230	2	163	1	137
ECU	3	2,079	0	0	0	0
Others	6	688	4	158	6	439
Total	683	86,102	780	118,027	580	76,970

Source: IFR Securities Data

the reference rate. The margin need not be constant over the life of an FRN. Sometimes a rising margin is combined with *call options* giving the borrower the right to redeem the bonds.

FRNs are usually senior unsecured obligations of the borrower, like other *Eurobonds*. Banks, however, have issued subordinated FRNs which augment their capital ratios but carry a higher margin. The key achievement is to have an instrument which counts as capital, but the interest expense of which is a tax-deductible item.

FRNs are typically of longer maturity than straight bonds. This has been because the perception of FRNs was that the reset interest rate combined with good secondary market liquidity made them effectively short-term instruments. From time to time investors rediscover that this is not always so. Some FRNs have been issued as *perpetuals* with no specified maturity date. Some of these issues have provisions for steeply rising margins which are designed to encourage the issuer to redeem them.

Variations
Variations often seen are the bull floater and the bear floater. A bull floater

145

Figure F3

FRNs AND VRNs: PATTERN OF ISSUANCE BY COUNTRY					
	No of issues 1995	US$ m 1995	No of issues 1994	US$ m 1994	No of issues 1993	US$ m 1993
Supranational	18	3,390	19	2,628	31	4,207
United States	111	23,374	93	24,035	56	11,491
Canada	11	1,625	9	6,242	8	849
Western Europe of which:	214	35,718	191	32,410	223	32,763
United Kingdom	45	5,637	56	9,898	40	6,277
Italy	24	5,285	25	6,991	34	5,711
France	34	4,332	29	3,792	45	6,875
Germany	53	12,680	28	3,635	60	7,468
Scandinavia of which:	25	3,952	40	11,574	62	11,874
Sweden	16	3,271	23	8,133	40	8,034
Finland	5	318	13	3,189	8	926
Eastern Europe	0	0	1	246	0	0
Australia/N. Zealand	6	1,303	23	5,101	4	701
Latin America of which:	3	352	28	3,875	11	1,228
Mexico	1	300	11	1,989	5	530
Argentina	0	0	7	829	2	200
Brazil	2	52	6	538	3	448
India & Asia of which:	282	15,086	249	19,387	97	9,036
Japan	240	10,683	143	7,351	69	5,987
Hong Kong	3	459	22	4,410	6	1,424
Korea	14	1,357	42	3,447	14	735
Thailand	10	820	19	1,856	1	100
Caribbean	10	1,040	11	1,659	1	99
Middle East	2	110	1	271	0	0
Africa	1	150				
Total	683	86,102	665	107,429	493	72,248

Source: IFR Securities Data

appeals to investors who expect rates to fall, because its **coupon** is calculated as the result of subtracting a variable market rate from a fixed rate. The coupon paid will be larger when the former is smaller. The bear floater appeals to the investor who expects rates to rise and its coupon is calculated as a multiple of a variable market rate less a fixed rate. It is not usually possible to issue both types of floater at once. The arithmetic for the borrower is driven by the swap market.

Example

Assume a bear floater where the coupon is calculated as "2 x 6 month LIBOR less 7%." Now, provided the fixed swap rate which the borrower can pay in the swap market is lower than the fixed rate used to calculate the floater's coupon, the borrower will have a net liability at a margin below the variable rate. If the swap rate in this case were 6.875%, the borrower would have a net liability of six-month LIBOR less about 12 basis points – remember annual bond basis points (30/360 day basis) are not as valuable as semi-annual money market basis points (actual/360 day basis).

FRNs have been issued with a cap or a floor – an embedded interest rate option. With a cap, the investor has in effect sold the borrower an option. If interest rates rise above the cap level, which may be thought of as a strike price, the borrower effectively exercises his option, and does not pay more than the cap rate. With a floor, the borrower has in effect sold the investor an option. If interest rates fall below the floor level, the investor in effect exercises his option and continues to receive interest at the floor rate even though market interest rates are below it. The notional value of these options should be added or subtracted from the price of a conventional FRN pricing for the same borrower to arrive at the value of the capped or floored FRN.

A collared FRN is best thought of as a structure where the borrower seeks to cap his maximum rate and, rather than pay an implicit premium through a higher coupon, pays for the cap by granting an option to the investor – the floor. Again, the theoretical value is calculated by valuing the cap and the floor separately, offsetting one value against the other and adding or subtracting, as the case may be, the net from the price of a conventional FRN for the same borrower.

A stepped FRN has a provision for the interest rate or margin to be increased after a set period of time. Often this is a feature found in perpetual and/or subordinated FRNs, where it is used to give the investor some assurance that the borrower will in fact exercise the accompanying call option. In this case, because the FRN has no mandatory repayment date, it may count as a form of capital, until the borrower calls it because the coupon has risen to an unattractive level.

Floating-rate preferred stock

Preferred stock with floating or variable dividends.

Floor

An **option** which secures for the holder a minimum rate of interest income at certain interest reset dates. If the chosen variable reference rate is below the strike rate on a reset date, the seller of the floor pays the difference to the holder (see Figure F4). A floor may be embedded in a security so that, for example, a FRN might have a minimum coupon rate. This is often combined with a cap or maximum rate. The individual options which conceptually make up a floor are known as "floorlets." See **cap** and **collar**.

Figure F4

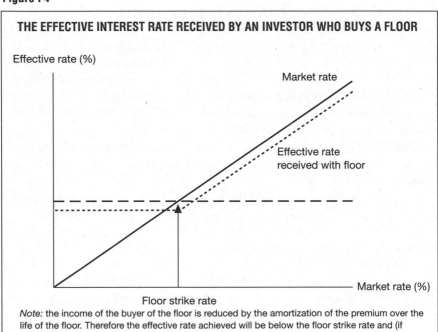

THE EFFECTIVE INTEREST RATE RECEIVED BY AN INVESTOR WHO BUYS A FLOOR

Effective rate (%)

Market rate

Effective rate
received with floor

Market rate (%)

Floor strike rate

Note: the income of the buyer of the floor is reduced by the amortization of the premium over the life of the floor. Therefore the effective rate achieved will be below the floor strike rate and (if higher) the market rate.

Floor broker

A trader on an exchange floor who executes orders for those who do not have access to the trading area.

Floor price

The minimum purchase or sales price that an option strategy provides.

Floor trader

A trader on an exchange floor who trades for his own account or that of his employer.

Floored put

Put option with a limit on the maximum amount payable.

Floorlet

The individual options that make up a floor are sometimes called "floorlets."

Floortion

Inelegant word for an option on a floor.

Flotation

The selling of shares in a new company on a stock market.

Flowback

The sale of securities which were originally bought by foreign investors back into the securities' domestic market. In so far as securities firms try to develop international markets for securities, they tend to see flowback as a mark of failure.

Fondo comune

Italian phrase for a mutual fund.

Fonds commun de créances

A type of French mutual fund.

Fonds commun de placements

Another type of French mutual fund.

Footsie

The FT-SE 100 Index.

Force majeure

A clause often seen in debt issues which gives the lead manager discretion to release the managers and underwriters of an issue from their obligations at any time before the closing date if there has been, in the opinion of the lead manager, such a change in national or international financial, political or economic conditions or currency exchange rates or exchange controls as would prejudice materially the success of the offering.

Usually the swap contracts related to a new issue do not have such a clause and are not linked to such a clause. Therefore, if the clause comes into effect a borrower is likely to end up with a swap but no issue to set against it.

Forced conversion

(1) A borrower usually may call a convertible security when the share price has traded at a certain level above the exercise price for a period of so many days. If a borrower does call the issue, investors must either convert their

securities into common shares or take a loss by accepting the call price.

(2) Warrants also have similar call provisions, but here the call decision will result in an inflow of cash for the borrower as the warrants are exercised.

Foreign bond

A security issued by a borrower in a domestic capital market other than its own. In the Japanese market, they are called "Samurai issues," in the US, they are called "Yankee issues," in the UK they are called "Bulldogs," in Portugal they are called "Navigator issues" and so on.

Forex

Foreign exchange.

Forex-linked bond

An issue in which the redemption amount is linked to the spot exchange rate of another currency against the currency of denomination at maturity.

Forfaiting

Non-recourse financing of export receivables.

Forint

The national currency of Hungary.

Form 10K

The annual financial report required to be filed with the US Securities and Exchange Commission (the SEC) by any corporation which is listed on an exchange, issues securities, has 500 or more shareholders or assets of $2 million. Once filed, the report becomes public information.

Form 10Q

The quarterly financial report required to be filed with the US Securities and Exchange Commission (the SEC) by corporations required to file a 10K report. The report summarizes financial information and compares it with the same quarter of the previous year. It need not be audited.

Forward contract

A forward contract obliges the forward buyer to purchase a specified financial instrument or commodity at a specified price on a specified future date, the settlement date. The seller of a forward contract is similarly obliged to deliver a specified financial instrument or commodity in settlement of his obligation. Generally no payments are made under a forward contract until the settlement date. Forward contracts therefore represent a credit risk for each party on the other, from the inception of the contract until the settlement date. Settlement of a forward contract may be by cash settlement. That is, no delivery takes place, but there is a cash payment from one party to the other of the difference between the contract value of the forward and the spot or current value on the settlement date. If the forward contract relates to a reasonable liquid instrument or commodity, then the forward price will be related to the cost of owning the underlying instrument or commodity, less any income such ownership may bring. In the absence of any storage or other costs, and in the absence of any income, then the forward price will generally exceed the spot price by an amount equivalent to the cost of owning or carrying the underlying for the period of the forward contract. This net difference is one of the things called **basis**.

Forward cover

The forward foreign-exchange contracts executed to protect against movements in exchange rates.

Forward curve

The future interest rate curve which is implied by the forward interest rates calculable today from the zero-coupon curve. See **expectations theory**.

Forward foreign exchange contract

A contract to buy or sell a currency at an exchange rate determined at the outset on a specified future date.

Forward outright rate

A forward foreign-exchange rate price expressed as an absolute rate, rather than as a difference from the spot price.

Forward points

The decimal figure to be added to or subtracted from the spot price in order to determine the forward price. These points are the product of interest rate differentials. Those who cannot remember if the forward price is at a premium or a discount to spot should remember that the forward bid–offer spread will be wider than the spot spread.

Forward rate agreement (FRA)

Short-term contract which secures a future interest rate.

Forward Rate Agreement of the British Bankers' Association (FRABBA)

Standardized terms and conditions for forward rate agreements traded in London which were published by the British Bankers' Association (BBA) which also published the British Bankers' Association Interest Rate Swap terms (BBAIRS)

Fourchette

French word for a fork, used to denote a spread or range.

Fourth company law directive

EU directive concerned with the format and content of company accounts

Fractional entitlements

In a rights issue, the fractions of shares to which a shareholder may be entitled as a result of the relationship between the number of shares owned and the ratio of the rights issue.

Franc

The national currencies of Belgium, France and Switzerland.

Franc zone

Those currencies which are linked to the French franc. They include some of the currencies in West and Central Africa, and the Pacific franc which is used in certain overseas departments of France. See **CFA Franc Zone** and **CFP Franc Zone**.

Fraption

Supposed to be an option on a forward rate agreement.

Fraudulent trading

In English law, the carrying on of a business either with the intention of defrauding those with whom the business deals, or when the business has no reasonable prospect of paying its liabilities as they fall due.

Freddie Mac

The US Federal Home Loan Mortgage Corporation and the securities issued by it.

Free of tax to residents abroad (FOTRA) stocks

Formerly important status enjoyed by certain UK government securities (gilts) which is now much less significant. The planned introduction of gilt strips has created a list of strippable stocks which pay interest gross to all holders. The Central Gilt Office's **Star Account** system allows foreign corporate investors, and others, to receive interest gross on all gilts.

Freimakler

German word for an independent dealer on a stock exchange.

Freiverkehr

German word for the "free market" segment on the German Stock Exchange.

French Government Bonds

In December each year the French parliament approves the Finance Act which authorizes the Minister of the Economy to borrow in French francs or in ECU to cover the needs of the *Trésor* (Treasury). This is a general authorization without a limit. All debt is issued by the *Trésor* and is in book entry form. OATs are identified by a SICOVAM number of four or five digits. Besides the Ministry of the Economy which has a general supervisory role over the markets, the following entities have regulatory responsibilities.

Banque de France

The newly independent *Banque de France* is responsible for defining and implementing monetary policy. It is also responsible for supervising the money market and has operational involvement through keeping Treasury bill current accounts via the Saturne system.

Comité de la Réglementation Bancaire (CRB)

The banking regulations committee is chaired by the Minister of the Economy. It formulates general banking rules, accounting rules, prudential and risk ratios, market rules and particularly rules governing the inter-bank market and markets in negotiable debt securities.

Comité des Établissements de Credit (CEC)

The lending institutions committee is chaired by the Governor of the *Banque de France*. It licenses lending institutions (other than those supervised by the *Commission Bancaire*) and money brokers (*agents des marchés interbancaires*) under the Banking Act and under regulations laid down by the *Comité de la Réglementation Bancaire*.

Commission Bancaire

Under the Act of 24 January 1984 the Commission is responsible for ensuring compliance by lending institutions operating in France with all legislation and regulations. The Commission has wide powers to obtain information, to impose measures and to punish erring institutions.

Conseil des Bourses de Valeurs (CBV)

The CBV (Stock Exchange Supervisory Council) draws up and enforces stock market regulations. For example, trading in the secondary market in government securities is governed by Title IX of the Conseil's general regulations.

Société des Bourses Françaises (SBF)

The SBF is responsible for daily operations and development of the market under the rules of the CBV.

Conseil des Marchés à Terme (CMT)

An advisory body for the futures market. It formulated general regulations which were published in March 1990 and which make up the regulatory document for the derivatives market.

Matif SA
Operates the market and the clearing mechanism for futures.

Commission des Opérations de Bourse (COB)
The commission is responsible for investor protection. It supervises investor information, operation of the securities market, listed financial products and traded futures. It approves prospectuses, and licenses mutual funds (Sicavs) and investment trusts.

Bons du Trésor à Taux fixe et Interêt Précomptés (BTFs)
BTFs are the treasury bills of the French market. They are issued in minimum denominations of Ffr1million. Initially maturities are from 13, 26 and 52 weeks. New issue maturities may be adjusted so as to attach new sales to existing issues. Sometimes, therefore, short-dated notes of 4 to 6 weeks are issued, or notes of 24 to 29 weeks, or notes of 42 to 52 weeks, in order to match an existing issue.

Interest is in the form of a discount and the bills are quoted on a yield to maturity basis on a 360 day year to two decimal places.

Bons du Trésor à Taux fixe et Interêt Annuel (BTANs)
BTANs are interest-bearing fixed rate Treasury notes. They are issued in minimum denominations of Ffr1million though smaller amounts may be added to an existing holding of the same issue. Maturities are either two or five year bullets. Every six months the Treasury issues new two-year and five-year BTANs and subsequent monthly issues add to the amount outstanding. Maturities and coupons are usually set to fall on the 12th of the month.

Coupons are paid annually and notes are quoted on a yield to maturity basis on a 365 day year. The notes are not listed on the Stock Exchange.

ECU denominated BTANs
First issued in February 1993. Issues have been syndicated rather than auctioned.

Obligations Assimilables du Trésor (OATs)
OATs are in minimum denominations of Ffr2000. Initial maturities are from seven to 30 year bullets. Coupons are paid annually. Notes are quoted on a price basis excluding accrued interest. Bonds are traded on screen and on the Stock Exchange.

ECU denominated OATs
Issued first in 1989 and regularly thereafter. Denominations are ECU 500.

Other OATs
Besides the fixed rate bullet maturity OATs there are some older less traded issues which are convertible or were issued with warrants.

Floating rate OATs
The existing different variable rate issues are known by their initials:

TMB

The rate is the arithmetic mean of the monthly average of the 13-week T-bill auctioned weekly throughout the year prior to the coupon payment.

TRB

The rate is reset quarterly as the yield of the 13-week T-bill auctioned prior to the payment of the coupon.

TRA

The rate is the arithmetic mean of the monthly average of yields on fixed-rate *Emprunts d'État* with maturities greater than 7 years. This rate is published by the *Caisse des Dépots et Consignations*.

TME

The rate is the monthly average yield on a weighted sample of 7–30 year bonds on the secondary market recorded over the 12 months prior to payment of the coupon.

TEC

The *Taux de l'Echéance Constante*, a 10-year constant maturity yield index is published daily in the form of the yield to maturity of a hypothetical OAT with a maturity of exactly 10 years. The yield is interpolated from the yields of the two nearest maturities of government bonds based on mid prices quoted at 10.00 am in Paris by OAT market-makers, rounded to two decimal places. A 10.5 year OAT has been issued with quarterly coupons set in advance based on the TEC. These bonds, like other floating rate bonds, are not very sensitive to absolute rate changes but to changes in the yield curve.

Emprunts d'Etat (EEs)

Issued regularly until 1985 and revived as the *Grand Emprunt d'Etat* known as the Balladur bond which had an initial issue amount of more than Ffr110 billion.

Stripped OATs

Since May 1991 the *Trésor* has permitted certain OATs to be stripped. The intention is to have liquid zero-coupon instruments maturing in April and October in several years. Since June 1993 the par value of a stripped coupon has been Ffr5 so as to achieve fungibility between all interest certificates of a given maturity derived from OATs of different maturities. Strips are quoted in terms of yield unlike other government securities which are quoted in terms of price. The par value of ECU stripped coupons is ECU1.25. SVTs may strip or reconstitute eligible OATs at any time.

Front contract

A futures or options contract that is the nearest to expiry of those on that underlying available on a given exchange. Also referred to as "front month."

Front office

The dealing room of a financial institution, contrasted with the "back office."

Frontrunning

When a trader deals for his own account in advance of known customer orders. The practice is usually illegal.

Frozen assets

Normally funds that are temporarily blocked, either due to court order or government regulation, often arising from war or major international dispute.

FSR

Fonds de Soutien des Rentes, the French government debt management fund.

FT All-Share Index

Index of some 650 UK companies quoted on the London Stock Exchange. It is an arithmetic capitalization weighted index calculated once a day. There are 38 sectoral sub-indices.

FT-30 Index

Financial Times Industrial Ordinary Share Index, known as the FT 30-Share Index. This is the oldest continuous index of UK equities. The base value of 100 was set in 1935. The index is calculated as a geometric mean and the index is not weighted. Once the key measure of investor sentiment, the FT-30 lost this role to the FT-100 Index which was introduced in 1984.

FTA

See **Financial Futures Market, Amsterdam.**

FT-SE 100 Index

Index of 100 leading UK shares listed on the London Stock Exchange often called "the Footsie." It is an arithmetic capitalization weighted index. Its constituents represent about 70 percent of the capitalization of the London Stock Exchange. The index is calculated each minute.

Fukuoka Stock Exchange

One of the five regional Japanese stock exchanges. It grew out of the Hakata Rice Exchange. Trading is by the **zaraba** method on the floor of the exchange.

Full service bank

A bank which offers services across all or most product ranges.

Full two-way payments

Provision of the International Swap & Derivatives Association (ISDA) standard master swap agreement which stipulates that, in a default, the net value of the swaps between two parties is calculated and is payable to the appropriate party even if that is the defaulting party.

Fully diluted

The calculation of how many shares in a company could exist if all outstanding options, warrants and convertible securities were converted into shares. This is necessary, particularly for earnings or net assets per share calculations.

Fully invested

A fund or portfolio which holds no cash or equivalents is said to be fully invested.

Fully paid

When a security has been completely paid for. The term is used when securities are issued in partly paid form with one or more subsequent payments required at stated intervals.

Fund management

The industry which invests money on behalf of others. It may be divided into institutional fund management on the one hand, and retail and mutual fund management on the other. The amounts involved in the former are often larger, but pension fund trustees and others are a more demanding group of clients who are well served by actuaries and consultants in the business of measuring the performance of each fund manager. Retail fund management may involve smaller amounts, with higher costs of acquiring new money, but once acquired, clients are more stable and are often more concerned with absolute returns rather than relative performance.

Funding risk

The risk that a borrower will not be able to raise funds as expected. Before derivatives, a borrower could not easily separate funding risk from rate risk. Swaps and futures allow borrowers to manage their debt and the rate risks therein separately from funding risk. Funding risk is magnified by the increasing homogeneity of bond markets and the rapidly growing mountain of government debt which requires refinancing. The Mexican crisis in 1994 illustrated the danger of panic spreading from one market to another. Funding risk can be expected to be a growing problem for borrowers in an increasingly volatile international capital market.

At a lower level, the small company may sometimes suffer from unpredictable bank behaviour. The willingness of banks to lend for certain purposes has been observed to vary in a cyclical manner. These cycles show a tendency to accelerate as corporate memory shortens. See **risk**.

Fungible

Securities which are fungible may be exchanged for each other on identical terms.

Furthest month

The latest contract month for which a derivative may be traded on an exchange.

FUTOP

FUTOP (Garantifonden for Danske Optioner og Futures) is the Danish derivatives clearing centre established by the National Bank of Denmark, the Danish Bankers' Association and the Danish Securities Dealers Association. The FUTOP Clearing Centre is a party to all registered contracts. The Copenhagen Stock Exchange A/S is the official marketplace for listed future and option contracts. Prices and volumes are published in the official list of the exchange. Over-the-counter contracts for non-guaranteed, unlisted futures and options are available in an unregulated market which is not covered by FUTOP's guarantee scheme.

Securities firms may be one of several types of member: handling agents, brokers, direct clearing members or general clearing members. An investor may trade with handling agents, brokers, or direct clearing members but may settle only through direct clearing members or general clearing members. Most members are either direct clearing members or are both handling agents and general clearing members. At June 1996, there were 19 members.

There are also specialized market makers (SMMs) who undertake to maintain firm bid and offer prices in the contracts for which they have registered. At June 1996, there were six SMMs and the following contracts were traded:

Futures and options on the 8% 2006 Government bond
Futures and options on the 8% 2001 Government bond
Futures on the 6% 2026 mortgage-credit bond
Futures on three-month CIBOR (Copenhagen interbank offered rate)
Futures and options on the KFX Stock Index
Futures and options on nine Danish stocks

Future

A future is an exchange-traded contract to buy at a specified date in the future a unit of a commodity or financial instrument, standardized as to amount, date and place of delivery. A future is in effect an exchange-traded forward contract. A future has three important advantages over a forward contract. First, being exchange-traded, the price is readily ascertainable. Second, futures are a robust mechanism for controlling and reducing credit risk. Third, futures are, for the most part, very liquid, traded instruments, so that the owner of a future can always sell it.

Clearing house

The counterparty to a futures contract is the exchange clearing house. This may be a preferable counterparty to many of the market participants. The clearing house can net the exposure of a member to the market and ensure that only net amounts need to be paid. A clearing house controls its exposure to members by requiring initial margin, and subsequently variation margin, to be deposited at the inception of a contract, and then in response to changes in the market value of that contract.

Standard terms

Futures contracts are standardized, particularly the following terms:

- amount
- settlement date
- last trading date
- minimum price movement
- eligible deliverable securities.

Trading

Trading may be by open **outcry** on the floor of an exchange or by an automated screen based trading system.

Delivery

Delivery is the obligation attached to a futures (or option) contract which has remained open at the end of trading in that contract and which is not specified to be cash-settled. At LIFFE, for example the Gilt, Bund and BTP futures are deliverable while the JGB future is cash-settled.

At some exchanges, delivery is by a named counterparty, who is assigned the obligation to deliver. Alternatively, as at LIFFE, delivery may be through the clearing house, and therefore anonymous.

What is delivered is the cheapest-to-deliver bond from the basket of deliverable bonds specified by the exchange. Before a contract comes to be traded, a basket of deliverable bonds is announced. These bonds will be of different maturities and coupons, though all will have a certain minimum amount in issue. To each bond is attached a price factor intended to equalize their value for delivery when applied to the nominal amount.

At the end of each contract's trading life, an Exchange Delivery Settlement Price (EDSP) for the future is set. The invoicing amount for delivery is therefore set as:

Invoicing amount = (EDSP x price factor x nominal value)
+ accrued interest

Example

Suppose that we are calculating the invoicing amount for a trade in a single Bund future for which the unit of trading is DM250,000. The EDSP is 97.875, the price factor for the CTD bond is 1.018976 and the accrued

159

interest is DM1,987.65. The invoice amount is calculated as:

$$((97.875/100 \times 1.018976 \times DM250,000) + DM1,987.65$$

which is:

$$DM251,318.34$$

Cheapest-to-deliver

The cheapest-to-deliver bond is the bond from the basket of deliverable bonds which provides the highest return on a cash and carry transaction. This is the calculation which ties the fair price of a future to the cash market in the underlying. So it is important to understand **cash and carry**.

Cash and carry

A cash and carry transaction is usually a long position in the underlying bond and a short position in the related future. The profit or loss calculation is as follows:

Cash inflow less cash outflow, or:

Short futures less long underlying bond, which is:

(Futures price x price factor + accrued interest at delivery + coupon income)
less
(Long bond clean price + accrued interest at purchase + financing cost)

(See also **basis trading.**)

Uses of futures

There are numerous ways to use futures and many possible users. Some of the more obvious users and their possible strategies are described in Figure F5.

Example from LIFFE

A fund manager has a holding of £100 million of the Treasury 8.5% 2007 United Kingdom gilt. He is bearish about the gilt market and wishes to hedge his position. He knows that notional value of the gilt future is £50,000 and that (for this example) the 8.5% 2007 gilt is the cheapest to deliver stock with a price factor of 0.9607523.

The number of contracts needed for the hedge is calculated as:

(Amount of holding/contract size) x price factor

which in this case is:

(£100,000,000/£50,000) x 0.9607523 = 1,922 contracts

Note that the number of contracts is calculated to the nearest whole number of contracts. It is not always possible to hedge a position exactly. A

Figure F5

USES AND USERS OF FUTURES		
User	*Strategy*	*Application*
Market-makers	Hedging cash book	Long bonds/sell futures Short bonds/buy futures
Institutional investors	Hedging Investing future cash	Long bonds/sell futures Buy futures (sell when bonds bought)
	Change asset allocation	e.g., Sell gilt futures and buy Bund futures
	Duration adjustment	Buy/sell futures to alter duration
Issues of debt	Hedging future borrowing	Sell bond futures and close when debt is issued
Traders	Directional trades Yield curve trades	Buy/sell bond futures Buy/sell bond futures and sell/buy short futures short-term interest rate
	Bond spreading	Buy/sell bond futures and sell/buy other bond futures

(Source: LIFFE)

second imperfection is that the asset being hedged may not be exactly replicated by the future. In this case, the gilt being hedged was also the cheapest to deliver. If it had not been or had been outside the deliverable basket altogether, there would have been a **basis risk** and the hedge would have been imperfect.

Futures trading volumes
The table shown in Figure F6 is arranged by nationality of the underlying and shows the leading government bond futures contracts in 1995.

Futures and options fund
A type of UK unit trust authorized by the Securities and Investments Board. In spite of the name, such a fund is not very aggressive. It may invest in transferable or approved securities as defined by the UK authorities, approved derivatives but only up to 10 percent of the fund, forward transactions in currencies or gold, units in collective investment schemes up to 5 percent of the fund, and gold up to 10 percent of the fund. All derivative transactions must be covered with cash, the underlying or other derivatives.

161

Figure F6

LEADING GOVENMENT BOND FUTURES CONTRACTS IN 1996

Contract	Size	Exchange	Volume traded
United States			
US Treasury Bond	$100,000	CBOT	84,725,128
US Treasury Note 10yr	$100,000	CBOT	21,939,725
US Treasury Note 5yr	$100,000	CBOT	11,463,640
United Kingdom			
Long Gilt	£50,000	LIFFE	15,408,010
France			
Notional Bond 10yr	Ffr500,000	MATIF	35,321,843
Germany			
German Bund	DM250,000	LIFFE	39,801,928
German Bund Future	DM250,000	DTB	16,496,809
German BOBL	DM250,000	DTB	18,269,169
Japan			
10yr Government bond	¥100,000,000	TSE	12,450,925
		LIFFE	
Italy			
BTP	ITL200,000,000	LIFFE	12,603,754
10yr Notional bond	UTL250,000,000	MIF	2,240,085
Other			
Australian 3yr T bond	A$100,000	SFE	9,217,667
Australian 10yr T bond	A$100,000	SFE	5,322,003
Canadian 10yr bond	C$100,000	MONTREAL	1,072,111
Danish long-term bond	DKK1,000,000	FUTOP	199,219
Spanish 10yr notional bond	PTS10,000,000	MEFFRF	18,535,566
Swedish 5yr Government bond	Skr1,000,000	OM	900,544
Swedish 10yr Government bond	Skr1,000,000	OM	865,822
Swiss Government bond	Sfr100,000	SOFFEX	913,446

(Source: Futures & Options World)

Futures exchange

Exchange where futures contracts in financial instruments, currencies or physical commodities are traded. There are numerous exchanges around the world.

Futures-style options

Options where the premium is not paid upfront but is paid through the margining system of the exchange. LIFFE options are an example of this.

G

Gamma

In the valuation of options, gamma is the measure of the rate of change of **delta** in relation to a movement in the **underlying**. Gamma will tend to be lower when an option is deeply **in-the-money** or deeply **out-of-the-money**. The gamma of an **at-the-money** option will be higher. As options approach expiry the gammas of deeply in or out-of-the-money options will tend to decline while the gamma of an at-the-money option will increase. This is because the delta of at-the-money options is volatile.

In a portfolio of options, gamma is an indicator of how frequently a delta-hedged portfolio will need to be rebalanced. In a portfolio with a high gamma, small movements in the value of the underlying will change the delta significantly, requiring the hedges to be adjusted. A portfolio with a low gamma will not need frequent rebalancing.

See **delta**, **kappa** and **theta**.

Gap

(1) The difference between the maturity of loans and deposits on the books of a bank or trading firm. It is a measure of potential interest rate risk.

(2) When a market moves quickly, the price of a security may be said to "gap" (up or down) if the difference between one quotation and the next is large. Gapping is a symptom of an illiquid or panic-stricken market.

Gap analysis

Originally the comparison of the principal amount of maturing assets and maturing liabilities period by period to calculate for each period the exposure to interest rate changes. Now used to describe the same analysis, but of all the cash flows in a trading book. These may be of principal or of interest and may arise from derivative transactions as well as on-balance sheet transactions.

Garman-Kohlhargen model

Modified version of the Black–Scholes option pricing model published in 1983, which may be used to value currency options with European exercise. The model has separate terms for the two interest rates.

Gauhati Stock Exchange

Indian stock exchange which trades stocks. See **National Stock Exchange of India.**

Geared futures and options funds (GFOF)

A type of UK authorized unit trust allowed to invest in transferable securities (as defined), approved derivatives, forward transactions in currencies and gold, in gold itself (up to 10 percent of the fund) and units in collective investment schemes (up to 5 percent of the fund). GFOFs may only invest 20 percent of the fund in "initial outlay" on derivatives. GFOFs may not borrow money.

Gearing

See **leverage**.

Geld und Brief

German words for bid and asked, sometimes abbreviated in price tables to "g" for bid and "b" for asked.

General collateral (GC)

In the repo market, collateral which meets the general requirements. See **repo**.

Generally accepted accounting principles (GAAP)

US standards set by the Financial Accounting Standards Board with the intention of achieving uniformity in financial reporting.

Gensaki

Japanese short-term money-market based on **repos**, open to corporations and financial institutions. The *Gensaki* rate is as important as yen LIBOR as an indicator of short-term interest rates.

Genußscheine

A German form of profit participation certificate without voting rights.

Geometric average

Calculated as the nth root of the product of n values. For example if n were 4 the average a would be calculated as

$$a = \sqrt[4]{(v_1 \times v_2 \times v_3 \times v_4)}$$

Unless all the value are equal, the result will be smaller than an arithmetic average. A geometric index is therefore easier to outperform which may account for its rarity.

Geregelter Markt

The regulated trade segment of the German Stock Exchange.

German Government Bonds

Bonds and treasury notes are issued as shares in a collective debt register claim entered in the Federal Debt Register in the name of *Deutscher Kassenverein AG, Frankfurt am Main*. Investors may have their holdings inscribed in their names in the Federal Debt Register.

Treasury Certificates are issued in book-entry form as shares in a collective certificate deposited with the *Deutscher Kassenverein AG*. Treasury Certificates are not converted into either physical securities or Debt Register claims.

The market is overseen by the *Deutsche Bundesbank*. *Bunds, Bobls*, and *Schätze* are listed on the eight German Stock Exchanges. BULIS and *Finanzierungs-Schätze* are not listed.

Besides the Federal Government, significant public sector borrowers include the Federal States (*Länder*), the *Treuhandanstalt*, the Federal Post Office (*Bundespost*), the German Unity Fund (*Fonds "Deutsche Einheit"*) and the Federal Railways (*Bundesbahn*).

The chief types of security are as follows.

Bundesanleihen (Bunds)

Generally fixed rate bonds with annual coupons, bullet maturities and no calls or puts. Minimum denomination is DM1,000. Some floaters have been issued which pay interest quarterly and which have call provisions.

The *Treuhandanstalt*, the German Unity Fund, the Economic Recovery Programme (ERP), the Federal Railway (the *Bundesbahn*) and the Federal Post Office (the *Bundespost*) also issue *anleihen*. The first three carry the explicit guarantee of the Federal Government. The agencies (*Bahn* and *Post*) are backed by the full faith and credit of the Federal Government.

Bundesobligationen (Bobls)

Fixed rate bonds with annual coupons, a five year bullet maturity and no calls or puts. Minimum denomination is DM1,000.

Bundesschatzanweisungen (Federal Treasury Notes or *Schätze*)

Fixed rate bonds with annual coupons and a four year maturity (since May 1991). Denominations are DM5,000.

Bundesbank Liquiditäts Unverzinsliche Schatzanweisungen (Discounted Treasury Certificates or BULIS)

Discounted bills with maturities from one to two years. Minimum denomination of DM500,000 (from March 1983 to December 1993 DM100,000). The *Deutsche Bundesbank* ceased issuing BULIS in September 1994.

Finanzierungs-Schätze (Treasury financing bills)

Discounted bills with maturities from one to two years. DM1,000 minimum denomination. Not listed. May not be sold to credit institutions or to foreign investors.

Bundesschatzbriefe (Federal Savings Notes)

Issued for six years with interest paid annually (type A) or for seven years with interest rolled up and paid at maturity (type B). Designed for private investors the type A notes have a DM100 minimum investment and the type B notes a DM50 minimum.

German Stock Exchange

The *Deutsche Börse AG* in Frankfurt was formed from the combination of the Frankfurt Stock Exchange (founded in 1585) and the DTB. In 1995 plans were announced to merge the operations of the Frankfurt, Munich and Düsseldorf exchanges. Share transactions must be routed through a bank which is a member of the exchange. Kursmaklers and freimaklers may not trade with members of the public. A single price is established each day for all listed shares. The most liquid shares are traded continuously. The IBIS computer assisted trading system is in addition to floor trading and allows exchange members all over Germany to trade in 36 liquid shares, 30 public bonds and some other securities in large size. An order transmission system, BOSS, aids the dealing process, conveying orders, confirmations and price data. Delivery of securities is usually through the securities clearing and deposit bank, the DKV (Deutscher Kassenverein AG), while payment is effected by direct-debit from accounts with the Bundesbank. There are many indices, of which the DAX (Deutscher Aktienindex) and the DAX-100 are the best-known. The DAX is made up of 30 shares, the DAX-100 of 100 shares.

Ghana Stock Exchange

Trading began in 1990. Shares but no debt instruments are listed. Trading is on three days each week under the call-over system with a limited auction element. The index is the GSE All-share Index. Settlement is not automated or centralized.

Gilt-edged market-maker (GEMM)

Gilt-edged market-makers (GEMMs) are primary dealers in the UK government bond market. They are required to quote firm two-way prices in all conditions at all times. GEMMs may deal directly with the Bank of England, they have access to a secured late-lending facility at the Bank of England and access to inter-dealer brokers (IDBs) in order to trade anonymously with other GEMMs. The 20 GEMMs in 1996 were:

> ABN Amro Hoare Govett Sterling Bonds Limited
> Aitken Campbell (Gilts) Limited
> Barclays de Zoete Wedd Gilts Limited
> Baring Sterling Bonds
> CS First Boston Gilts Limited
> Daiwa Europe (Gilts) Limited
> Deutsche Bank Gilts Limited
> Goldman Sachs Government Securities (U.K.)
> HSBC Greenwell

J.P. Morgan Sterling Securities Ltd.
Kleinwort Benson Gilts Limited
Lehman Brothers Gilts Limited
Merrill Lynch Gilts Limited
NatWest Gilts Limited
Nikko Gilts Limited
Salomon Brothers UK Limited
Societe Generale Gilts Limited
SBC Warburg Securities (Gilt – Edged) Ltd.
UBS Gilts Limited
Winterflood Gilts Limited

The Bank of England is anxious that these firms should be robust, and regularly reports their aggregate capital which was, for example £ 815 million at 31 December 1995. Their aggregate profitability has been volatile with an aggregate operating loss in 1994 of £60 million, being followed by an operating profit in 1995 of £13 million. The Bank of England noted that "a profit was reported by nearly half the GEMMs which were active throughout 1995." In fact the seven most prominent GEMMs have a market share of about 70 percent according to the Bank of England. These leading firms are BZW, Goldman Sachs, HSBC, Lehman Brothers, Salomon Brothers, NatWest and SBC Warburg.

Gilt-edged security

Domestic sterling-denominated security issued by the UK Treasury. At 29 December 1995 the nominal and market value of the sterling government bonds listed on the London Stock Exchange were as in Figure G1.

Figure G1

STERLING GOVERNMENT BONDS LISTED ON THE LONDON STOCK EXCHANGE: NOMINAL AND MARKET VALUE AT 29 DECEMBER 1995			
	No. of securities	Nominal value (£m)	Market value (£m)
Shorts (0–7 yrs)	31	78,516.8	83,253.0
Mediums (7–15 yrs)	26	74,193.0	80,896.2
Longs (over 15 yrs)	9	37,323.6	39,294.8
Undated	8	3,207.6	1,387.6
Index-linked	14	24,401.7	37,640.2
Variable rate	1	5,700.0	5,707.4
Bonds	5	11,061.0	11,231.8
Total	**94**	**234,403.7**	**259,411.0**

Source: London Stock Exchange

All gilts have a title. Some of these have no practical significance (e.g., Treasury, Exchequer, Funding) but some titles are significant. "Convertible" stocks give holders the right on specified terms and specified dates to convert all or part of their holding into one or more other specified stocks. "Conversion" is the title of stocks which came into being as a result of a conversion. "Loan" means that an investor may hold the stock in the form of bearer bonds.

"Double-dated" stocks (e.g., 8% Treasury Loan 2002-2006) give the government the right to redeem the stock at par on giving three months' notice at any time after the first date. Such stocks must be redeemed by the second date.

New issues are sometimes in the form of "partly paid" stocks where the stock is paid for in two or three stages with interest accruing on the amount paid.

The different types of gilt are shown in Figure G2.

Figure G2

DIFFERENT TYPES OF GILT

Conventional stocks   These have a fixed coupon paid semi-annually and usually one fixed repayment date.

Undated stocks   There are eight un-dated stocks which have a fixed rate of interest but no repayment date. Three of these, 2 1/2% Consolidated Stock, 2 1/2% Annuities and 2 3/4% Annuities have interest paid quarterly.

Index-linked stocks   Both the interest payments and the amount payable on redemption are adjusted in line with UK inflation as measured by the Retail Prices Index eight months in arrears. Stockholders are protected against changes in the coverage of the index or its calculation. If the Bank of England considered that a fundamental change had been made which was materially detrimental to the interests of investors, then holders would be offered the right to require the Treasury to redeem their stock not later than seven months from the last month of publication of the old index.

Floating rate stocks   Interest payments are reset every three months by reference to sterling money market rates.

Ginnie Mae

The US Government National Mortgage Association and the securities it issues.

Glass-Steagall Act

US Act of 1933 which separated the functions of banks and securities firms..

Global custody

Those services which an institutional investor might require to administer a portfolio of international securities. They might include settlement, safe-keeping, dividend and interest collection, foreign exchange, tax reclamation, portfolio valuation and reporting services.

Global master repurchase agreement

Standard contract documentation for repos published in 1992 by the US Public Securities Association (PSA) and the Council of Reporting Dealers repo sub-committee of the International Securities Market Association Limited (ISMA).

Global note

Temporary certificate representing a whole issue which is in place for a period after the closing usually to meet certain legal restrictions such as the US 40-day lock-up requirement, or because definitive certificates have not been printed.

GLOBEX

The GLOBEX® Trading System is an international automated order entry and matching system operated by Reuters for use by the **Chicago Mercantile Exchange (CME)**, the *Marché à Terme d'Instruments Financiers* **(MATIF)** and other exchanges which may join the system. In mid-1996 there were 420 GLOBEX terminals around the world.

The CME's GLOBEX session is referred to as Electronic Trading Hours (ETH), pit trading is referred to as Regular Trading Hours (RTH). GLOBEX allows a 23-hour trading day for CME futures and options; trading on GLOBEX begins shortly after and ends shortly before Regular Trading Hours on the CME. The GLOBEX session marks the start of a new trading day for the CME so that Tuesday's GLOBEX session is the start of Wednesday's trading day. Daily settlement prices are calculated at the close of RTH.

The contracts traded on GLOBEX may be grouped into three categories: currencies, interest rates and indices.

Currency futures and options on the Australian dollar, Brazilian real, British pound, Canadian dollar, Deutschemark, French franc, Japanese yen, Mexican peso and the Swiss franc. There are futures contracts on Deutschemark Forward, Deutschemark Rolling Spot®, Japanese yen Forward and Japanese yen Rolling Spot®.

There are futures and options on Eurodollars and the Eurodollar Mid-curve. There are futures on Federal Funds Rate, LIBOR, one-year T-bill, and the 90-day T-bill. There are also futures and options on Argentinian, Brazilian and Mexican Brady bonds.

The index products are futures and options on the S&P 500, S&P 500/Barra growth, S&P 500/Barra Value, S&P Midcap 400, GSCI, IPC Stock Index (Mexico), the Major Market Index, Nasdaq 100 and Russell 2000.

There is also cross-exchange access to the MATIF contracts on PIBOR, the CAC 40 and the ECU bond.

Going long

The purchase of a security or commodity, implicitly without hedging the position, so that the purchaser will benefit from a rise in price and suffer from a fall when he comes to close his position.

Going public

Offering shares for the first time to the public.

Going short

The sale of a security or commodity not owned, implicitly without hedging the position, so that the seller will benefit from a fall in price and suffer from a rise when he comes to close his position.

Gold

About 85,000 tonnes of gold are estimated to be held in private hands with a further 36,000 tonnes held by central banks and other institutions. The attitude of central banks to gold varies. Some central banks have been sellers of the metal. Others have maintained their holdings. The Bundesbank, for example, holds about 95 million ounces.

Global gold production totalled 72,495,000 troy ounces in 1995. It has been projected to increase to 83,000,000 troy ounces in 1999. Exact figures are unlikely because a percentage of gold production, estimated at 5 to 10 percent in some countries, simply goes missing. The table in Figure G3 shows projections for production in 1999 by the Gold Institute in Washington, based on information from gold mining companies.

Gold participation certificate (Gold PC)

Participation certificate issued by the US **Federal Home Loan Mortgage Corporation** with enhancements. Gold PCs have an FHLMC guarantee of full and timely payment of both interest and scheduled principal; and their published pool factors are based on actual, rather than predicted prepayments.

Gold standard

The fixing of the value of a currency in terms of gold. The UK left the gold standard finally in 1931, the US in 1971.

Gold tranche

That part of an IMF country quota, usually 25 percent, which has to be paid in gold.

Figure G3

1999 PROJECTIONS FOR GOLD PRODUCTION

Country	Output in 000's troy ounces	% increase over 1995
South Africa	14,551	–13%
United States	12,743	+21%
Australia	11,220	+38%
CIS	7,500	+3%
China	5,966	+36%
Canada	5,787	+21%
Brazil	2,815	+30%
Indonesia	2,673	+12%
Ghana	1,843	+10%
Papua New Guinea	1,789	+2%
Peru	1,768	+7%
Chile	1,575	+10%
Philippines	1,126	+23%
Argentina	988	+3429%
Zimbabwe	881	+5%
Venuzuela	880	+60%

Source: *World Gold Mine Production 1995–99*, The Gold Institute)

Golden hello

Payment offered to induce a potential new employee to join a firm.

Gold-linked note

Note with payments of interest, principal or both linked to the price of gold.

"Good till cancelled"

An order to buy or sell securities, which if it is not executed at once remains in effect until the order can be executed or is cancelled.

Goodwill

Intangible asset. It may arise when a company pays more than net asset value for another company when this surplus is attributed, sometimes charitably, to the intangible assets of the acquired company. In some accounting jurisdictions, goodwill arising on acquisitions may be written off against reserves, in others it must be written off over time as a charge to profits. Companies subject to the latter treatment are perhaps more thoughtful about paying large premiums above net asset value to acquire businesses. Brands and other similar intangible but important assets are often not recognized in a company's accounts.

Gourde

The national currency of Haiti.

Governing law

The jurisdiction to which the parties in a transaction agree to be subject. Usually chosen because of the experience of the judicial system, and the clarity of the laws and their interpretation.

Government Bonds

Many countries issue government bonds and many encourage foreign investors. The volume of government debt has been growing rapidly in recent years both absolutely and in relation to GDP. The 13 largest borrowing countries were estimated to issue more than US$1,500 billion of debt in 1996. The levels of activity of the major governments may be summarised as follows:

Country	Forecast new borrowing 1996 in US$ bn
United States	601
Japan	366
Italy	182
France	100
Germany	85
United Kingdom	40
Spain	37
Canada	32
Belgium	28
Netherlands	25
Sweden	19
Denmark	18
Australia	7

Source: J.P. Morgan

The following table shows the relative trend expressed as a percentage of GDP.

Country	Net Public Debt/GDP %		
	1975	1985	1995
Belgium	48.9	112.5	128.4
Italy	53.2	79.9	109.2
Canada	7.3	34.7	66.2
United States	27.3	33.0	51.5
Spain	3.5	27.5	50.1

Germany	1.0	20.8	49.0
United Kingdom	42.8	30.6	38.8
France	-1.0	10.8	35.0
Sweden	-28.8	14.3	26.8
Japan	-3.0	25.9	11.1

Source: OECD

Each government bond market has evolved differently. Even the arithmetic can be different – not just between markets but between yield calculations and accrued interest calculations in the same market. Market conventions in certain government bond markets are set out in the following table.

Country	Prices	Coupon payment	Yield calculations	Accrued interest calculations
USA	fractions	semi-annual	Act/Act	Act/Act
Japan	decimals	semi-annual	Act/365	Act/365
UK	fractions	semi-annual	Act/365	Act/365
France	decimals	annual	Act/Act	Act/Act
Italy	decimals	semi-annual	Act/365	30/360
Spain	decimals	annual	Act/365	Act/Act
Canada	decimals	semi-annual	Act/Act	Act/365
Ireland	decimals	annual & semi-annual	30/360	30/360
Germany	decimals	annual	30/360	30/360
Netherlands	decimals	annual	30/360	30/360
Belgium	decimals	annual	30/360	30/360
Austria	decimals	annual	30/360	30/360
Sweden	decimals	annual	30/360	30/360
Denmark	decimals	annual	30/360	30/360
Finland	decimals	annual	30/360	30/360
Switzerland	decimals	annual	30/360	30/360

See also **Auctions, Bonds, French Government Bonds, German Government Bonds, Italian Government Bonds, Japanese Government Bonds, US Government Securities, gilt-edged securities, basis trading, yield, term structure of interest rates, repos.**

Government broker

Formerly the agent of the Bank of England who acted on behalf of the UK government in the gilt market. Almost the last person to wear regularly a top hat in the City of London.

Government National Mortgage Association (GNMA)

Known as Ginnie Mae, it is a US-government corporation which guarantees privately issued securities backed by pools of federally insured or guaranteed mortgages.

Governmental Accounting Standards Board (GASB)

US authority which sets accounting standards for State and local government bodies.

Grace period

(1) The time between the start of a loan and the first repayment of principal.

(2) The time allowed for the breach of a covenant in an agreement to be remedied.

Gramm-Rudman Hollings Act

US act passed in 1985 requiring the gradual reduction and eventual elimination of the US Federal budget deficit!

Grantor

The writer of an option

Green Book

See **Yellow Book**.

Green shoe

An option granted to the lead underwriter by an issuer allowing the underwriter to purchase more shares to cover the short position created by over-allotting the offering. This was first done in an issue for the Green Shoe Manufacturing Company.

Greenbacks

US banknotes first printed during the Civil War, and now used to denote US banknotes in general.

Greenmail

The practice of acquiring a block of shares in a company, and then making oneself so objectionable to the management of the company that they arrange for you to be bought out at a profit. Typically, the process involves the threat of a hostile takeover bid which stimulates the activities of arbitrageurs.

Gresham's Law

Bad money drives out good. Named after Sir Thomas Gresham, who became rich lending money to Elizabeth I of England. His sign, a grasshopper, still hangs in Lombard Street. He helped to finance the Cathay Company which set out to find a northwest passage from England to China and found Canada instead.

Grey Book

Bank of England's supervisory rules for the wholesale markets in foreign exchange, sterling, and bullion which are not regulated under the Financial Services Act.

Grey market prices

The equivalent of when-issued trading in the Euromarkets. Originally begun by Stanley Ross, whose firm Ross & Partners had one of the most used bond broker's screen pages on Reuters in the early 1980s. Lead-managers of new issues had not been used to seeing their pricing judged so quickly, and initially resented such trading.

Gross

A payment made without the deduction of tax is said to be made gross.

Gross domestic product

The value of a country's output, income or expenditure, excluding overseas transactions.

Gross domestic product deflator (GDP deflator)

A measure of inflation in an economy expressed as the percentage difference between real Gross Domestic Product (GDP), i.e., GDP at constant prices, and nominal GDP, i.e., money GDP (or GDP at current prices).

Gross national product (GNP)

Gross domestic product (GDP) plus income earned from investment or work abroad.

Gross positions

The sum of a trader's position in each instrument without netting between, say, puts and calls or long and short positions.

Gross redemption yield

The yield on a security which is before the deduction of any tax on interest payments and which includes the effect of any premium or discount in the purchase price. The yield is calculated using the technique of discounted cash flows. The gross redemption yield is that rate which equates all future gross cash flows to the current market price. See **yield**.

Gross-up clause

The clause in a loan agreement or bond issue document which provides for additional payments to be made by the borrower to the lender (or investors) to raise their interest income to the level which it would have been but for the imposition of withholding or other taxes. Often the issuer of securities has an alternative option to redeem them at **par** rather than pay a higher interest cost.

Group of Fifteen (G15)

Formed in 1989 as an offshoot of the non-aligned movement. It is made up of Algeria, Argentina, Brazil, Egypt, India, Indonesia, Jamaica, Malaysia, Mexico, Nigeria, Peru, Senegal, Venezuela, Yugoslavia and Zimbabwe.

Group of Five (G5)

France, Germany, Japan, the UK and the US.

Group of Seven (G7)

The Group of Five plus Canada and Italy.

Group of Ten (G10)

Belgium, Canada, France, Germany, Italy, Japan, the Netherlands, Sweden, Switzerland, the UK and the US. Saudi Arabia is an Associate Member.

Group of Thirty (G30)

Group of leading policy-makers, academics and bankers which studies and reports on international financial questions.

GSCI™

Goldman Sachs Commodity Index, a production-weighted commodity price index. It is a cash index based on futures prices and is therefore an investable index. The index, along with most commodities, is strongly positively correlated to inflation and strongly negatively correlated to stock and bond returns. Futures and options on this index are traded on the CME. The GSCI at January 1997 was in percentage dollar weights (see Figure G4).

Guandong United Futures Exchange

Formed from the merger in 1994 of the Guanzhou Commodity Futures Exchange and the South China Commodity Futures Exchange. Trading is by computer and clearing through an independent clearing house. The exchange trades futures on aluminum, copper, gasoline, diesel, heating oil, white sugar, soya bean, soya bean meal, corn, and polished long-grain non-glutinous rice.

Figure G4

GOLDMAN SACHS COMMODITY INDEX COMPONENTS AND WEIGHTS

Subsector Commodity	Dollar weight (%)
Energy	63.18
Crude Oil	21.62
Unleaded Gas	11.19
Heating Oil	10.67
Natural Gas	19.89
Industrial Metals	6.27
Aluminium	2.87
Copper	1.97
Lead	0.30
Nickel	0.44
Tin	0.11
Zinc	0.69
Precious Metals	2.20
Gold	1.77
Platinum	0.24
Silver	0.19
Agriculture	18.91
Wheat	6.58
Corn	3.81
Soybeans	2.19
Cotton	2.48
Sugar	2.18
Coffee	1.34
Cocoa	0.26
Livestock	9.44
Live Cattle	5.83
Lean Hogs	3.60

Guarantee

Undertaking in writing by one party to ensure the performance of a particular obligation by another party.

Guaranteed investment contract (GIC)

Contract encountered in the US, and obtained from an insurance company which typically offers a high return but the investor is locked in for the life of the contract.

177

Guaranteed Mortgage Certificate (GMC)

Bond issued by the US Federal Home Loan Mortgage Corporation (FHLMC), backed by a pool of conventional mortgages. Unlike a pass-through, the FHLMC guarantees that some minimum principal amount will be paid each year and the investor has a put option prior to maturity.

Guaranteed warrant

Warrant where performance is guaranteed by a third party rather than the Options Clearing Corporation. Often of longer maturity than exchange-traded contracts.

Guayaquil Stock Exchange

The Bolsa de Valores de Guayaquil CC is the second exchange of Ecuador, after the Quito Stock Exchange. Shares and bonds are traded. The exchange began to expand in 1993, when trading volumes began to increase.

Guilder

The national currency of the Netherlands, the Netherlands Antilles and Surinam.

Gulf riyal

The national currency of Qatar and Dubai.

H

Haircut

The capital required for a trading position. In the US, this differs according to the nature of the instrument and the volatility of its price.

Half a bar

Dealers' slang phrase for half a million. Common in London dealing rooms.

Hamburg Stock Exchange

The Hanseatische Wertpapierbörse Hamburg is the oldest stock exchange in Germany, having been founded in 1558. The operation of the market is as described under **German Stock Exchange**.

Hammering

The announcement of the failure of a member firm on the London Stock Exchange.

Hammersmith & Fulham swap case

UK court case in 1989–91 concerning a local government body which was held to have acted *ultra vires* in executing almost £3,000 million of swap contracts, when its own total debt was £390 million. Many of the transactions were speculative positions, which turned to loss when UK interest rates rose. The final decision after appeals was that all the swap contracts were invalid. The losses were borne therefore by the bank counterparties, and not by the taxpayers of Hammersmith & Fulham. The story did not enhance London's reputation.

Hand signals

Gestures used on the floor of an exchange by traders (see Figure H1).

Handel

German word for trade.

Handymax Index

Shipping index launched by the Baltic Exchange in London in December

Figure H1

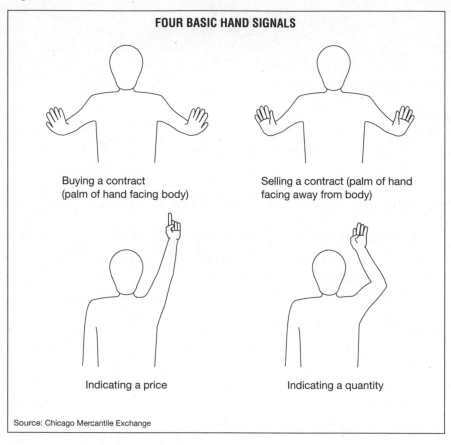

FOUR BASIC HAND SIGNALS

Buying a contract
(palm of hand facing body)

Selling a contract (palm of hand
facing away from body)

Indicating a price

Indicating a quantity

Source: Chicago Mercantile Exchange

1996. It is based on a 43,000 tonne deadweight carrier with four 25 tonne cranes and on four time charter rates. See **Baltic Freight Index (BFI)**.

Hang Seng Index

Index of leading share prices on the Hong Kong Stock Exchange.

Hanover Stock Exchange

The Niedersächsische Börse zu Hanover is a provincial German stock exhange. The operation of the market is as described under **German Stock Exchange**.

Hard currency

A currency thought to be a safe store of value on account of the political and economic stability and the austere financial policies that a country exhibits.

Harmless warrant

A bond warrant which is issued with a callable host bond. The host bond may be called in part by lot or entirely. Thus the issuer avoids double funding risk, because he is able to call the host bonds as new bonds are created by exercise of the warrants. A variation is to have warrants where the exercise price may only be paid in host bonds, so that host bonds are surrendered to match the new bonds created. Such warrants may or may not be detachable from the host bond.

Head and shoulders

A pattern seen on charts of securities prices thought by chartists to indicate a likely price reversal.

Heaven and hell bond

High-risk security where the redemption value is linked in a geared manner to the change in a foreign exchange rate. The redemption value may vary from almost nothing to twice the purchase price or more.

Heavy share

A share which has a high unit price in relation to the average price of shares in the market. Sometimes thought to be at a disadvantage to lower priced shares though there is little evidence for this. Share splits designed to deal with the problem have no theoretical justification, but they happen anyway. An exceptional case is the share price of the US company Berkshire Hathaway which rose to a height that made the purchase of even one share too expensive for many private investors. The company issued 'B' shares which were fractions of a full share.

Hedge

A transaction intended to reduce or neutralize an existing risk.

Hedge accounting

Accounting principles which look at the net effect of a series of related transactions, and try to account for them in a way which matches related gains and losses and does not distort the financial statements.

Hedge fund

Speculative mutual fund or limited partnership, formed with the intention of taking aggressive and usually unhedged positions in a wide range of instruments and derivatives.

Helsinki Money Market Centre

Payments clearing system owned by the Bank of Finland and major Finnish market participants.

181

Helsinki Stock Exchange

The Finnish stock exchange was founded in 1912. Trading has been decentralized and automated since 1990 using the HETI system. Each trading day begins with a period in which orders are matched followed by the free trading period. Most trading is in shares with small amounts of bonds, subscription rights and other instruments. All transactions are cleared through the exchange's clearing centre on the DVP principle on T+3.

Herstatt risk

The risk which arises when foreign exchange transactions are settled in different time zones. For example, in a DM/US$ FX deal, the D-mark payment must be made in the European banking day before the US dollar countervalue has been received in New York.

The term comes from the failure in 1974 of the German bank Herstatt which was closed by the Bundesbank having received D-marks in European time but having not yet made US dollar payments in New York. See **risk**.

Higher of proceeds and market

The accounting rule applied to liabilities such as short positions and sold options. It is the mirror image of the rule applied to assets: "the lower of cost and market."

High-low option

A type of **lookback option** which pays out the difference between the highest price and the lowest price at which the underlying has traded during the life of the option.

Hindsight currency option

A lookback currency option. See **lookback option**.

Hiroshima Stock Exchange

Japanese exchange established in 1949 and one of the five regional exchanges. The exchange trades shares, convertible bonds, bonds with warrants and equity warrants. Trading is by the *zaraba* method on the floor of the exchange.

Historical volatility

The variance or standard deviation of the change in price of the underlying during a particular past period. It is often used as an indicator of future volatility – though it ain't necessarily so.

Hit

A bid is hit when it is dealt on. An offer is lifted when it is dealt on.

Hoeckman

Jobber on the Amsterdam Stock Exchange.

Hokkaido Grain Exchange

Merged with the Tokyo Grain Exchange in April 1994.

Holder

The owner of a security or option.

Hold-in-custody repo

A classic **repo**, where the supplier of the collateral does not physically deliver it to the counterparty, but keeps it in a segregated account or delivers it to a clearing bank for safe-keeping. See **repo**.

Holding company

Company which holds shares in other companies but is not usually itself an operating company.

Holding cost

The costs of maintaining a position. This may include interest costs, margin calls, or storage and insurance costs in the case of commodities.

Holding period

In **value-at-risk** analysis, the volatility estimate used will depend on the length of time for which a position is likely to be held. A long holding period will suggest higher risk of loss and a higher volatility assumption.

Hong Kong Futures Exchange

Incorporated originally in 1976 as the Hong Kong Commodity Exchange. Futures and options are traded on the Hang Seng Index and futures are traded on the Commerce & Industry, Properties, Finance, and Utilities sub-indices. There are futures on specific stocks, the first three of which were HSBC Holdings, Hong Kong Telecommunications and Cheung Kong (Holdings). There are futures on three-month HIBOR and Gold, as well as rolling DEM and YEN futures. Trading is by **open outcry**, except for trading in currency products. The exchange has a link with the PHLX, which allows PHLX currency options to be traded in Asian business hours.

Hong Kong Stock Exchange

Trading is order-driven through the AMS computerized system with an automatching facility. Settlement and clearing are through CCASS on T+2. The main indices are the Hang Seng Index, a capitalization-weighted index of 33 shares, the Hang Seng Midcap 50 Index, which is made up of the 50 most actively traded shares, and the Hang Seng China Enterprises Index, made up of all **H-shares** listed on the exchange.

Horizontal spread

An options strategy, where a trader buys one option and sells another with the same strike price but with a different expiration date. See **calendar spread**.

Hors-côte

French word for Unlisted.

Host bond

A bond to which some other security or warrant was attached at the time of issue. A host bond will naturally trade at a discount to its issue price, once the warrants have been detached and may therefore cease to be a current coupon bond very soon after issue. This may slightly affect its value in some markets.

Hryvna

National currency of the Ukraine until the 17th century, and reintroduced in 1996 when it replaced the karbovanets (or coupons).

H-shares

The shares of Chinese enterprises listed on the Hong Kong Stock Exchange.

Hurst exponent

A way of measuring deviation from the bell-shaped graph of a normal distribution was devised by a British scientist studying flooding of the Nile in 1907. He found that two successive floods or droughts were slightly more frequent than one would have expected. The Hurst exponent is a measure of how much a graph was produced by a purely random process which will tend to fall into the pattern of a normal distribution. It is the probability that one event will be followed by a similar event. If a graph has an exponent of 0.5, it is produced by a random process. If it is more than 0.5, it is leptokurtotic and is the result of a process which tends to go in runs. The graph will have "fat tails."

The discovery that, like the Nile, stock prices also tend to be leptokurtotic was significant. It tended to undermine the stronger versions of efficient market theory, and to undermine the use of standard deviation as a measure of risk in the capital asset pricing model.

Hybrid security

Security combining two or more features of bonds or notes, swaps, forwards, futures or options. They may be divided into hybrids where the redemption amount is variable, which can be lethal, and hybrids where only the interest rate is variable, which are just exciting.

Hyderabad Stock Exchange

An Indian stock exchange which will become part of the unified Indian stock exchange. See **National Stock Exchange of India.**

Hyperinflation

Rapid inflation tending towards economic collapse. Rapid inflation is probably in excess of 50 percent per month.

Hypothecate

To place a charge on an asset. The exact meaning of this and related terms will vary with each legal system.

Hypotheken bank

German mortgage bank.

I

IASC

International Accounting Standards Committee. Founded in 1973 by accountants from nine countries, it now has 119 member bodies from 87 countries. Its rules may in time become a world standard.

Iceland Stock Exchange

Established in 1985 in Reykjavik, the largest group of listed securities is debt securities followed by shares and UCITS. Trading is by computerized order-driven system. Securities are in physical form, and settlement is on T+1.

Icing stock

Slang term from the **repo** market which means reserving or putting on hold stock at the request of someone planning to acquire that security through a **repo**.

IDEM

See **Italian Derivatives Market (IDEM)**.

In option

A type of **barrier option,** which is like an ordinary option only when the price of the underlying reaches an agreed barrier price before expiry.

Ijara

Islamic financial technique similar to lease financing.

Illiquid

A security which is not actively traded and may be difficult to buy or sell.

Immunization

An asset management strategy which matches the Macaulay duration of a bond portfolio to the duration of a specified set of future liabilities, and the present value of the portfolio to the present value of the liabilities. The portfolio should then produce the target rate of return whatever changes occur in market rates. See **dedication**.

Implied forward interest rate

Future interest rate implied by the current term structure of interest rates (yield curve), which is in fact not an accurate predictor of future rates.

Implied repo rate

The financing rate at which a long cash–short futures arbitrageur would neither gain nor lose on a transaction. The implied repo rate can also be thought of as the rate of return earned on the funds used to purchase the cash security in a **cash-and-carry** trade. See **barrier trading** and **repo**.

Implied volatility

The volatility assumption implied by an existing option price. See **historic volatility**.

Implied yield

A future yield derived from present yields, and based on the assumption that the yield curve on one particular day is a reliable indication of its future shape. See **expectation theory**.

Income right

An instrument which entitles the holder to an annuity.

Income statement

Profit and loss statement. If a balance sheet is a picture at a single date, an income statement may be thought of as the story of a period between two balance sheet dates.

Income warrant

Warrant which pays the holder interest on the nominal value of the warrant until such time as it is exercised or expires.

Income yield

Another term for interest yield, current yield or running yield. See **yield**.

Inconvertible currency

Currency which cannot be freely exchanged.

Increasing rate debt

Security which may be extended in maturity at the borrower's option but at an ever-increasing interest rate. May also refer to perpetual debt, which when issued by banks may count as part of their capital base, but which has a rapidly increasing coupon after a number of years, such that the borrower is highly likely to refinance it. If the borrower is unable to do so, the high coupon is likely to support the price of the debt in the market.

Increasing rate preferred stock

Type of preferred stock, often issued at a discount-to-face value, which pays dividends which increase over time.

Indemnity

An undertaking to preserve a person from loss if a specified event happens.

Indenture

US term for the document which describes the terms of a bond issue, the obligations of the issuer and the duties and powers of the Trustee. May also be used to describe a mortgage document.

Index

A measure of the total return accruing to the holders of a class of asset. Indices may be very focused on a small class or may be worldwide in scope. Indices are widely used to follow markets and to measure the performance of investment managers. Fund managers whose jobs depend on relative performance tend to replicate the content of indices quite closely in their portfolios. Their relative lack of success in outperforming indices has led to the growing popularity of tracker funds which try only to mimic an index and not to outperform it. See **share index**.

The arithmetic of indices

An index is calculated by weighting a number of prices or rates according to a predetermined set of rules and then calculating an average. The two crucial choices are to do with weighting and the average calculated.

Indices may give weights to each constituent price or they may be equally weighted. For example, all the FT Actuaries share indices are weighted by market capitalization, while the oldest FT index, the FT-30, is unweighted. Weighted indices are more common than unweighted indices.

The second choice is to do with averages. The choice is between calculating an arithmetic average and a geometric average. An arithmetic average is calculated as the sum of n values divided by n. For example

$$(v_1 + v_2 + v_3 + v_4 \ \ldots \ + v_n)/n$$

A geometric average is calculated as the nth root of the product of n values.

$$\sqrt[n]{(v_1 \times v_2 \times v_3 \ \ldots \ \times v_n)}$$

Unless all the values are equal the result of the geometric average calculation will be smaller than an arithmetic average. The latter is now more common though both methods are still used. For example the FT-30 Index is based on a geometric average while the FT All-Share Index is an arithmetic mean.

Return calculations

Typically total returns are calculated assuming that each security is bought at the begining of the period and sold at the end of it. Normally bidside valuations are used. A security's total rate-of-return is the percentage change in its total value over the measurement period. Where total returns are market-capitalization weighted the security's beginning-of-period market value is used. The components of total return are: price change; principal payments; coupon or dividend payments; accrued interest; reinvestment income; currency movements (where applicable).

The following characteristics are desirable in an index.

Comprehensiveness
An index should include all the opportunities that are realistically available to market participants under normal market conditions. It should not be subject to opinions about which securities to include on a particular day.

Replicability
The total returns reported for an index should be replicable by market participants. Information about the composition of an index and its historical returns must be readily available.

Stability
An index should not change composition very often, and changes should be well-understood and predictable. Investors should not be forced to execute a significant number of transactions just to keep pace.

No barriers to entry
The markets or market segments included in an index should not have significant barriers to entry.

Expenses
It is normal for investment activity to result in expenses relating to withholding tax, safekeeping and transactions. These expenses should be predictable and not excessive.

Objective selection criteria
There should be a clear set of rules governing the inclusion of securities in an index.

Index amortizing (rate) swap
An interest-rate swap where the notional principal decreases as interest rates fall, replicating the behavior of mortgage-backed securities when the underlying fixed-rate mortgages begin to be refinanced at lower rates.

Index and Options Market (IOM)
A division of the **Chicago Mercantile Exchange (CME).**

Index arbitrage

Trading to exploit discrepancies in pricing between a stock index and related derivatives.

Index Compagnie des Agents de Change (CAC40)

The CAC40, as it is known, is an index compiled from the share price of 40 leading French companies and was introduced in June 1988. Futures based on it were introduced by the *Marché à Terme d'Instruments Financiers* (MATIF) in August 1988 and CAC40 options by the *Marché des Options Négociables de Paris* (MONEP) in November 1988.

Index fund

An investment fund which is intended to replicate the return of a market index. Also called a "tracker fund."

Index futures

Futures on an index, usually an equity index. Most of the main equity indices have related futures.

Indexed currency option note

A combination of a conventional fixed-rate security and a currency option applied to the principal amount at maturity.

Index-linked debt

Index-linked securities may have payments of interest, principal or both tied to an index. Usually, this is an index of inflation and the bonds carry an interest rate set at a margin above the index.

In 1996 the US Treasury secretary announced plans to issue inflation protected bonds with a 10-year life. The initial plan was to start a program of quarterly issuance in January 1997 but issuance was subsequently postponed.

Figure I1 gives a summary of the issuance of government index-linked bonds at March 1996.

Indicative price

A price which a dealer makes, but which is not a firm price at which the trader undertakes to deal.

Indicative rating

When a prospective new issuer of securities discusses their possible rating with the rating agencies, the issuer will be given an indicative rating which helps the transaction to progress, but which is not a formal rating. See **rating bond.**

Figure I1

GOVERNMENT INDEX-LINKED BONDS ISSUED AS AT MARCH 1996						
	Australia	*Canada*	*Israel*	*New Zealand*	*Sweden*	*UK*
Total $bn	2.7	4.3	27.9	0.1	5.7	71.1
% of total marketable debt	3.8%	1.4%	79.0%	0.7%	4.5%	17.8%

Source: Bank of England

Indonesian Commodity Exchange Board

Founded in 1986, the exchange trades physical rubber and coffee contracts. Trading is by **open outcry**. Clearing and settlement is through the Indonesian Commodities Clearing House.

Industrieanleihen

German word for corporate bonds.

Inflation risk

The risk that a nominal rate of return on an investment is reduced or removed altogether in real terms by the effect of inflation. See **risk**

Information memorandum

Document prepared to inform prospective investors or lenders about an issue of securities or loan and about the issuer or borrower.

Inhabereffekten

German word for bearer securities.

Inhaberschuldverschreibungen

German word for unsecured domestic bearer bonds.

Inheritance tax (IHT)

UK tax levied on the amount, if any, by which the estate of a deceased person exceeds £215,000 (in 1997). There are certain exemptions, including total exemption if an estate is left to the deceased's spouse.

Initial margin

The amount of money required required to be paid to the clearing house of a derivatives exchange to establish a position in a derivative. The amount of initial margin required varies between exchanges, and is calculated by each exchange using its own risk measurement model. Further margin calls follow on any day when the market value of the position requires it.

Initial public offering (IPO)

The first offering to the general public of a company's equity.

Inscribed form

A way of describing securities held on a book-entry system and not in physical form.

Insider dealing

The exploitation of privileged information for profit. The degree to which this is a crime, and the degree to which, if a crime, the authorities have succeeded in enforcing the law varies from country to country. In the UK, there is at least clarity as to the law. The relevant legislation is the Criminal Justice Act 1993. There are three offences: dealing in securities with the benefit of information which is not generally available, encouraging someone else to do so, and passing the information to someone else. Those convicted may be jailed for up to seven years and subject to an unlimited fine. Inside information relates to a particular security or issuer, is specific or precise, has not been made public and would have , if it were made public, a significant effect on the price. It is not necessary for the use of this information to be profitable: people have been convicted for insider dealing which lost money. A person has inside information if he has it as a result of being a director, employee or shareholder, or as a result of his employment, office or profession, or if the direct or indirect source of the information has it by virtue of these things.

Insolvency

The condition of being unable to pay one's liabilities as they fall due. A company is also insolvent if its assets are less than the amount of its liabilities.

Installment loan

Loan repayable in installments.

Instrike

The barrier price at which an **in option** becomes like an ordinary option.

Insurance financial strength rating

Moody's Investors Service rating system for insurance companies which judges the ability to pay policyholder obligations.

Intangible assets

Things such as the cost of patents, the value of brands and trade marks, and goodwill which are not physical assets.

Inter-American Development Bank (IADB)

Development Bank for Latin American countries. Members include Japan and 14 European countries, as well as the USA and 26 countries of Latin America.

Interbank rate

The rate at which banks bid for and offer deposits to other banks. In London these two rates are known as LIBID and LIBOR respectively, whatever the currency involved. See **AIBOR, ATHIBOR, BIBOR, DIBOR, FIBOR, KIBOR, LIBOR, LXBOR, MIBOR, NIBOR, PIBOR, RIBOR, SIBOR, TIBOR,** and **VIBOR.**

Interbanken Information System (IBIS)

German equity trading system.

Inter-dealer broker (IDB)

Intermediary between market-makers. IDBs are matched-book or blind brokers since they act as principals, but only between two matching counterparts, in order to provide anonymity to each side.

Interesse maturato

Italian phrase for **accrued interest.**

Interest coupon

The coupon attached to a certificate which gives the holder the right to interest payments at specified dates.

Interest cover

A measure of a borrower's ability to service its debt. Usually calculated as earnings before interest and tax (EBIT), divided by the annual interest payable.

Interest rate risk

The possible loss which would arise from a change in interest rates. This risk may be divided into absolute risk, relative risk and security-specific risk.

Absolute risk is often analyzed first in terms of a parallel shift in interest rates which supposes that rates at all maturities change by the same amount, so that the new interest rate curve is parallel to the old one. A more complex analysis is needed to assess the loss which might occur if the yield curve changed in a non-parallel fashion. The range of possible shapes of the new curve is not endless; the steepness may change or short-term rates may rise sharply but medium and long-term rates tend to be close to each other.

Relative interest-rate risk arises when a position in one instrument or market is hedged in a similar but not identical instrument or in a related market. The risk that the relationship between the instruments or markets may change and cause loss may be quantified by examining the volatility of data series and looking at the correlation between them. This methodology is part of what is known as value-at-risk analysis.

Security-specific interest-rate risk may arise from some feature of the security in the case of a structured transaction or may be a consequence of an adverse change in the credit of the obligor. This is more likely to be thought of as credit risk.

Interest rate swap

An agreement between two parties to exchange interest payments calculated on a given notional principal amount. These interest payments are most often fixed on one hand and variable on the other, but variable/variable structures are also encountered. Interest rate swaps are off-balance sheet transactions which do not involve the payment or receipt of the principal amount: this is not the case with currency swaps. The two key functions of such swaps are to act as a link between the rates in different markets, for example, money markets, loan market and bond markets, which did not previously exist and, second, to allow a company to manage its interest-rate exposures, whether as borrower or investor, separately from decisions about the underlying assets or liabilities. Most swaps are documented under agreements based on the ISDA swap master agreement. This brings a degree of standardization to this OTC market, and helps counterparties to manage their risk on each other by providing for the netting of all exposures arising on contracts executed under the same master agreement. See **swap**.

Interest-only mortgage

A mortgage where the borrower is only bound to pay interest until the maturity date of the loan when the whole principal amount is due for repayment. Usually such loans are pre-paid in whole or in part at the discretion of the borrower.

Interim dividend

Dividend declared during a company's financial year in contrast to a final dividend paid after the year-end.

Interim statement

Summary accounts covering a portion of a financial year.

Intermarket Clearing Corporation (ICC)

A subsidiary of the Chicago-based Options Clearing Corporation (OCC) which clears and settles futures contracts.

Intermediation

The act of standing between two parties to facilitate transaction. The traditional function of banks which has been eroded in recent years.

Internal rate of return (IRR)

The interest rate that equates the present value of a future stream of payments to the price of the security. It is the same as yield to maturity. See **yield**.

International Bank Credit Analysis (IBCA)

A London-based rating agency.

International Bank for Reconstruction and Development (IBRD)

Proper name of the World Bank. It has 149 member countries which must also be members of the IMF. It was founded to help refinance the reconstruction of Europe after World War II, and now provides loans to developing countries. The World Bank has been a leading borrower in the international capital markets, and has a reputation for helping to develop new techniques. It is said to have been a party to the first currency swap and, more recently, has pioneered the global bond issue.

International Commodities Clearing House (ICCH)

London-based independent central clearing and guarantee organization through which contracts traded on futures and options exchanges in London and elsewhere are settled.

International Finance Corporation (IFC)

Affiliate of the World Bank (see **International Bank for Reconstruction and Development (IBRD)**) which assists private enterprises in developing countries.

International Financial Services Centre

Zone in Dublin's Custom House Dock which benefits from tax concessions granted to financial institutions engaged in international business.

International Monetary Fund (IMF)

International organization formed to enhance world monetary stability. Its lending is usually linked to strict reform of a country's fiscal imbalance.

International Monetary Market (IMM)

A division of the Chicago Mercantile Exchange (CME), specializing in currency and Eurodollar futures. The IMM was the first financial derivatives exchange in 1972. Many over-the-counter derivatives transactions are arranged to match IMM settlement dates.

International Organization of Securities Commissions (IOSCO)

International association of securities regulators.

International Petroleum Exchange (IPE)

Energy futures and options exchange in London. Contracts traded are futures and options on Brent crude oil and Gas Oil. The daily average of contracts traded in January 1996 was equivalent to 77 million barrels per day. Total world production of oil at the same time was 70 million barrels per day. There are 45 floor member companies as well as local members. The IPE is a **recognized investment exchange**, regulated by the **Securities and Futures Authority** which is a **self-regulating organisation** under the UK Financial Services Act.

International Primary Markets Association (IPMA)

International organization of institutions engaged in managing issues of securities in the Euromarkets. It has more than 100 member banks. IPMA publishes a set of recommendations which represent standards of good practice, relating to the syndication and documentation of new issues of debt and equity securities.

International Securities Markets Association (ISMA)

Established in 1969, with headquarters in Zurich, ISMA has about 500 member firms.The objective of ISMA is to promote orderly trading and the general development of the Euromarkets. Under UK regulations, ISMA is a **recognised investment exchange**.

International Swap and Derivatives Association (ISDA)

Formerly the International Swap Dealers Association, ISDA is the professional association for swap traders which has published codes of practice and "master agreements" for use in swap transactions. The activities of the association have widened to other derivatives in recent years. It has been an effective lobbying body educating legislators and regulators. It publishes statistics which give an indication of overall volumes traded in OTC derivatives.

Internet

Much useful information may be obtained from the Internet. Derivative exchanges have been particularly quick to use the medium, even if they cannot all resist an elaborate first page which is slow to download. Figures I2 and I3 give selective lists of addresses.

Figure I2

EXCHANGES: SOME INTERNET ADDRESSES	
Chicago Board of Trade	http://www.cbot.com/
Chicago Mercantile Exchange	http://www.cme.com/
Hong Kong Futures Exchange	http://www.hkfe.com/
LIFFE	http://www.liffe.com/
MATIF	http://www.matif.fr/
MEFF Renta Fija	http://www.meff.es/
NYMEX	http://www.ino.com/gen/nymex/html
Singapore International Monetary	
Exchange Limited	http://www.simex.com.sg
Sydney Futures Exchange	http://www.sfe.com.au/
Tokyo Grain Exchange	http://www.toppan.co.jp/tge

Figure I3

CENTRAL BANKS, ETC: SOME INTERNET ADDRESSES	
The Bank of England	http://www.bankofengland.co.uk
Ministère de l'Économie, Paris	http://www.cat.finances.gouv.fr
The US Treasury	http://www.ustreas.gov

In-the-money

An option with intrinsic value, which would therefore be profitable to exercise. A **call option** is in-the-money when the strike price is below the current market price of the underlying. A **put option** is in-the-money when the strike price is above the current market price of the underlying. It is rarely the case that the holder of an in-the-money option should exercise it before the last possible date. This is because options also have **time value** in addition to **intrinsic value** and should be more valuable when sold than when exercised.

Intrinsic value

An option has intrinsic value if it could be exercised profitably. This value is equal to the difference between the strike price and the current market price of the underlying.

Investment grade

Securities rated Baa or above by Moody's or BBB or above by Standard & Poor's are known as investment grade securities. See **bond rating**.

Investment Management Regulatory Organisation (IMRO)

Self-regulatory organization under the UK Financial Services Act 1986 (FSA) responsible for institutional investment managers and unit trust managers.

Investment Services Directive

European Union (EU) directive establishing common standards for investment services firms other than banks, effective from 31 December, 1995.

Investment trust

In the UK, an investment trust is a limited company which invests in securities and is regulated by the Companies Acts, Stock Exchange regulations and tax legislation. The company is run by directors, and the shares are traded on the Stock Exchange. Price is determined by supply and demand and the shares may stand at a premium or a discount to net asset value per share. Investment trusts are restricted in the advertising they are permitted to do. Unlike a unit trust, an investment trust has a fixed number of shares in issue and is therefore closed-ended rather than open-ended. Investment trusts may borrow, unlike unit trusts. One of the features of investment trusts is that they may issue different types of share. Split-capital trusts have issued zero-dividend preference shares, stepped preference shares and others. In the UK approved investment trusts are taxed in the same way as unit trusts: gains in the trust are tax free, dividend income is not subject to tax, and the company's net income is subject to corporation tax.

Investor Protection Committee

UK body representing other associations of institutional investors.

Investors' Compensation Scheme

The UK Securities and Investments Board set up the scheme to compensate individual investors who suffer loss from the conduct of authorized investment firms. It is financed by a levy paid by investment firms.

Iota

Also known as *rho*, it is a measure of the sensitivity of an option to movements in interest rates. Currency options may have two iotas/rhos because option value is affected by changes in the interest rates in each currency. See **delta, gamma** and **theta**.

Irish Futures and Options Exchange

IFOX closed at the end of August 1996. Its 24 members traded only 7,000 contracts in 1995. It traded three Irish government bond futures and an interest rate future.

Irish Stock Exchange

The exchange has existed since 1793. Between 1973 and 1995, the exchange was merged with the London Stock Exchange, but has now reasserted its independence. Equities are traded by an order-driven, broker-to-broker system. There are market-makers in government bonds (gilts). The ISEQ Index is made up of all the shares on the official list.

Irredeemable

A UK gilt-edged security which may be redeemed at the UK government's option, but which need not ever be redeemed. The outstanding irredeemable gilts have low coupons, and are unlikely to be redeemed in present circumstances. See **gilt-edged security**.

Islamic Banking

Banking operations carried on in conformation with Islamic principles which prohibit usury. Christian principles used also to prohibit usury.

Issue date

The date of an issue of securities from which interest accrues.

Issue price

The percentage of nominal value at which a new issue of securities is sold. In some markets there is a prejudice against securities issued at a premium because the inevitable capital loss at redemption may not be offsettable against the tax paid on the interest income. Many securities are issued at a discount, with the most extreme form being zero-coupon bonds where all an investor's return derives from the difference between the issue price and the eventual redemption price.

Istanbul Stock Exchange

The Turkish exchange trades chiefly bearer shares and bonds. Trading is divided between the national market, the main stockmarket, the regional markets, for medium-sized and small companies, and the wholesale market for large lot trading. In 1995 a new companies market was introduced as a potential fourth segment. Settlement is through Takasbank, formerly the ISE Settlement and Custody Company, which is recognized as an approved depository by the UK's SFA, and as an eligible foreign custodian by the US's SEC. Settlement is on T+2. The chief indices are the ISE Composite Index, the ISE Price Index and the ISE Performance Index. The first is weighted by the publicly held portion of each of the 100 shares in the index. The other two are short-term government bond and bill indices.

Italian Government Bonds

Italian Government securities are issued by the Treasury initially in book entry form. After one coupon period they may be converted into bearer form. Bonds are listed on the Italian Stock Exchanges after six months when they become bearer securities. Most trading is OTC.

Italian Capital Markets are regulated by the CONSOB (Companies and Stock Exchange Commission). A screen-based automated quotation system, the MTS (*Mercato Telematico Secondario*), has been in operation since 1988, which since January 1992 has been managed by SIA (*Societá Interbancaria per l'Automazione*).

Certificati di Credito del Tesoro (CCT)
Floating rate securities with maturities ranging between 5 and 10 years. Interest is paid semi-annually.

Certificati del Tesoro con Opzione (CTO)
Fixed interest securities with 6 years bullet maturity, but puttable after 3 years, There have been no issues of CTOs since June 1992.

Buoni del Tesoro Poliennali (BTP)
From 3 to 30 years bullet maturity, fixed interest rate securities.

Buoni ordinari del Tesoro (BOT)
Discount bills with 3, 6 or 12 months maturity.

Certificati del Tesoro in ECU (CTE)
Five-year bonds with fixed interest rate paid annually.

Buoni del Tesoro in ECU (BTE)
Fixed coupon certificates with maturity slightly over one year.

Italian Derivatives Market (IDEM)

IDEM began operation in 1994. It is a screen-based system operating both with market-makers and by order matching. The clearing house, the Cassa di Compensazione e Garanzia is the counterparty to each trade. The exchange trades futures and options on the MIB 30 Index, and options on individual equities.

In 1996, 60 **SIMs**, 13 banks and 13 stockbrokers were trading on IDEM. Of these, eight were market-makers in MIB 30 futures, eight in MIB 30 options and nine in stock options. Market-makers in the futures contracts must make bid and ask prices for at least 10 contracts for the nearest two contracts. Market-makers in MIB 30 options must quote bid and ask prices continuously for 10 call and 10 put options for five exercise prices in the nearest three contracts. Market-makers in stock options must provide quotations on request within five minutes for at least 10 contracts for each put and each call series for the last five strike prices.

Italian Financial Futures Market

The Mercato Italiano Futures (MIF) was founded in 1992. Trading is via the

Circuito Telematico, the screen-based government bond trading system. Futures contracts are traded on five and 90-year notional BTPs (government bonds) and there are options on the 10-year future.

Italian Stock Exchange

The Milan Stock Exchange was the major market where floor-based trading took place. Since 1994, securities have been traded electronically under a national computerized, order-driven system. The system is operated by CED Borsa, a company owned by market members, which also operates the RRG system which matches trades and nets payments. Settlement is through the Bank of Italy's Stanze di Compensazione. The CONSOB remains, with the Bank of Italy, the regulating authority. Securities traded include ordinary, preference and savings shares, government securities, commercial and convertible bonds and warrants.

The MIB Index is calculated in both historical form, based at 1,000 on 2 January 1975, and in current form (*corrente*) based at 1,000 at the beginning of each calendar year. The MIB 30 Index is based on the 30 most liquid stocks, it is capitalization weighted and accounts for more than 70 percent of the market's capitalization.

Itayose

A method employed to determine opening and closing prices on the Tokyo Stock Exchange, so that, for instance, all orders to buy or sell at the market opening price are satisfied at one price.

J

Jaipur Stock Exchange

Indian exchange which began operation in 1989. Shares, preference shares, bonds and mutual fund units are traded. The exchange has a weekly account system. Screen-based trading is planned. See **National Stock Exchange of India.**

Jakarta Stock Exchange

PT Bursa Efek Jakarta was reopened in 1977. Shares, preferred shares, convertible securities and corporate bonds are traded on the exchange. Since 1995 trading has been automated. Settlement is through the PT KDEI, the Indonesian clearing and depository system. The Composite Share Price Index includes all the shares listed on the exchange. There are 10 industrial sector indices.

Jamaica Stock Exchange

The exchange began operations in 1969. Since 1991 the exchange has cooperated with the exchanges of Barbados and Trinidad and Tobago in the cross trading of listed securities. Trading is by **open outcry**. Settlement of all trades in a trading week are settled on the last working day of the following week. The main index is the Jamaica Stock Exchange Market Index.

Japanese Government Bonds

The Japanese government bond market is the second largest in the world after the US market. The market expanded quickly in the 1980s with the introduction of reforms and derivatives. The market has some unusual characteristics. For example, much of the trading in the secondary market is concentrated in a single issue.

Japanese Government Bonds (JGBs) are of three different legal origins. In the beginning JGBs were issued for "construction" purposes and were mostly placed with banks. Such bonds, known as Construction Bonds, are still issued under Article 4 of the Public Finance Law. After the first "oil shock" of 1975 larger government deficits required "deficit financing bonds" to be issued with the specific approval of the Diet (Parliament). Deficit Financing Bonds are issued under a specific law for each fiscal year where there is a deficit that cannot be financed with Construction Bonds. There are also Refinancing Bonds which are issued under Article 5 of the Law Concerning Special

Account of Government Bonds Consolidation Fund.

JGBs are a charge on the National Debt Consolidation Fund Special Account which is run by the Ministry of Finance (MOF). JGBs may be in registered or in bearer form. Compulsory registration in the name of the beneficial owner occurs on every interest payment date. This registration is required to take place before the seven business day suspension period which preceeds each interest payment date.

The Ministry of Finance acts through the Finance Bureau to manage new issues for the Government and through the Securities Bureau to regulate the securities market. The Banking Bureau, the Tax Bureau and the International Finance Bureau are also concerned in the operation of the market. The Bank of Japan has a supervisory function.

All 10 and 20 year JGBs are listed on the Tokyo Stock Exchange. The market in publicly issued bonds may be divided into four sectors:
 – super long term bonds (20 year)
 – long term bonds (10 year, much the largest part of the market)
 – medium term bonds (2, 3, 4 and 6 year)
 – discount bonds (zero coupon, 5 year).

All the fixed rate issues are semi-annual coupon bonds. JGBs have bullet maturities.

Treasury Bills

Issued in discount form since 1986. The Bank of Japan uses them for open market operations.

Financing Bills

60-day maturities issued by the Government mostly to the Bank of Japan and then sold on to financial institutions when needed to manage market liquidity. There is no secondary market.

Jellyroll

Using options with the same strike prices, but different expiry dates to roll a synthetic position in the underlying to a more distant expiry date.

JJ Kenny Index

US index of short-term tax-exempt municipal note yields.

Jobbers

Formerly dealers on the London Stock Exchange.

Johannesburg Stock Exchange

The exchange was founded in 1887. Trading has been automated since 1996 with an order-driven system supplemented by market-makers. Shares, preference shares, debt securities and options are traded on the exchange. Options are traded on individual shares, on the All Shares Index and the All Gold Index. The main indices are the JSE-Actuaries Overall Index, the All Gold Index and the Industrial Index.

Joint account

Agreement to share risk between two or more parties.

Joint and several

Where there is more than one guarantor of an obligation, the term means that if one guarantor were to default, the others would still be liable for the full amount. In an extreme situation, a single guarantor would be liable for the whole obligation if all the others defaulted. Underwriters of new issues of Eurosecurities are jointly and severally liable to underwrite and, if necessary, to pay for the securities issued.

Joint lead manager

Participant in a syndicated transaction, who is not the book-runner, but ranks ahead of the co-lead managers, and therefore has a larger underwriting commitment.

Jump

A price movement larger than a random process would generate

Junior debt

Debt which ranks below secured or senior debt for repayment in the event of a default. Also called subordinated debt.

Junk bond

Securities with credit ratings well below investment grade. Volatile in price, as investors are overtaken by alternating bouts of optimism and pessimism.

Kabushiki kaisha

Japanese phrase for a jointstock company.

Kanara Stock Exchange

Indian stock exchange in Mangalore. See **National Stock Exchange of India**.

Kangaroo bond

Australian dollar-denominated bond issued in the US.

Kanmon Commodity Exchange

Japanese commodity exchange in Shimonoseki, founded originally in 1805 and refounded in 1953. Trading by *Itayose* method is in red beans, soya beans, yellow corn, raw sugar, and refined sugar. There are futures contracts in Azuki red beans, US soya beans, yellow corn and refined sugar.

Kansai Agricultural Commodities Exchange

Exchange in Osaka formed in 1993 by the merger of the Osaka grain, the Osaka sugar and the Kobe grain exchanges. Trading is by the single price session method and is in azuki beans, imported soya beans, raw sugar and refined sugar. There is an option contract in raw sugar.

Kansas City Board of Trade (KCBOT)

A US derivatives exchange originally founded in 1856. Grain futures have been traded since 1876. Stock index futures trading began in 1982. Trading is by **open outcry**. Clearing is by the KCBT Clearing Corporation. Futures are traded in Wheat (No. 2 Hard Winter), the Value Line Index and the Mini Value Line Index. There are options on the Wheat and Mini Value Line futures.

Kappa

The sensitivity of option prices to a change in implied volatility. See **delta**, **gamma** and **theta**.

Karachi Stock Exchange (Guarantee) Ltd.

Pakistan stock exchange, trading shares by open auction. Settlement is weekly.

Kassakurs

On German stock exchanges, the official price established daily at which small orders for shares are settled.

Kassenobligationen

German word denoting medium term securities.

Kassenverein

German bank which is part of the German clearing system.

Keepwell agreement

Undertaking given by a parent company to keep a subsidiary solvent. Usually it is not a specific guarantee but a general commitment to maintain the subsidiary in such a way as to be able to meet its obligations.

Keiretsu

Japanese conglomerates with cross-shareholdings with banks

Kengyo

Japanese word for the ancilliary activities of a securities house subject to approval of the Ministry of Finance.

KIBOR

Kuwait interbank offered rate.

Kicker

A feature of a loan or investment which may give the lender or investor an enhanced yield in favorable circumstances (US slang).

Kiken shisan hiritsu

Japanese phrase for **risk asset ratio.**

Kingai-shin

Type of Japanese **investment trust.**

Kiwi bond

New Zealand dollar-denominated **Eurobond.**

Knock-in option

See **barrier option.**

Knock-out option

See barrier option.

Kobe Raw Silk Exchange

Exchange in Kobe, Japan first established in 1928, reached merger agreement with the Kansai Agricultural Commodities Exchange. Trading by *Itayose* method in raw silk and raw silk futures.

Kobe Rubber Exchange

Founded in 1952, trades by single price session method in rubber. Futures contract in No. 3 Ribbed Smoked Sheet Rubber. Natural Rubber Index launched in 1995.

Kommunalobligation

German word for the type of bond issued by German banks in order to finance public sector loans and secured on such loans.

Kondratieff cycle

Long-term economic cycles, named after the economist who developed the idea.

Korea Stock Exchange

Stock Exchange in Seoul where stocks and bonds are traded. Trading is order-driven with the majority of trades executed through the SMATS system, rather than manually on the floor of the exchange. Shares are divided into first and second sections with plans for a third section for small or medium-sized companies. The main indices are the Korea Composite Stock Price Index (KOSPI), the KOSPI 200 Index, the Adjusted Stock Price Average and the Bond Index. Stock Index futures have been traded since May 1996.

Koruna

The national currency of Czechoslovakia.

Krona

The national currency of Sweden and Iceland.

Krone

The national currency of Denmark and Norway.

Kuala Lumpur Commodity Exchange

Founded in 1980 in Kuala Lumpur, Malaysia. Trading is in the following commodity futures: Crude Palm Kernel Oil, Tin, Cocoa, and Rubber SMR 20.

Kuala Lumpur Stock Exchange

Formed originally in 1964, the stock exchange trades shares, divided between the Main Board and the Second Board, preference shares, loan stocks, bonds, and warrants. Trading is automated. The clearing house is Securities Clearing Automated Network Services (SCANS). The exchange's indices include the KLSE Composite Index (86 shares), the KLSE EMAS Index (the Main Board all-share index), and the KLSE Industrial Index (30 shares), as well as sub-indices by industry.

Kursmakler

German word for an official exchange broker.

Kursmaklerkammer

Public body which represents the *kursmaklers*. It is responsible for editing the Official List among other responsibilities.

Kurtosis

The extent to which changes in a variable (or the logarithm of the variable) differ from those of a variable with normal distribution. In particular, risk managers are concerned with leptokurtosis, or "fat-tailed" distributions, i.e., the risk of occasional large price moves. Thin-tailed distributions, that is distributions with a fat midrange, are referred to as platykurtotic.

Kuwait Stock Exchange

Founded in 1984. Only citizens of Bahrain, Saudi Arabia, Kuwait, Oman, the United Arab Emirates and Qatar may buy shares on the exchange but others may invest in listed unit trusts.

Kwacha

The national currency of Malawi and Zambia.

Kwanza

The national currency of Angola.

Kyat

The national currency of Burma.

Kyoto Stock Exchange

Founded in 1949, share trading is by the **zaraba** method on the floor of the exchange. It is one of the five regional exchanges in Japan.

L

La Plata Stock Exchange

The Bolsa de Comercio de La Plata in Buenos Aires trades shares and commodities.

Ladder option

An option contract which provides that when the price of the underlying reaches certain preset levels, the payout ratchets upwards.

Lahore Stock Exchange

The Lahore Stock Exchange in Pakistan trades shares, *modaraba* certificates, foreign exchange bearer certificates, dollar bearer certificates, certificates of investment and bonds. Trading is by **open outcry**. Trading is either spot business or ready business which settles once a week. Settlement is through a clearing house. The chief indices are the LSE 101 Index and the State Bank of Pakistan General Index of Share Prices.

Lambda

The leverage factor, i.e., the percentage change in the price of an option divided by the percentage change in the price of the underlying.

Large exposures directive

European Union (EU) directive which limits the total exposure a bank can assume when dealing with one company or one group of connected companies.

Last notice day

The final day on which notices of intent to deliver on futures contracts may be issued.

Last trading day

The final day during which trading may take place in a particular contract.

Law Society

The Law Society of England and Wales is the governing body for solicitors. It is also a recognized professional body (RPB) under the SIB regulatory framework, and therefore regulates the conduct of investment business carried on by solicitors in England and Wales.

Lead manager

Description of a role in the issue of new securities. A lead manager may be the **bookrunner**, in which case he will control the issue, or he may be a joint lead manager, a co-lead manager or a regional lead manager in which case the designation will reflect a larger underwriting than mere managers but not effective control of the issue.

Leasing

See **finance lease** and **operating lease**.

Leg

Slang for a part of a transaction, usually a single stream of payments. In an interest rate swap, for example, one might speak of the floating leg and the fixed leg. A leg over is something quite different (see **Legged over**).

Legal lending limit

The maximum amount which a bank may lend to a single borrower. In the US a nationally chartered bank may lend up to 15 percent of its capital and reserves in unsecured loans to a single borrower, or up to 25 percent in secured loans.

Legal reserves

Reserves recorded in a balance sheet as a result of legal requirements. In the US legal reserves are required by the Federal Reserve System to be kept as either cash in a bank's vault or in a an account with a district Federal Reserve Bank.

Legal right of set-off

The right to offset balances held on account of a party against amounts owed to you by that party. When a company goes into bankruptcy such a right might preserve a bank from loss.

Legal risk

The risk that the law may be interpreted differently in the courts from the manner assumed. A notable example of this risk was in the Hammersmith & Fulham case in the UK (see **Hammersmith & Fulham swap case**). See **risk**.

Legal tender

Coin or currency accepted in the settlement of private and public debts.

Legged over

Slang phrase, derived from an obscenity, used to describe being tricked or otherwise persuaded into a bad dealing position.

Lek

The national currency of Albania.

Lemon

Slang word for a bad deal.

Lempira

The national currency of Honduras.

Lender of last resort

The role of the central bank in each country to supply liquidity to the banking system and to preserve the banking system in times of crisis. As banks become more adventurous in their trading activities, it is becoming less obvious that a central bank should use taxpayers' money to rescue a bank from the consequences of poor trading.

The size of such loan operations can be very large. It was reported that in 1985 the Federal Reserve Bank of New York lent US$22 billion to the Bank of New York to cover a temporary overdraft, caused by a computer failure affecting the bank's government securities clearing business.

Generally, a central bank will try to determine whether the failure of a troubled bank would threaten the whole banking system, and whether a trouble bank is illiquid but solvent, or is both illiquid and insolvent. A bank whose failure would not threaten the system, and which was both illiquid and insolvent might be left to fail. See **Barings**.

Leone

The national currency of Sierra Leone.

Leptokurtosis

See **Kurtosis**.

Letras del tesoro

Spanish treasury bills with three, six and 12-month maturities.

Letter of credit

A long-established aid to trade. A bank issues a document guaranteeing payment on behalf of its client to a third party on stated conditions. These conditions are usually related to the production of documents relating to the shipment of goods, so that a letter of credit is sometimes called a documentary credit. It should be noted that banks deal in documents not in goods. The bank will pay out against documents conforming to the requirement of the credit, and will not be responsible if the goods are unsatisfactory. An irrevocable letter of credit may not be withdrawn before a specified date. A confirmed letter of credit is confirmed by a bank in the beneficiary's own country. This is often useful if the issuing bank is unknown to the beneficiary who is therefore unable to judge the credit quality of the bank. Letters of credit in the UK are handled in accordance with the "Uniform Customs and Practice for Documentary Credits" issued by the International Chamber of Commerce.

Letter of renunciation

UK term for the form attached to an allotment letter which is used to transfer or to renounce the rights conferred by the allotment letter.

Letter repo

Hold-in-custody. See **repo**.

Leverage

(1) The ratio of debt to equity, known in the UK as gearing. This it defined as:

$$\frac{\text{total liabilities} \times 100}{\text{equity}}$$

where total liabilities are large-term debt plus short-term liabilities. This is balance sheet gearing. Income gearing is:

$$\frac{\text{interest expense} \times 100}{\text{operating profit}}$$

(2) Any method of magnifying the gain or loss on a position. Derivatives provide leverage because they increase the quantity of the underlying which may be controlled with a given sum of money.

Leveraged buy-out

Purchase of a company which is predominantly financed with debt.

LIBID

London interbank bid rate. The rate at which banks offer to take deposits and therefore lower than LIBOR.

LIBOR

London interbank offered rate. The rate at which prime banks offer to make Eurocurrency deposits.

Life-to-call

The time remaining until a borrower's first option to call or redeem a security.

Life-to-put

The time remaining until an investor's first option to put or have redeemed a security.

LIFFE

London International Financial Futures and Options Exchange.

Lift

To accept an offer price (i.e., to buy), the opposite of hit which is to accept a bid price (i.e., to sell).

Lima Stock Exchange

La Bolsa de Valores de Lima in Peru was first established in 1860. The exchange trades ordinary shares, labor shares, bills of exchange, bonds and mortgage drafts. Trading is by **open outcry** and by an electronic trading system.

LIMEAN

The average of the bid (LIBID) and offer (LIBOR) rates in the London Eurocurrency deposit market.

Limit

The maximum change in price allowed in a trading day on an exchange. Trading is suspended once the limit is reached. See **circuit breakers**.

Limit order

Order to buy or sell at or better than a particular price.

Limited convertibility

Partial restriction on the conversion of a currency. Often such rules apply to residents, but not to non-residents.

Limited two-way payments

A clause in a swap master agreement which provides that in a default the non-defaulting party is treated more favorably. The clause is less used now than formerly.

Line of credit

A facility given by a bank to a customer, allowing the customer to borrow up to a certain amount. Such facilities may be committed for a period of time or uncommitted, in which case the line of credit may be cancelled at any time.

Lineaire Obligaties

Belgian government bonds, see *Obligation linéaire*.

Liquidation

The process whereby a third party, the liquidator, sells the assets of a company in order to satisfy as far as possible the claims of the company's creditors.

Liquidity risk

The risk that a financial instrument cannot be sold quickly or close to its theoretical market value. Also, the risk that a financial institution will not be able to raise funds when needed. See **risk**.

Lira

The national currency of Italy, Turkey, Malta and the Vatican City.

Lisbon Stock Exchange

The Bolsa de Valores de Lisboa in Portugal has trading in shares, bonds, unit trusts and related rights. The automated trading system is called TRADIS. Settlement for all securities in the system is through the Central de Valores Mobiliaros e Sistema de Liquidaçao e Compensaçao, the Central Securities Depository and the Nationwide Clearing and Settlement System. The chief indices are the BVL Index – General, the BVL 30 Index, the BVL National Continuous Index and, for bonds, the BVL ORF Index.

Listed option

An option contract which is traded on an exchange.

Listed security

A security which has satisfied the requirements of an exchange to be listed on that exchange. This usually implies a minimum standard of financial information, though not necessarily a minimum standard of value or credit worthiness. Such a security need not be actively traded on the exchange where it is listed. Certain institutions are allowed only to buy listed securities.

Listing

The admission into the official list of an exchange of a particular security.

The issuer of the security is bound by the rules of the exchange as to reporting financial information and other matters. This security may not necessarily be traded on the exchange though most exchanges publish lists of prices.

Listing particulars

Information required by a Stock Exchange for any listed security.

Livraison

French word for delivery.

Ljubljana Stock Exchange

Slovenian exchange founded in 1924, closed in 1941, and reopened in 1989. Trading is both on the floor and by an electronic trading system. The exchange trades government bonds, municipal bonds, ordinary shares, preference shares, options, foreign-currency treasury bills and precious metals. The main index is the Slovenian Stock Exchange index of 13 listed shares. Settlement is through the Central Slovenian Clearing and Depository House.

Lloyd's of London

Medium-sized insurance business in London, founded in an 18th century coffee house. Until recently all the capital of the business was supplied by private individuals or names, grouped into syndicates, who assumed unlimited liability to pay losses on the business they underwrote. Because of the fragmented syndicate structure, the claims-paying ability of Lloyd's has not been rated.

In the 1980s and early 1990s, a series of natural-disaster- and pollution-related claims led to large losses. The fragmented capital structure was expensive to administer, and the fiduciary responsiblities of those involved were not clearly understood by them. The revelation of malpractices within Lloyd's and related law suits forced a fundamental review of its business practices. The introduction of limited liability corporate participation in Lloyd's heralded the end of personal underwriting with unlimited liability.

Loan stock

Security with a fixed rate of interest which, unlike a debenture, may be unsecured.

Loan-to-value ratio

In asset-backed financing, the ratio between the amount of debt and the value of the asset.

Local

A dealer who trades for his own account on a derivatives exchange.

Local authority bond

Security issued by a local government body in the UK. These bonds are not guaranteed by the government. Maturities are generally from one to five years.

Lock-up period

With new issues of securities, the period after the closing, during which physical securities may not be obtained by investors, and the whole issue is represented by a global note.

Lognormal distribution

A security is said to have a lognormal distribution if the logarithm of the price has a normal distribution. If such a distribution is plotted in price terms, the curve will appear to be positively skewed in a manner similar to the observed price behavior of stocks.

Lombard rate

The German Bundesbank sets the Lombard rate which is the rate on short-term loans collateralized with securities.

London Clearing House

Founded in 1888 to clear trades in sugar and coffee, it now clears trades for four London exchanges, LIFFE, IPE, LME and LCE.

London Code of Conduct

Guidelines on the conduct of derivatives business published by the Bank of England.

London Commodity Exchange (LCE)

The LCE incorporates the Baltic Futures Exchange and was called London FOX before 1993. It shares its market floor with the IPE. The exchange trades futures and options in cocoa, Robusta coffee, No 5 white sugar, BIFFEX (Baltic Freight Index), wheat, barley and potatoes. All contracts except the sugar contracts are traded by **open outcry**. Sugar is traded electronically. Clearing is through the **London Clearing House**.

London International Financial Futures and Options Exchange (LIFFE)

LIFFE is the London derivatives exchange. Settlement is through the London Clearing House. LIFFE has a link with the CBOT to trade the long-term bond futures and with the CME to trade three-month DM futures and options. The contracts traded are as follows:

Short-term interest rates: futures and options on three-month sterling, Euromarks, Eurolire, Euroswiss, and futures on ECU and Eurodollars.

Government bonds: futures and options on long gilts, German Bunds and Italian BTPs, and futures on Japanese JGBs.

UK Stock Indices: futures and options on the FT-SE 100 Index, and futures on the FT-SE Mid 250 Index. The FT-SE 100 options may be American or European style, and a FLEX product is also offered.

Equity options are traded on over 70 UK shares.

London Metal Exchange (LME)

Established in 1877, the LME trades particularly in lead, zinc, tin, aluminum and nickel, but also in copper. Options are available on most LME contracts. Trading may be for up to 27 months forward in aluminum, copper and zinc. Trades are settled through the London Clearing House.

London rules

A method of handling the bank-related business of a troubled company. The Bank of England acts as a neutral intermediary and a consensus is sought among the lending banks based on a standstill at the time trouble first becomes clear and trying to treat banks equally and other creditors fairly.

London Stock Exchange

Formally constituted in 1802 after more than a century of informal trading. Shares, UK gilts, fixed interest securities, preference stock, loan stock, Eurobonds and traditional options are traded on the exchange. Trading is elctronic.

In shares, trading is based on the competing market maker system though it is planned to change this to an order driven system. Market-makers are obliged to quote two-way prices in **normal market size (NMS)**, which differs for each share, on the **Stock Exchange Automatic Quotations System (SEAQ)**. The SEAQ Automated Execution facility, SAEF, is intended to settle small trades, and the Stock Exchange Alternative Trading Service (SEATS) is used for those shares which do not see enough trading volume to support a market-maker. Settlement is on T+ 5. The exchange's new Crest system first went live in July 1996. It is a paperless book entry system. The Alternative Investment Market is the small company market with lighter listing requirements than the main market.

London Traded Options Market (LTOM)

Options exchange merged with LIFFE in 1992. See **London International Financial Futures and Options Exchange.**

Long

Owning a financial instrument, commodity or currency.

Long bond

The on-the-run 30-year US treasury bond.

Long coupon

An interest period which is longer than usual. For example, a bond might be issued with a long first coupon period in order to achieve a higher nominal coupon than would otherwise be possible.

Long gilt

(1) UK government security with the longest maturity.
(2) At LIFFE, the long gilt is a notional gilt with a 9% coupon. Deliverable gilts may have from 10 to 15 years to maturity.

Long position

Owning a security or commodity, the opposite of short.

Long-term equity anticipation securities (LEAPS)

CBOE equity index based options. See **Chicago Board Options Exchange (CBOE)**.

Long-term prime rate

Japanese rate which is the Japanese banks' prime lending rate and is set at 0.9 percent above the five-year bank debenture rate.

Lookback option

An option which operates retroactively to give the holder the right to buy or sell the underlying at its minimum or maximum price in the lookback period

Lookforward option

An option which gives the holder the right to the difference between the strike price set at the beginning of the period and the highest (or lowest) price during the period.

Lot

Trading unit on a derivatives exchange.

Low exercise price option (LEPO)

Swiss Options and Financial Futures Exchange (SOFFEX) instruments based on 11 bearer stocks. Both puts and calls are designed to have very high **deltas**, and to behave in a manner very close to that of the **underlying** share.

Ludhiana Stock Exchange

Indian stock exchange. See **National Stock Exchange of India**.

Luxembourg Stock Exchange

Société de la Bourse de Luxembourg was founded in 1927. The first **Eurobond** was listed in 1961. Trading on the exchange is divided between gold trading, bond trading and equity related trading. By far the largest category of security listed is bonds, which are more than 60 percent of the total. Trading is now mostly automated. Settelement is through the Chambre de liquidation, the exchange's clearing house, or through another recognized clearing system such as *Centrale de Livraison de Valeurs Motilières (CEDEL)* or **Euroclear**. The main indices are the Luxembourg shares index and the Luxembourg shares return index.

LXBOR

Luxembourg interbank offered rate.

M

Macaulay Duration

See **duration**.

Madhya Pradesh Stock Exchange

Established in 1916 in Indore, India. Trades shares. Has agreed to the creation of a single stock exchange for India. See **National Stock Exchange of India**.

Madras Stock Exchange

Has agreed to the creation of a single stock exchange for India. See **National Stock Exchange of India**.

Madrid Stock Exchange

Founded in 1831, it is one of the four Spanish stock exchanges. Trading is by **open outcry** and increasingly on the continuous market. The four stock exchanges have formed the Mercado Continuo, the continuous market, which operates on the CATS system developed by the Toronto Stock Exchange. Trading is at three levels, the mercado de lotes (large lots), the mercado de picos (small lots) and términos especiales (special conditions). Most trading is in the first category. Settlement is on T+5 and there is a book entry system in place since 1992 run by the Spanish Central Depository. The main indices are the IBEX-35, a capitalization weighted index of the 35 most liquid shares traded on the continuous market, and the Madrid Stock Exchange Index. See the stock exchanges of **Bilbao**, **Barcelona** and **Valencia**.

Maebashi Dried Cocoon Exchange

Founded in 1952, it is one of Japan's 12 commodity exchanges. Trading, by the *Itayose* method, is confined to futures in raw, dried cocoons, the raw material for raw silk.

Magadh Stock Exchange

Recognised in 1986, the exchange which is in Bihar has agreed to the creation of a single stock exchange for India. See **National Stock Exchange of India**.

Maginot spread

The difference in yield between *German Bundesanleihen (Bunds)* and

French OATs *(Obligations assimilable du Trésor)*. Sometimes called the BOAT spread.

Maintenance margin

The additional margin required by an exchange to compensate for price changes after a derivatives position has been opened. Positions usually are marked-to-market at least daily. If the loss on a position exceeds the amount of margin previously posted, a margin call is issued.

Major Market Index (MMI)

Index of blue-chip US stocks.

Make-up day

The day when banks compile returns for central bank reporting. Nothing to do with mascara or magazines.

Makler

German word for broker.

Malta Stock Exchange

Began trading in 1992, by the call-over system. While the number of listed shares is small, government bonds are also traded. The Central Securities Depository maintains a register for each listed security.

Mambo Combo

An option position combining an in-the-money put and an in-the-money call where the holder is long or short of both options.

Managed float

More float than management, a managed float is when the authorities in a country try to smooth out foreign-exchange market changes to reduce the disruptive effect of price fluctuations.

Management buy-in (MBI)

Purchase of a business by an outside management team, usually with additional finance from banks or other investors.

Management buy-out (MBO)

Purchase of a business by its existing management.

Management fee

A portion of the total fees earned by the managers of a new issue of securities. Originally quoted separately from the underwriting fee and selling concession, it is more common to see a combined fee now. The way in which Eurobonds were distributed strongly influenced the fee structures that evolved. The final investor paid the issue price, the bank which sold it to the investor was paid a selling concession, the underwriters who took market risk earned an underwriting commission, the managers earned an additional fee and the lead manager(s) might also retain a *praecipuum*, an overriding share of the management fee. As time passed the underwriting and management fees merged and the lead manager's praecipuum was abandoned.

The commission arithmetic of a five-year issue intended for retail placement might be as shown in Figure M1.

Figure M1

COMMISSION ARITHMETIC OF A FIVE-YEAR ISSUE INTENDED FOR RETAIL PLACEMENT	
	%
Issue price paid by investor	100.000
less: Selling concession	1.250
Price paid by selling group member	98.750
less Management/underwriting commission	0.625
Price paid by manager	98.125

The issuer would still not receive 98.125 percent of the issue amount because issue expenses, lawyers' fees, paying and fiscal agency fees would all be deducted either at the outset or over the life of the transaction.

This type of fee structure now survives only in those parts of the Euromarkets which are predominantly retail-investor based (e.g., the Swiss and Luxembourg franc bond markets). Commissions in the main sectors of the Euromarket now reflect the more institutional and trader-driven character of the market. The fixed price re-offer issue technique also reflects this change.

The "bought deal" with a small group of banks underwriting the whole issue has made unnecessary the elaborate fee structure which used to be thought necessary to reward all the different participants.

Typical fees for fixed-rate issues in the main international bond markets are as shown in Figure M2.

Management group

The primary underwriters of a new issue of securities. The members may be five to six or 50 to 60, with the average, which differs from market to market, somewhere in the middle.

Manager

A manager has three functions which are to manage, underwrite and sell an issue. In many cases, managers do very little of any these three duties, some-

Figure M2

TYPICAL FEES FOR FIXED-RATE ISSUES BY MARKET						
Market: Maturity	Euro %	Global %	Yankee %	Samurai %	Swiss %	Luxem- bourg %
2	0.1250	0.1250				
3	0.1875	0.1875	0.5000	0.8000	1.5000	1.3750
4	0.2250	0.2250			1.7500	1.6250
5	0.2500	0.2500	0.6000	0.9500	2.0000	1.7500
7	0.3000	0.3000	0.6250	1.0000	2.5000	1.8750
10	0.3250	0.3250	0.6500	1.0500	2.7500	2.0000
30	0.4500	0.4500	0.8750		3.3750*	

* 20 years or more

times being content to underwrite a few bonds and place fewer still. The largest part of the three duties is carried out by the lead, joint-lead and perhaps co-lead managers.

Mandate

Authorization from a borrower to a bank or securities firm to proceed with a new transaction on the agreed terms. A mandate will often be expressed in terms of the all-in cost (variously defined) of the transaction, net of all swaps or other related transactions. The borrower will usually undertake not to launch a similar transaction while the one contemplated is in the market.

Mandatory convertible bond

Bond issued by a bank which is classified as capital because it must be repaid, either with the cash proceeds from a sale of new shares or with the new shares themselves.

Mandatory quote period

On the London Stock Exchange, the period during which market-makers must make bid and offer prices available to the market.

Manila International Futures Exchange Inc

Began trading in 1986. There are three trading systems: agricultural contracts are traded by the one-price-group trading system; the financial contracts are traded by **open outcry** while interest futures are traded using a modified system which combines one-price-group and board-trading systems. Clearing is through the Manila International Futures Clearing House. The contracts traded are Sugar, Coffee, Copra, Soya Beans, Dry Cocoon, Interest rates, and Currencies (USD/JPY, USD/DEM, GBP/USD, USD/CHF, USD/Peso).

Manufactured dividend

Payment made during the term of a **repo** transaction by the borrower of collateral to the lender equivalent to the dividends or coupons which otherwise would have been received by the lender.

Maple leaf

Canadian gold coin.

Maracaibo Stock Exchange

Incorporated in Venezuela in 1986, the exchange uses an automated trading system, SETCOM, to trade registered shares, government bonds, private bonds, treasury bonds, commercial paper and participation stocks.

Marché à Terme d'Instruments Financiers (MATIF)

The French futures and options market for financial instruments and commodities established in 1986. Trading is by **open outcry** during normal trading hours and by **GLOBEX** outside those hours. MATIF has a link with the Deutsche Terminbörse designed to give the members of each access to the other's contracts. MATIF trades the following contracts: futures on three-month PIBOR, the long-term notional bond, three-to-five year medium-term government bond, ECU bond, French treasury bond, CAC-40 Stock Index, White sugar, potatoes, wheat and Rapeseed. Options are traded on the long-term notional bond futures, ECU bond futures, three-month PIBOR futures, and USD/DEM.

Marché à Terme de la Pomme de Terre

Potato futures exchange in Paris operating under the umbrella of the MATIF.

Marché des Options Négociables de Paris (MONEP)

The French stock options market.

Marché monetaire

French phrase for the money market.

Marché primaire

French phrase for the primary market.

Marché secondaire

French phrase for the secondary market.

Margin

A deposit required to be placed with an exchange or clearing house to secure a derivatives position.

Margin borrowing

US term for borrowing secured on shares or other securities. The amount which a bank may lend in this way is limited by the Federal Reserve's **Regulation U**. Lending by brokers and securities firms is limited by **Regulation T**.

Margin call

A demand by a futures exchange or by an individual broker for clients to increase their margin payments in response to a change in the value of their positions.

Market amount

The minimum transaction amount which is usual for dealing in a market.

Market auction rate preferred stocks

Variation of floating-rate preferred stock.

Market capitalization

The total market value of a company's equity, calculated by multiplying the market price by the number of shares in issue.

Market risk

Risk, also called "price risk", arising from possible changes in the value of a position. See **risk**.

Market segmentation theory

Theory relating to interest rates which holds that the short and long-term markets are separate. Individual investors have fixed maturity preferences, and do not readily abandon them. Consequently, the two markets move largely independently of each other.

Market-Maker Information and Trading System (MIDAS)

The German securities price information and settlement system.

Market-maker

A dealer who regularly quotes bid and offer prices. Each market has its own conventions as to what a market-maker must trade in, for what size and at what bid–offer spread a market maker must quote and what obligations or privileges are conferred with market-maker status.

Marketable collateral

Security, used as collateral in a contract, which can be sold easily.

225

Markka

The national currency of Finland.

Mark-to-market

The process of adjusting the price of a security or other position to reflect its market value, often done daily. The process gives rise to unrealized profits or losses. Generally, but not everywhere, these are recognized in the profit and loss statement. This is now the normal practice in most trading activities in most countries. The difficulty arises where the desire to control traders is frustrated by inadequate systems, accounting conventions which do not allow the recognition of unrealized gains, or fiscal obstacles. The benefit of reflecting mark-to-market values in accounts is that the accounts are more meaningful. The disadvantage is that reported earnings may become more volatile. Many banks produce accounts where part of the balance sheet is recorded at cost and part at market value.

Masse monétaire

French phrase for money supply.

Master swap agreement

Agreement between two swap counterparties governing all the swaps transacted between them. The International Swap & Derivatives Association (ISDA) Master Agreement is the most common model. The existence of a single contract governing many transactions makes it more likely that each party will be able to net its exposure to the other and thus reduce its credit risk.

Master trust

A single asset pool used as collateral for a series of securitized transactions.

Matador

A foreign bond denominated in Spanish pesetas.

Matched book

Any trading book where the positions are matched so that there is little or no market risk remaining. Used particularly of deposit books and repo/reverse repo books.

Matched repos

Securities acquired through reverse repurchase agreements and matched with a repurchase (**repo**) agreement on the same security for the same period of time.

Matched sale

Reverse repo.

Match-fund

To match a loan (asset) with a deposit (liability) of the same maturity. This action reduces funding risk, but might also reduce profitability.

Material adverse change

Clause designed to protect a lender from unexpected breaches of other covenants in a loan agreement. In it, a borrower warrants at the signing of a loan agreement that there has been no significant change which might affect the position of the lender since the date of the last audited annual accounts. It adds to the power of the clause if the borrower can be made to repeat the warranty at regular intervals.

Matilda

Australian-dollar-denominated bond sold at the same time in the Australian domestic market and abroad.

Maturing adjustable preferred stock

Another variation of floating-rate preferred stock.

Maturity

The period of time during which an instrument or transaction is outstanding.

Maturity date

The date on which the nominal amount of a loan or bond becomes due and payable.

Maturity value

The value of a security when it is to be repaid in the future. This will be different from its market value which reflects current market conditions, and may well be different from its issue price, because, for example, it was issued at a discount or different from its nominal value, for example, because it will be repaid above par as in the case of an index-linked security.

Mauritius Stock Exchange

Dealing is by open outcry, and by a version of the 'casier' system which determines an equilibrium price for each share in each trading session. Ordinary and preference shares, bonds and treasury bills and unit trusts are traded. A second market for small companies was planned.

Maximum margin

Typically used in the context of note issuance facilities or Eurocommercial paper facilities to denote the highest rate at which tender panel bids will be accepted, or the rate at which underwriters commit to buy notes or paper in the absence of investors.

Maximum price fluctuation

The maximum amount by which a contract price may change during one trading session on an exchange.

Medellín Stock Exchange

Colombian stock exchange established in 1961. Trading is by call-over for shares and by an electronic system for fixed-income securities (the Mercado Electrónico Continuo). Shares, certificates of deposit, exchange certificates, bonds, commercial paper and securitization certificates are traded.

Medium-term note (MTN)

See **Euro-medium-term note (EMTN)**.

Memorandum and articles of association

The two key legal documents establishing a UK-registered company. The memorandum of association deals with a company's relations with the outside world. It sets out the company's name, its registered office, its objects, its authorized capital and whether or not the company is a public limited company. The articles of association deal with a company's internal affairs and set out the powers of directors, the rights of shareholders, borrowing powers, the procedure for issuing and transferring shares and the proceedings at meetings.

Mendoza Stock Exchange

Argentinian stock exchange which began trading in 1961.

Mercado Abierto Electrónico

Argentinian electronic exchange which began trading in 1989. In 1994, under an agreement with the Bolsa de Comercio de Buenos Aires, the MAE concentrated on government and corporate bonds.

Mercado Continuo Español Sociedad de Bolsas SA

See **Madrid Stock Exchange**.

Mercato Interbancario dei Depositi

Italian screen-based market for interbank deposits.

Mercato Ristretto

Italian restricted secondary market for trading in smaller companies.

Mercato Telematico dei Titoli di Stato (MTS)

Italian primary bond dealers' screen-based market

Mercato Telematico delle Opzioni su Futures (MTO)

Italian market for the options on government securities futures.

Merchant banks

Once the élite among English financial institutions, now largely bought by
. foreign banks or marginalized. Despite being famed for their contacts and
skills, those merchant banks which were sold did not sell for very much
above net asset value. Of the remaining independent banks, the four most
important, Schroders, Flemings, Hambros and Rothschild, have together
about US$3.5 billion of capital, less than many single US investment banks.
Of necessity, they now specialize in advising and in fund management rather
than in lending or trading.

MERFOX

Argentinian agricultural derivatives exchange which trades at the Bolsa de
Comercio. Futures and options are traded on live steers auctioned at the Lin-
iers cattle market in Buenos Aires.

Mexican Stock Exchange

The Bolsa Mexicana de Valores (BMV) was founded in 1894. Shares, commercial paper, corporate debentures and mutual funds are listed. The main
index is the Price and Quotations Index for shares. Trading is by **open outcry**.

Mezzanine finance

In acquisition finance, that part of the financing which is ranked behind the
secured debt but ahead of the equity. Often takes the form of subordinated
convertible debt.

MIBOR

Madrid or Milan interbank offered rate.

MidAmerica Commodity Exchange (MidAm)

A affiliate of the Chicago Board of Trade, originally founded in 1868 as
Pudd's Exchange, it was incorporated in 1880 as the Chicago Open Board of
Trade and took its present name in 1972. Trading is by **open outcry** and set-
tlement is through the Board of Trade Clearing Corporation. On the
exchange futures are traded in Corn, Soya Bean, Soya Bean Meal, Oats,
Wheat, Live Cattle, Live Hogs, NY Gold, NY Silver, Platinum, Treasury
Bonds, Treasury notes (five and ten-year), Treasury bills, Three-month
Eurodollars and currencies. There are options on futures on Wheat, Corn,
Soya Beans, NY Gold and the US Treasury Bonds.

Middle office

The risk control and valuation function in a financial institution which is often situated between the dealers (**front office**) and the operations people (**back office**).

Middle price

The arithmetic mean of the **bid price** and the **offer price**. Also called "mid-price" and "mid-rate."

Minas, Espírito Santo, Brasília Stock Exchange

Brazilian stock exchange established in 1926.

Mini-max bond

A collared floating rate note (FRN)

Minimum price fluctuation

The smallest change of price allowed by the rules of an exchange.

Minimum quote size (MQS)

London Stock Exchange term for the minimum size for which a market-maker must quote on Stock Exchange Automated Quotations System (SEAQ) and is each stock's normal market size which differs from share to share.

Minimum rate

In the case of a FRN with a collar or floor, this is the rate below which the coupon will not fall, however low market rates may be.

Minneapolis Grain Exchange

Founded in 1881 the exchange trades by **open outcry** in futures and options on Hard red spring wheat, White wheat, Oats, White shrimp and Black tiger shrimps.

Mio

Million . Care is needed with all abbreviations of million and thousand; "m" can be either.

Mismatch

Opposite of match. May also refer to FRN issues where the interest rate period and the payment frequency do not coincide.

Mitlelstand

German word for the three million small and medium-sized businesses which are estimated to account for about half Germany's industrial production and perhaps two-thirds of jobs.

Modern portfolio theory (MPT)

Theory which assumes that markets are efficient and that the market price incorporates all publicly known information. It suggests that a diversified portfolio of risky assets will be less risky than the sum of the risks of the individual assets would suggest.

Modified duration

A measure of the percentage price sensitivity of a bond to changes in yield. Unmodified duration is used to immunize a portfolio. Modified duration is preferred when measuring a security's price volatility. See **duration**.

Monetary union

An agreement between countries to exchange their own currencies for a common currency. Implicit in such a change is the sacrifice of monetary independence which many consider implies a parallel political union. In a European context, the Bundesbank was quoted as envisaging monetary union coming about by a process of convergent *Anschluss*. The implicit unification of Europe under a European central bank based in Frankfurt seems more popular with bureaucrats than with people.

Money back warrant

Warrant which may be exercised or redeemed at its face value

Money-market basis

The way to calculate interest on money market instruments (such as CDs, FRCDs, FRNs and sometimes short-dated bonds). The rate of interest is multiplied by the actual number of days elapsed and divided by the number of days in the accounting year, e.g., 360 (many European markets) and 365 (UK).

Money-market fund

Mutual fund investing only in money market instruments and bank deposits.

Money-market preference share

Another type of preference share with a coupon reset mechanism based on short-term interest rates.

Montreal Exchange

Canada's first stock exchange chartered in 1874. On the exchange are traded common shares, preferred shares, warrants, rights, PEACs (payment

231

enhanced appreciation capital securities), SPECs (speciality equity claim securities), equity options, bond options, Canadian bankers' acceptance futures, 10-year government bond futures and options on 10-year government bond futures. The principal index is the XXM which is made up of the 25 largest capitalization shares quoted on at least two Canadian stock exchanges.

Moody's Investors Service

Credit-rating agency, subsidiary of Dun & Bradstreet.

Mortgage pass through security

Security where investors receive a proportionate interest in each cash flow generated from a pool of residential mortgages.

Mortgage-backed security

A bond backed by an undivided interest in a pool of mortgages. Cash flow from the underlying mortgages is used first to pay interest and then to make principal payments by drawing bonds for redemption

Moscow Central Stock Exchange

Founded in 1990 with trading beginning in 1991. Securities and currency futures are traded by **open outcry** and electronically.

Moscow Commodity Exchange

Originally founded in 1789, closed in 1917 and reopened in 1990. Trading in the spot market is by auction and by **open outcry** in the futures market. Futures contracts are on USD/Rouble, DEM/Rouble, White Sugar and Soft Wheat (Third Class Grade).

Moscow International Stock Exchange

Also founded in 1990 and began trading in 1991. Shares, debt securities, options and unit trusts are traded.

Multicurrency clause

Clause in a loan agreement which allows the borrower to draw funds in any currency he chooses and to switch currencies on an interest roll-over date.

Multilateral netting

Netting of obligations between several parties and a central clearing house. See **bilateral netting**.

Multiple option financing facility (MOF)

Flexible financing facility where one or more lenders offer to sell a variety of short- or medium-term instruments on behalf of a borrower and promise to lend themselves if none of the other options is possible.

Murabaha

Common form of Islamic trade finance.

Musharaka

Form of Islamic long-term trade finance structured as a joint venture.

Mutual fund

Collective investment vehicle.

Mutual offset system

A system of substitution between futures exchanges. A trade executed on one exchange may be used to offset or establish a position on another exchange. Also called inter-exchange transfers.

N

Naamlooze Venootschapp (NV)

Dutch equivalent of a public limited company.

Nagoya Grain and Sugar Exchange

Japanese exchange originally founded in 1877 as the Nagoya Rice Exchange. Trading by the *Itayose* method is in Red Beans, White beans, Sweet Potato Starch and Refined Sugar.

Nagoya Stock Exchange

Founded originally in 1886 and refounded in 1948, shares, bonds, bonds with warrants, convertible bonds and options on the Option 25 Index are traded. The most active shares are traded on the exchange floor, while the others are traded electronically. Most transactions are settled through the clearing department of the exchange (regular-way transactions) but cash, specified-day and when-issued settlement is also possible. The Option 25 Index is a price-weighted index of 25 shares from 20 sectors.

Nagoya Textile Exchange

Established in 1951, trading by the *Itayose* method is in futures on Cotton Yarn, Woollen Yarn and Staple Fibre Yarn (dull).

Nairobi Stock Exchange

Kenya's stock exchange was founded in 1954. Shares and bonds are traded by **open outcry**. The main index is the Nairobi Stock Exchange Index.

Nakadachi

Member of the Osaka Stock Exchange who acts as broker for regular members of the exchange. He may not accept orders from the public or deal on his own account.

Naked option

An uncovered option position.

Naked position

An unhedged risk position.

Names

UK term for individuals who accept unlimited liability as members of the Lloyd's insurance market. Many names have suffered large losses and the number of them is much reduced. See **Lloyd's of London**.

Namibian Stock Exchange

Based in Windhoek, the exchange began trading in 1992. Shares, debt securities and unit trusts are traded. The Stock Exchange has a central depository but not all securities are registered there.

Nanjing Petroleum Exchange

The exchange (NANPEX) in the People's Republic of China began operations in 1993. Trading was by **open outcry** in Gas Oil and Gasoline futures. In 1994 trading in energy futures was banned by the Chinese government.

Napoleon

French gold coin.

National Association of Securities Dealers Automated Quotations (NASDAQ)

US over-the-counter stock quotation system of the National Association of Securities Dealers (NASD). It began operations in 1971 and is the second largest stock market in America behind the NYSE. The large majority of securities traded is in the common stock of US companies, but there are also foreign securities, American depository receipts, units, warrants, preferred shares, and convertible debentures. Trading is by competing multiple-market-makers. The average number of market-makers per security is 12, and some of the most active shares have as many as 40 or more market-makers. Besides the NASDAQ system, there is also a Small Order Execution System (SOES) which provides automatic execution for trades of up to 500 shares at the best price available. Clearing and settlement is through the Automated Confirmation Transaction (ACT) system. The exchange publishes numerous indices of which the main indices are the NASDAQ Composite Index which contains all the common stocks listed on NASDAQ, the NASDAQ industrial index, the NASDAQ-100 Index which contains the largest non-financial stocks, and the NASDAQ-Financial index which contains the largest financial stocks.

National Association of Securities Dealers (NASD)

Primary regulator of the US over-the-counter securities market. NASD is a self-regulatory organization, the largest in the US, which licenses broker-dealers, issues rules governing trading, the listing of new issues and the treatment of customers.

National debt

The total outstanding value (usually expressed in nominal terms) of a central government's debt. A State's total liabilities include unfunded pension obligations, as well as the debts of government agencies and local government bodies.

National Mortgage Market Corporation

Agency established by the State Government of Victoria, Australia, in order to develop a secondary mortgage market.

National Stock Exchange of Costa Rica

The Bolsa Nacional de Valores in Costa Rica was formed in 1976. Ordinary shares, public bonds and private debentures are traded by an automated trading system. Settlement may be in one of three ways: same day, "spot-price" on T+1 and fixed-term transactions up to 360 days forward.

National Stock Exchange of India (NSE)

Incorporated in 1992, the NSE began its debt trading activities in June 1994 with equity capital being traded from November 1994. The exchange is electronic with members trading through their remote terminals. At the end of 1996 there were 1010 such terminals in 50 cities throughout India. Of these the largest concentrations were in Mumbai (304), Delhi (269), Calcutta (120), Madras (69), Ahmedabad (56), Pune (36) and Hyderabad (34). Some 1500 shares and 528 debt securities are traded on the exchange. The index is the NSE-50 Index, a market capitalization weighted index. The constituent shares must meet criteria based on market capitalization and on trading frequency and cost. The Index's base was set at 1000 on 3 November 1995.

The National Securities Clearing Corporation Limited (NSCCL) is a wholly-owned subsidiary of the NSE. It was incorporated in August 1995, and became active from April 1996. It has formed a Settlement Guarantee Fund. Settlement procedures were in transition at the end of 1996 but the NSCCL had achieved significant improvements in settlement accuracy.

The National Securities Depository Limited (NSDL) was promoted by the NSE, the Industrial Development Bank of India and others to act as a central depository which would enable the NSCCL and the NSE to achieve automatic payment against delivery. Trading in depository securities began on 26 December 1996 with the first trade in Reliance Industries.

A futures and options segment on the NSE is planned. The NSCCL will clear and settle these trades also.

See the stock exchanges of **Ahmedabad, Bangalore, Bhubaneswar, Bombay, Calcutta, Cochin, Coimbatore, Delhi, Guahati, Hyderabad, Jaipur, Kanara, Ludhiana, Madras, Madhya Pradesh, Magadh, Pune** and **Uttar Pradesh.**

Nearby basis

The difference between the cash price of the underlying and the nearby futures contract price.

Nearby month

In futures or options markets, the near-term delivery months.

Nebenbörse

Swiss secondary market for shares in Zurich.

Negative carry

When the income accruing from a position is less than the cost of financing that position the position is said to have negative carry.

Negative convexity

An interest-rate sensitive position has negative convexity when it does not rise in value for a fall in interest rates at the relevant maturity by as much as suggested by the position's duration and may fall more in price for a rise in rates of the same amount. Motgage-backed securities often have negative convexity, because when interest rates fall, the underlying mortgages are often repaid, being refinanced more cheaply elsewhere.

Negative pledge

Undertaking in a loan or bond document given by a borrower not to grant security to any other lender. It may be phrased so that giving security is allowed so long as the lender is also given acceptable security. As with all covenants, the scope of the clause materially affects its strength and may be varied according to the types of debt to which it applies, the inclusion of some or all companies in a group and exemptions for transactions in the normal course of business.

Negative yield curve

A yield curve where short-term interest rates are higher than long-term interest rates.

Net asset value (NAV)

A company's or fund's net assets divided by the number of outstanding shares.

Net present value (NPV)

The discounted value of all cash flows associated with an investment. See **yield**.

Netting

Generally the reduction of risk by offsetting transactions so as to arrive at a smaller risk. Payment-netting addresses the risk inherent in making payments to one or more counterparties by netting cash payable and receivable on a single date, and requiring each party to pay only the net amount. Such payment-netting may be bilateral between two parties, or multilateral between many. Risk-netting addresses the credit risks inherent in many transactions by establishing that each party has a right of offset, so that at a default by one party, only the net exposure is at risk and claimable by one party against the other. See **bilateral netting** and **multilateral netting**.

New Cedi

The national currency of Ghana.

New Israeli shekel

The national currency of Israel.

New money

In a US Treasury refunding, the amount by which the value of the new securities to be sold exceeds that of those maturing.

New rupiah

The national currency of Indonesia.

New South Wales Treasury Corporation spread

Known as the TCorp spread, it is a benchmark for pricing longer-dated Australian dollar swaps.

New York Clearing House

Largest and oldest clearing house in the US which was founded in 1853. It is owned by 11 money centre banks and operates the Clearing House Interbank Payments System or CHIPS, and the New York Automated Clearing House.

New York Cotton Exchange

Founded in 1870, it established a division, the Financial Instrument Exchange (FINEX®), in 1985. In 1988 the New York Futures Exchange became an affiliate of the NYCE. In 1994 FINEX opened a trading floor in Dublin. There are futures and options on Cotton, Frozen Concentrated Orange Juice, the US Dollar Index ®, and futures on US Treasury Auction Five-Year and Two-Year Notes. There are futures and options on DEM/ITL, GBP/DEM, DEM/JPY, DEM/SKR and DEM/FFR and futures on JPY, GBP, SFR, DEM, and CAN. Trading is by **open outcry**.

New York Futures Exchange

Incorporated in 1979, the NYFE became an affiliate and then a subsidiary of the NYCE. Contracts traded include futures and options on the Commodity Research Bureau Futures Price Index, the CRB Index, the NYSE Composite Index®.

New York Mercantile Exchange

The largest physical commodity futures exchange in the world, founded in 1872 as the Butter and Cheese Exchange of New York, NYMEX merged with the Commodity Exchange (COMEX) in 1994. The exchange has two divisions: the NYMEX Division which lists futures and options on Light Sweet Crude Oil, Heating Oil, New York Harbor Gasoline, Natural Gas and Platinum and futures on Propane, Palladium, Sour Crude Oil and Gulf Coast Gasoline. Options on the difference between heating oil and crude oil and between gasoline and crude oil were introduced in 1994. These are known as **crack spread** options.

The COMEX Division lists futures and options on Gold, Silver, Copper and the Eurotop 100 Index. Trading is by **open outcry** and, after trading hours, by the electronic system NYMEX ACCESS. All trades clear through the NYMEX clearing house or the COMEX clearing association.

New York Stock Exchange

The origins of the exchange go back to a group of brokers meeting under a Buttonwood tree on lower Wall Street at the end of the 18th century. Their first premises were the Tontine Coffee House. The New York Exchange Board was formed in 1817, and changed its name to the New York Stock Exchange in 1863. On the exchange, shares, bonds, options and many other varieties of security are traded. Most trades are processed electronically by a system which links the specialists on the exchange floor with the member firms. Settlement may be by one of five methods: regular way, which is T+5 for corporate stocks and municipal bonds and T+1 for government bonds; cash, which is same day settlement; next day, which is T+1; seller's or buyer's option, which may be T+6 to T+60 for corporate or municipal bonds, or T+2 to T+60 for US government bonds; or when issued, for new issues. The option contracts traded are on the NYSE Composite Index and the NYSE Utility Index, and regular way and long-term options on stocks. The main indices are the NYSE Composite Index, the New York Stock Exchange Utility Index, the Dow Jones Averages and the Standard and Poor's Composite Index of 500 Stocks.

New Zealand Futures and Options Exchange

The NZFOE was established in 1985, and has been owned by the Sydney Futures Exchange since 1992. There are four classes of dealer: public brokers authorised to deal on behalf of others or themselves; introducing brokers who are authorized to deal on behalf of others or themselves, but are not permitted to hold client money or property and may not be trading permit holders; principal traders who generally trade only on their own account; and trading permit holders, who may deal directly on the automated trading system of the NZFOE. Most exchange members belong to more than one category. Trading is automated by a system which links dealers in Auckland, Wellington, Christchurch and Sydney. All contracts are cleared by the Sydney Futures Exchange Clearing House. The exchange lists futures and options on the NZSE-10 Index, an index of 10 shares which together represent more than 72 percent of the market capitalization. There are also futures and options on the NZSE-40 Index which is highly correlated to the NZSE-10 Index. There are futures and options on three-year and 10-year government stock, as well as on 90-day bank bill rates. There are also a currency future on the US dollar, a New Zealand wool future and options on six individual equities.

New Zealand Stock Exchange

The exchange was founded in 1915. Trading is screen-based and is in equities and debt securities. Settlement is through the broker-to-broker accounting (BBA) system. The main indices are the NZSE-40 Index, the NZSE-10 Index, the NZSE-30 Selection Index and the NZSE Smaller Companies Index. Three shares on the exchange account for almost half the market capitalization. They are Telecom Corporation of New Zealand, Carter Holt Harvey Ltd, and Fletcher Challenge Ordinary.

NIBOR

Norwegian interbank offered rate.

Nigerian Stock Exchange

Formerly the Lagos Stock Exchange and founded in 1960, the exchange has branches and trading floors in six cities. Ordinary shares, preference shares, debt instruments and government securities are traded on the exchange. Trading is by the callover/auction system. The main index is the Nigerian Stock Exchange Common Stocks (All Share) Index.

Niigata Stock Exchange

One of the five regional Japanese stock exchanges, it was established in 1949. Trading is by the *Zaraba* method.

Nikkei Stock Index 225 (Nikkei 225)

Japanese stock index, based on an unweighted average price of 225 stocks traded on the Tokyo Stock Exchange.

Nikkei Stock Index 300 (Nikkei 300)

Japanese stock index, based on 300 stocks traded on the Tokyo Stock Exchange.

No-load fund

Mutual fund which does not carry an initial charge. Such funds do, however have annual management charges and often, for a period of years, make exit charges if an investor withdraws money from the fund.

Nominal interest rate

The stated interest rate which may not be the effective interest rate, and is in contrast to the real interest rate which is the amount by which the effective interest rate exceeds the rate of inflation.

Nominee

One who holds a security in his own name for the benefit of another.

Non-callable

A security which does not give the issuer the option to redeem the bonds before the specified maturity date.

Non-competitive auction

That part of an auction where non-competitive bidders accept the average price bid by competitive bidders, usually with a maximum amount stipulated by the authorities. See **auction**.

Non-cumulative

Used in connection with **preference shares** where the dividend payment is contingent on the issuer's profitability. If such a dividend is not paid when due, it does not remain a liability of the issuer and is not paid at a date in the future unlike cumulative dividends.

Non-recourse finance

Financing based on an asset or on a contractual cash flow, without recourse to the original owner of the asset or cash flow if it proves insufficient to service and repay the financing.

Non-refundable

Debt which may not be repaid from the proceeds of further borrowing.

Non-voting share

Share which does not entitle the owner to the right to vote as the holders of ordinary shares may vote.

241

Nordquote

A trade-supporting information system carrying information on shares quoted on the four Nordic exchanges of Copenhagen, Helsinki, Oslo, and Stockholm.

Normal distribution

A probability distribution in which about two-thirds of total observations fall within one standard deviation on either side of the mean, and about 95 percent of total observations fall within two standard deviations on either side of the mean. An unsatisfactory model for the price changes of most securities.

Normal market size (NMS)

UK term for the value calculated for each **Stock Exchange Automated Quotations System (SEAQ)** stock, based on the annual turnover in that stock. The number of shares thus calculated ranges from 500 to 200,000.

Normal yield curve

The yields of securities, which when plotted on a graph of yield against maturity form a line which is slightly upward sloping to the right, reflecting the fact that interest rates for longer maturities are "normally" higher than for shorter maturities.

Nostro account

In correspondent banking, a bank account held with a foreign bank. A good quick test of the basic competence of a bank branch's management is the extent to which the branch has unreconciled nostro accounts. The term for someone else's account with you is a **vostro account**.

Note

In general, a note is a promise to pay a sum of money in the future. In many markets, it has a specialist meaning. For example, in the US treasury market a note is a fixed rate government security of up to 10 years' maturity.

Note issuance facility (NIF)

A medium-term arrangement whereby a group of banks undertakes to distribute short-term notes for a borrower.

Notional principal amount

Reference amount used to calculate payment amounts in swaps.

Notionnel

The French government bond futures contract traded on the MATIF. The 10 year notional bond has a 5.5% coupon from the December 1997 maturity onwards. Previously the coupon was 10%. The remaining life of deliverable bonds from the same date is 8.5 to 10.5 years (previously 7–10 years). The minimum total outstanding required to admit a new deliverable bond is Ffr40 billion (previously Ffr5 billion).

Novation

Replacing an original agreement with a new agreement. This may be done so as to include a new transaction under the same agreement or to change a party to an existing transaction.

Nugget

Australian gold coin.

O

Obbligazione

Italian word for a bond.

Obbligazione a tasso variabile

Italian phrase for a floating-rate bond.

Obligaciones del estado

Ten- and 15-year fixed-rate Spanish government bonds with an annual coupon.

Obligation

French word for a bond.

Obligation assimilable du Trésor (OAT)

French treasury bond issued in French francs and in ECU with both fixed and floating-rate coupons.

French franc denominated OATs

OATs are in minimum denominations of Ffr2,000. Initial maturities are from 7–30-year bullets. Coupons are paid annually. Notes are quoted on a price basis excluding accrued interest. Bonds are traded on screen and on the Stock Exchange. At 30 November 1996, Ffr1,888 billion of OATs were outstanding with an average remaining life of eight years and 194 days.

ECU denominated OATs

Issued first in 1989 and regularly thereafter. Denominations are ECU 500. At 30 November 1996, there were ten issues totalling ECU 19.0 billion outstanding. The largest of these was the 6% of April 2004 with ECU 3.2 billion.

Other OATs

Besides the fixed-rate bullet maturity OATs, there are some older less-traded issues which are convertible or were issued with warrants.

Floating rate OATs

There were no issues of floating-rate OATs between 1990 and 1996. Plans were announced in March 1996 to issue new variable rate OATs based on a new index, the TEC. The existing different variable rate issues are also known by their initials.

TMB

The rate is the arithmetic mean of the monthly average of the 13-week T-bill auctioned weekly throughout the year prior to the coupon payment.

TRB

The rate is reset quarterly as the yield of the 13-week T-bill auctioned prior to the payment of the coupon.

TRA

The rate is the arithmetic mean of the monthly average of yields on fixed-rate Emprunts d'État with maturities greater than seven years. This rate is published by the Caisse des Dépots et Consignations.

TME

The rate is the monthly average yield on a weighted sample of 7–30 year bonds on the secondary market, recorded over the 12 months prior to payment of the coupon.

TEC

In March 1996, the Trésor announced the creation of "Taux de l'Echéance Constante," a 10-year constant maturity yield index. The TEC is published daily in the form of the yield to maturity of a hypothetical OAT with a maturity of exactly 10 years. The yield is interpolated from the yields of the two nearest maturities of government bonds based on mid prices quoted at 10.00am in Paris by OAT market-makers, rounded to two decimal places. It was planned to issue 10.5 year OATs with quarterly coupons set in advance based on the TEC. At 30 November 1996, Ffr64.9 billion of a single issue had been sold – the OAT TEC 10 of 10.2006. These bonds, like other floating-rate bonds, are not very sensitive to absolute rate changes. However these bonds are sensitive to changes in the yield curve. They will gain in value from any steepening of the curve and will fall on any flattening of the curve.

Figure O1 summarizes the amounts of OATs outstanding at year-end and their place in the total of negotiable debt issued.

Figure O1

OATS OUTSTANDING 1991–96 IN BILLIONS OF FRENCH FRANCS						
	*1996**	*1995*	*1994*	*1993*	*1992*	*1991*
OATs	2,012	1,655	1,421	1,215	978	761
Other long-term debt		119	138	138	79	149
BTF	298	292	239	189	259	139
BTAN	803	760	682	592	456	418
Total negotiable debt	**3,112**	**2,826**	**2,480**	**2,134**	**1,772**	**1,467**

Source: Ministère de l'Économie et des Finances

* Figures at 30 November 1996

Obligation linéaire/Lineaire Obligaties (OLO)

Belgian government bond. Introduced in May 1989 as fungible issues issued by public tender. Issues are often launched in up to 10 tranches. Maturities range from three to 20 years. OLOs are not callable, may be held only in registered or book-entry form and are exempt at source from withholding tax. Listing takes place one day after each auction. There are both fixed-rate and variable-rate issues of OLOs. OLOs may be stripped, but only by the clearing system of the National Bank of Belgium, and the resulting securities are traded by five specially approved primary dealers.

Occidente Stock Exchange

Colombian stock exchange based in Cali. Bonds, certificates of deposit, bank acceptances and ordinary shares are traded.

Odd lot

An amount of securities which is either smaller than the normal amounts dealt in a market or is an odd number. In some markets, such lots may be dealt at wider prices than generally quoted, particularly in the case of small amounts.

Off-balance sheet liabilities

Obligations not on the balance sheet were once hardly recorded, but are now generally the subject of detailed notes in the financial statements. Such transactions may include some lease obligations, asset-based finance, swaps, futures, options, and forward foreign exchange. The level of disclosure required varies from country to country.

Offer for sale

Issue of a security by public subscription.

Offer price

Asked price, the price at which a dealer is ready to sell.

Offering circular

Prospectus describing an issue of securities and the issuer.

Offering memorandum

Prospectus describing an issue of securities and the issuer.

Office of the Commissioner for Securities and Commodities

Hong Kong regulatory authority.

Official list

The list of securities, usually with their prices, published by a stock exchange.

Official receiver

UK official charged with the administration of compulsory liquidations and bankruptcies.

Offre publique d'achat

French phrase for a takeover bid.

Offre publique d'échange

French phrase for a share exchange offer.

Off-the-run issues

US treasury issues which are not the most recently issued in each maturity range and therefore are less liquid.

OM Stockholm

Options and derivatives market funded by Olof Stenhammar. OM intends to be a main market place for Nordic instruments. See **OMLX**.

Omega

Either the currency risk when translating the value of a currency option position in another currency, or the third derivative of the option price related to the price of the underlying

OMLX

London based exchange which is a part of the OM group.

On-the-run issues

US treasury issues which are the most recently auctioned, and therefore highly liquid.

Open interest

The sum of outstanding "long" or "short" positions in a given option or futures contract. An indicator of the depth of the market.

Open market operations

Central bank operations in the markets intended to achieve objectives of monetary policy.

Open outcry

Trading method on the floor of an exchange in which buyers and sellers call out their bids and offers face to face, often using hand signals because of the noise.

Open position

A trader's risk position.

Open repurchase agreement (open repo)

A **repo** transaction with no definite term continued from day to day by mutual agreement. Also known as a demand **repo**.

Opening call

Process followed at the opening of trading on a derivatives exchange. Each contract month of a particular underlying is traded in sequence within a short period of the opening.

Opening price

The price of the first trade of the day.

Oporto Derivatives Exchange

Bolsa de Derivados do Porto (BDP), Portuguese stock exchange which by an agreement with the Lisbon Stock Exchange surrendered all its cash trading activities and assumed the responsibility for the term markets and derivatives. The first futures were based on a 10-year fixed-rate treasury bond and on the PSI-20 stock index.

Option

An option gives the holder the right, but not the obligation, to buy (in the case of a "call" option) or sell (a "put" option) a specified instrument, currency or commodity (the underlying) during or at the end of a given period at a specified price (the "strike" or "exercise" price). The option may be for physical delivery of the underlying or cash settlement. The option buyer pays the grantor a premium for this right. See **Black–Scholes Model, delta, gamma, theta, kappa, tau, rho, bear spread, bulk spread, butterfly spread, put-call parity, straddle, strangle** and **volatility**.

Option class

Options of the same type – calls or puts – but with different strike prices and expiry dates listed on the same underlying.

Option series

Options of the same type with the same strike price and expiration date.

Optional redemption

Borrower's option to repay early an issue of debt securities. Such options are usually exerciseable at a premium above par which reduces towards the end of a security's life.

Options Clearing Corporation

The entity which guarantees listed security options in the US.

Optionsscheine

German word for a warrant.

Orange County

US local government entity which became bankrupt in 1994. The Treasurer of Orange County had invested in highly-geared derivative-based investments which lost almost USD1.7 billion. Some of thse securities were issued by Sallie Mae and other highly-rated issuers. The story highlights the difference between credit risk and market risk – the latter magnified by derivatives.

Order-driven

Stock exchange system in which prices react to orders, in contrast to quote-driven and other trading mechanisms.

Ordinary share

A share with all the rights of a share and no specific restriction, called "common stock" in the US.

Organization for Economic Co-operation and Development (OECD)

Founded in 1960 to promote economic growth in member countries. Also known for its economic research and publications. The members are Australia, Austria, Belgium, Canada, Denmark, Finland, France, Germany, Greece, Iceland, Ireland, Italy, Japan, Luxembourg, Mexico, the Netherlands, New Zealand, Norway, Portugal, Spain, Sweden, Switzerland, Turkey, the UK and the US.

Organization of Petroleum-Exporting Countries (OPEC)

A group of the major oil exporting countries which is based in Vienna. The members are Algeria, Gabon, Indonesia, Iran, Iraq, Kuwait, Libya, Nigeria, Qatar, Saudi Arabia, the United Arab Emirates and Venezuela.

Original issue discount (OID) bonds

Securities issued at a discount to par with low or no coupons, also called "deep-discount bonds."

Original maturity

The maturity of a security when first issued.

Osaka Securities Exchange

Japanese exchange originally founded in 1878 and refounded in 1949. Members of the exchange are served by *Nakadachi* members who fill the role of **inter-dealer brokers**. Stocks, bonds, futures and options are traded on the exchange. The exchange is particularly noted for its derivatives trading. The OSE has claimed that 99 percent of options and 78 percent of futures traded in Japan are traded on the OSE. There are both futures and options on the Nikkei 225 Index and on the Nikkei Stock Index 300. Stocks are assigned to the First or Second Sections. Generally all new listings are assigned to the Second Section except where a stock is already listed on the First Section of the Tokyo or Nagoya exchanges, or is a very big company. The largest 150 stocks are traded on the exchange floor while lesser stocks and all futures and options are traded by a computer-assisted trading system. All listed-stock trades are settled through the Osaka office of the Japan Securities Depository Centre (JASDEC). The chief indices are the OSE 300 Common Stock Index, the OSE Adjusted average for 250 Issues (the stocks in the First Section) and the OSE Adjusted average for 40 Issues (the stocks in the Second Section).

Osaka Textile Exchange

Established in 1984, to replace the Osaka Sampin Exchange and the Osaka Chemical Textile Exchange. Trading is by competitive auction to achieve a single price. There are futures contracts on Cotton Yarn (20S), Cotton Yarn (30S), Cotton Yarn (40S), Staple Fibre Yarn, and Woollen Yarn.

Oslo Stock Exchange

Norwegian stock exchange founded in 1881, and merged with the stock exchanges of Bergen and Trondheim in 1991 as the Oslo Børs. Bonds, shares, options and futures are traded. Clearing for option trades is through the Norsk Opsjonssentral (NOS) which acts as a clearing house and guarantor. Equities trades are recorded by the Norwegian Registry of Securities (Verdipapirsentralen or VPS), which is a computerized registration system. Futures traded are on the OBX Index, the seven-year Norwegian government bond and the 10-year Norwegian government bond. There are options on individual stocks, the OBX Index and the long OBX Index (options out to two years). The main indices are the Oslo Stock Exchange Index and the OBX Index which is a capital weighted index based on the 25 most actively traded stocks on the exchange.

OTC

See **over-the-counter**.

Out option

A type of **barrier option** which has an expiry price as well as an **expiry date**.

Out-of-the-money

An **option** without **intrinsic value**.

Outperformance option

An option where the payout is determined by the amount by which the price of one **underlying** outperforms the price of a second underlying.

Outright transaction

Foreign exchange transaction that is not part of an FX swap operation.

Outstanding contract

A contract which has not expired or been closed out.

Outstrike

The price at which the terms of a non-standard option change, or it expires.

Overcollateralization

Security in excess of the debt secured, offers protection to the lender from a fall in the value of the security.

Overfunding

Tactic sometimes used by the Bank of England to influence the money supply by selling more gilts than is at once necessary to fund the government's deficit.

Overlay risk management

Risk management, for example currency risk management, as a separate activity from the management of risk in individual securities.

Overnight limit

Net position that a dealer is permitted to carry over into the next dealing day.

Overnight money

Money placed in the money market for repayment the next day.

Overnight repo

Repo which matures on the business day after its **value date**.

Over-the-counter option

An option not traded on a public exchange.

Over-the-counter (OTC)

Lightly regulated trading separate from established exchanges. Contracts so traded can be tailored to a counterparty's needs. See **in-the-money** and **at-the-money**.

P

Pa'anga

The national currency of Tonga.

Pacific Stock Exchange

Formed on the merger of the Los Angeles and San Francisco Exchanges in 1956. The PSE has equity trading floors in Los Angeles and San Francisco and an options trading floor in San Francisco. Common shares, preferred stocks, warrants, bonds, and equity options are traded. The exchange trades on the specialist system. Most trades are processed electronically. There are equity options on individual shares, longer options termed LEAPS® on individual stocks and options on the Wiltshire Small Cap Index.

Pac-man defence

Term used in the US to describe a takeover defence tactic where a company subject to a hostile takeover attempt itself launches a bid for the other company.

Pagaré

Spanish word for a promissory note.

Pagares de empresa

Spanish phrase for commercial paper.

Palestine Securities Exchange

Embryonic exchange based in Naples.

Panama Stock Exchange

The exchange began operations in 1990, Domestic equities and domestic debt instruments are the chief instruments traded. Trading is by **open outcry**. Settlement is on T+3 via the Central Securities Depository. The exchange does not publish an index.

Panda

Chinese gold coin.

Paper

Slang term for securities, which may only exist in dematerialized form.

Paper gain

Unrealized gain.

Paper loss

Unrealized loss.

Par

The nominal value of a security, in percentage terms 100 percent.

Par bond

A bond trading at or close to par.

Par yield curve

Yield curve established by estimating the coupon rates for bonds to be priced at **par** for each maturity. The point is that bonds trading substantially above or below par may distort the yield curve because of possible differences between the tax treatment of income and the tax treatment of capital gains or losses. Bonds trading above par have suffered traditionally from the reluctance of some investors to accept a sure capital loss on bonds held to redemption without some extra yield as compensation.

Paraguay Stock Exchange

See **Asunción Stock Exchange** (*Bolsa de Valores y Productos de Asunción*).

Parallel loan

Early form of **arbitrage** transaction where two companies, usually in different countries, each made loans to the other's subsidiary in the lender's country. The transaction was used to circumvent exchange control restrictions. The idea of exploiting each party's access to a currency needed by the other lay behind the first **swap** transactions.

Parallel shift

A change in the level of interest rates across all maturities, so that the shape of the yield curve does not change. This is a relatively easy risk to measure, in contrast to the risk of possible changes in the shape of the yield curve.

Paraná Stock Exchange

The Bolsa de Valores do Paraná, a Brazilian provincial stock exchange, was established in 1948. A small number of companies is listed.

Pari passu

Frequently encountered clause in bond documentation which establishes the equality in preference of all securities in an issue and of all unsecured issues.

Paris

Dealers' slang for the FFR/USD spot rate.

Paris Club

Informal forum, chaired by the head of the Trésor in Paris, for discussions with debtor countries about rescheduling.

Paris Stock Exchange

In 1991, a single national stock exchange was formed when securities traded on the regional exchanges were added to the list in Paris. Ordinary shares, preferred shares, investment certificates, and bonds are traded. Trading is either on the cash market, (the *marché au comptant*) or on the monthly settlement market (the *règlement mensuel*). Trading takes place on a centralized order-drive, electronic system. Shares are registered on the SICOVAM central depository in book entry form. The main indices published are the CAC-40 Index, the SBF 120 Index, the SBF 250 Index and the Second Market Index.

Paris Traded Options Market (MONEP)

Marché des Options Négociables de Paris opened in 1987. Now trades options on stocks and two options on the CAC-40 Index, short-term and long-term. See **MATIF**.

Parquet

French word for a dealing floor. Literally, the well of a courtroom. An individual floor trader on the **MATIF** in Paris is called "négociateur individuel de parquet."

Partial lookback option

A **lookback option** where the lookback period is shorter than the life of the option.

Participating option

One of a number of possible structures where the holder obtains only a percentage of any favorable price movement.

Participating preference share

A type of **preference share** which confers the right to a share in the profits of the issuing company above a certain level.

Participation certificate

(1) Certificate representing participation capital, a separate class of share capital, which usually carries economic rights similar to ordinary shares but without voting rights. They are often issued in the form of bearer participation certificates or BPCs.

(2) In the US, a certificate representing a beneficial interest in mortgage loans.

Partly paid

A bond which requires the holder to pay only part of the face value at the time of issue with provisions for the balance to be paid in one or more parts on specified later dates.

Passive management

Investment strategy which sets out to achieve a certain return or to match a particular index by designing an appropriate portfolio which is not intended to be altered over a given time horizon. The contrast is with active management which tries to use currency or security selection to achieve superior returns. See **active management**.

Pass-through security

Certificate representing an ownership interest in a pool of mortgages.

Pataca

The national currency of Macao.

Path-dependent option

An option where the value depends not just on the value on expiry but also on the price pattern or path which led to it. **Asian** (average rate), **barrier** and **lookback** options are path-dependent.

Pay later option

See **deferred premium option**.

Paydown

In a US treasury refunding, the amount by which the value of the maturing securities exceeds that of the new securities being auctioned.

Payer's swaption

Option which entitles the holder to pay a fixed rate in a swap of a given maturity.

Paying agent

A bank or group of banks responsible for paying the interest or principal due on an issue on presentation by investors of coupons or bonds.

Pay-in-kind bond (PIK)

Bond which pays interest to holders in the form of securities. The interest on such bonds is not a call on the issuer's cash, and the investor is protected from reinvestment risk.

Pay-in-kind preferred (PIK preferred)

Form of preference share where payments are made in the form of additional PIK securities. Often used in the case of companies with projected cash deficits for a number of years.

Payment date

Date when a payment is due to be made. In the case of a new issue it is the date when the syndicate members must pay for the securities allotted to them and when all primary market transactions are settled.

Payment netting

Netting applied to payments due to be made on a single date. It may be bilateral or multilateral.

Payoff

(1) The return on an instrument or position.
(2) The value of an option at expiry.

Payout ratio

The percentage of the underwriting fee that is paid out by the lead manager to the syndicate after the costs of stabilization have been deducted.

Pension Benefits Guaranty Corporation

US agency which guarantees defined-benefit pensions where the plan has been closed or the company concerned no longer trades.

Pension fund

Fund, usually enjoying tax-exempt status, formed to provide pensions for the fund's beneficiaries. In some countries these funds are very large and play a leading role as institutional investors, often taking principled positions on questions of corporate governance. As countries face the problems of funding welfare services in the future and as life-time employment becomes less common, it is likely that personal pension funds will grow, partly replacing the large funds. The purposes for which they may be used may be extended to cover illness and even unemployment, thereby reducing charges on the state.

Pension livrée

French securities sale and repurchase agreement. See **prêt de titres**.

Per annum (p.a.)

Latin phrase meaning each year.

Performance bond

Usually a stand by letter of credit issued by a bank which guarantees the bank will pay to the beneficiary an agreed sum if the bank's client does not perform a contractual obligation.

Permanent interest bearing shares (PIBS)

UK securities issued by building societies, mutual mortgage lenders, which pay interest so long as the society is solvent and likely to remain so but have no redemption date. The building societies operate under the Building Society Commission which imposes harsher ratios than are imposed on banks in the UK.

Pernambuco and Paraiba Stock Exchange

The Bolsa de Valores de Pernambuco e Paraiba is a Brazilian provincial stock exchange which lists equities.

Perpetual

Bond which has no final maturity date, but which may have call provisions. The investor may be given some comfort that the call provision will be exercised if the coupon is set to rise steeply after a certain number of years.

Personal Investment Authority (PIA)

UK self-regulatory organisation which oversees the provision of financial products to individuals.

Peseta

The national currency of Spain.

Peso

The national currency of eight countries: Argentina, Chile, Colombia, Cuba, the Dominican Republic, Mexico, the Philippines and Uruguay.

Pfandbrief

Bond issued by one of a specially authorized group of German banks and collateralized by pools of mortgages (Mortgage Pfandbriefe) or loans to public sector entities (Public Pfandbriefe). The security is not allocated to individual issues but is maintained on an independent register. Twenty-four pure private mortgage banks, three mixed private mortgage banks, 12 regional Landesbanken and six "public sector banks with special functions" are permitted to issue Pfandbriefe. No issuer of such debt has ever defaulted on its obligations.

At the end of 1995, DM1,258 billion of Pfandbriefe were outstanding. This amount was about 35 percent of the entire German bond market (Bunds were 28 percent) and twice the size of the UK gilt market.

Philadelphia Board of Trade

The futures subsidiary of the Philadelphia Stock Exchange incorporated in 1985. Trading by **open outcry** is in futures on the National OTC Index, AUD, GBP, CAN, DEM, ECU, FFR, SFR and JPY.

Philadelphia Stock Exchange

With origins in the 18th century, the PHLX can claim to be the first stock exchange in the US. Equities, index options, over 290 equity options and currency options are traded. Trading is by the specialist system. There are currency options on the major currencies, long-term currency options and cross-rate options. There are index options on the National OTC Index, the Gold/Silver Index, the Value Line Composite Index, the Utility Index, the Bank Index, the Big Cap Sector Index, the Semiconductor Index and the Phone Index.

Philippine Stock Exchange

Incorporated in 1992 when the Manila Stock Exchange (MSE) and the Makati Stock Exchange (MKSE) merged. Common stocks, preferred stocks and bonds are traded. Trading is automated, but using a different system on each exchange floor; the Maktrade system on the MKSE, and the ATS system on the MSE. Settlement is through the Equitable Banking Corporation or Rizal Commercial Banking Corporation. A central depository system was launched in early 1997.

Physical delivery

Settlement of a futures contract by delivery of the underlying.

Physical security

Security with physical form, rather than one which is dematerialized in a computerized register.

Physical strip

Originally US treasuries were stripped by physically detaching the interest coupons and trading them in that separate, physical form. Now treasuries are stripped in their registered form. See **strip**.

PIBID

Paris interbank bid rate.

PIBOR

Paris interbank offered rate. In French it is known as *Taux interbancaire offert à Paris* or TIOP.

Pick-up

The amount by which the yield of one security exceeds that of another comparable one. Usually used in the context of switching securities in a portfolio.

PIMEAN

Paris interbank mean rate, the average of bid and offer rates.

Pin risk

The risk of an at-the-money option just before expiry when it is difficult to know whether it will be exercised or not. See **risk**.

Pip

1/100th of 1 percent.

Pit

Trading area on the floor of an exchange where a particular security is traded.

Pit broker

Broker who executes orders for others on the trading floor of a futures exchange.

Place

To sell a security to an investor believed to be a holder rather than a trader of the security.

Placing memorandum

Document describing the details of an issue of securities intended to be sold by private placement.

Placing power

The ability to find investors for securities, about which otherwise honest investment bankers sometimes tell terrible lies.

Plain vanilla

Simple instrument or transaction with no exceptional features.

Planned amortization class (PAC)

A class of collateralized mortgage obligation which has a scheduled sinking fund mechanism likely to give the investor the planned amortization, except at times of very high prepayments. Other classes of security carry the main risk of early redemption.

Plus (+)

US government securities prices are usually quoted in 32nds. To quote in 64ths, pluses are used. A bid of 3+ is 'the handle' or big figure plus 3/32 + 1/64, which equals the handle plus 7/64.

Point

Can be variously used so care is needed.
(1) As in basis point which is 1/100th of 1 percent.
(2) In security trading, 1 percent of the face value of a note or bond, as in "the price fell a full point."
(3) In foreign exchange markets, a change of 1 in the last figure of a price quotation.

Point and figure chart

Price chart, in the form of columns of "Xs" and "Os", where X represents a given rise and O a given fall.

Poison pill

A feature in a security issued or an action by the target of a takeover bid designed to make the target unattractive to the bidder.

Political risk

The risk associated with investment in unstable countries where a change of government might lead to radical changes of policy. See **risk**.

Pollution futures

Futures market in pollution permits.

Ponzi scheme

US name for a fraudulent scheme where the first investors are paid large but fictitious "profits" with money received from other investors. Publicity draws in more investors whose money is used to pay "profits" to earlier investors. The process can continue for some time because people are greedy and gullible but its end is certain. Named after Charles Ponzi, a swindler.

Pool

A group of assets, usually formed to be the basis for an issue of asset-backed securities. Often used of mortgages.

Portfolio insurance

Trading technique aimed at protecting the value of a portfolio with options. May not work when most needed if the underlying markets are gapping downwards in thin trading.

Portfolio optimization

Process of selecting securities in a portfolio so as to meet objectives relating, for example, to **yield, coupon, duration,** or **convexity**. The obstacles to this may be restrictions on what is available or acceptable in terms of credit, **diversification**, maturity or duration.

Positive carry

When the cost of financing a position is less than the income accruing from the position, it is said to have "positive carry."

Posizione scoperta

Italian phrase for a short position.

Pound

The national currency of Cyprus, Egypt, Lebanon and Syria.

Pound sterling

The national currency of the UK.

Power option

An option where the payoff is determined by raising the value of the underlying to some power. For example the value of a power option at expiry might be calculated as P^2-E where P^2 was the square of the price of the underlying at expiry, and E was the exercise price of the option.

Praecipuum

Now largely obsolete, the praecipuum is that part of the management fee taken by the lead manager and not distributed to the other managers.

Prague Stock Exchange

The exchange was re-opened in 1993. Shares, investment funds and bonds are traded in a listed market and an unlisted market. Trading is intermittent and is order-driven. Trades are cleared through the Clearing Centre of the Czech National Bank and recorded by the Securities Register Ltd. The main index is the Stock Exchange Index – PX 50 made up of the 50 most traded shares on the exchange weighted by market capitalization.

Pre-emption right

The right of a shareholder to subscribe for new shares before any shares are offered to other potential investors. The purpose of such rights is to prevent the dilution of a shareholding against the shareholders' will.

Preference share

A class of equity capital that ranks ahead of ordinary shares in respect of dividends and the distribution of assets on the dissolution or winding up of a company. Unlike ordinary shares, preference shares have a fixed liquidation value and often carry a fixed dividend. Dividends may be cumulative or non-cumulative. Known as "preferred stock" in the US.

Preferential creditors

Certain creditors may have a special priority conferred on them by law. In the UK, for example, preferential creditors rank ahead of holders of floating charges and all unsecured creditors. Preferential creditors in the UK include income tax and value added tax liabilities as well as wages owed to employees.

Preliminary prospectus

A **prospectus** which includes all the necessary information about a new issue of securities and the issuer except the final terms. It is subject to revision.

Pre-market trading

Trading before a market has officially opened.

Premier cours

French phrase for **opening price**.

Premium

The price of an **option**. Premium can also mean the amount by which the price of an option exceeds its **intrinsic value**.

Premium put convertible

Bond which entitles the holder either to convert into equity, or to require the issuer to redeem the bond for cash at a premium. The investor may receive a low coupon until he decides to convert or put the bond. The yield to put is higher than the running yield, because of the put premium, and is effectively the minimum yield, which the investor is guaranteed. For an issuer, the put option is dangerous, because it may be exercised at a time when the company is troubled, the share price low, and the company least able to repay a liability it had thought of as quasi-equity.

Prepayment

Payment made prior to its scheduled date.

Prepayment model

Model of prepayment rates for **mortgage-backed securities** in the US. Models may use various different repayment experiences.

Prepayment risk

The risk that a security will be repaid early, leaving the investor with an unexpected reinvestment risk. See **risk**.

Present value (PV)

The value of a payment or a series of payments discounted at a given interest rate.

Prêt de titres

French securities lending mechanism. See *pension livrée*.

Prezzo di apertura

Italian phrase for **opening price**.

Prezzo limite

Italian phrase for price limit.

Prezzo medio

Italian phrase for average price.

Price value of a basis point (PVBP)

A way of expressing the price sensitivity of a fixed-income security to a change in interest rates.

Price/earnings (P/E) ratio

A share price divided by the earnings per share. Earnings per share is net profit divided by the average total number of outstanding shares during the period. P/E ratios vary from country to country partly because accounting conventions differ and so produce different earnings figures.

Primary dealer

Dealers in government securities recognized by the authorities and often given special responsibilities and privileges. Example include gilt-edged market- makers (GEMMs) in the UK and *spécialistes en valeurs du trésor (SVTs)* in France.

Primary market

The market in new issues of securities. Primary market transactions are settled on a single date, the payment date of the issue, rather than a set number of days after the trade date as in the **secondary market**.

Primary underwriter

Securities firm which undertakes to underwrite a new issue of securities before a syndicate has been formed to share the risk of underwriting. The commitments undertaken by the members of the syndicate are secondary underwriting commitments.

Prime bank

A bank of the highest standing. This used to mean AAA-rated banks until most of the banks lost their AAA status. It is important for a customer to know whether a bank considers its undoubted credit standing to be a priceless part of its franchise, or merely another asset to be traded and exploited until it is exhausted. It may be argued that there are issues of public policy involved in the change from stable, cautious commercial bank to volatility-loving bonus-paying trading firm. It used to be said that confidence comes on foot, but goes on horseback.

Prime rate

The rate of interest at which US commercial banks offer to lend money to their best customers.

Private bank

Now used to describe a bank, or part of a bank, which offers banking and related services to high-net-worth individuals. Originally a bank owned by a small number of private individuals who were personally liable to the full extent of their personal wealth for the debts of their bank.

Private placement

Issue of securities that is offered to one or more large or sophisticated investors as opposed to being publicly offered. Private placements by virtue of their large denomination and private nature are generally exempt from those securities laws intended to protect retail investors. In the US, for example, they do not have to be registered with the **Securities and Exchange Commission (SEC)** and are not subject to the provisions of the Securities Act of 1933.

Privatization

The sale of government-owned shares in nationalized industries or other commercial enterprises to private investors. Privatization may be either a way of introducing commercial realism to sheltered, subsidized State enterprises, or it may be a way of funding a short-term government budget deficit. The former UK Conservative prime minister, Harold Macmillan, denounced it as "selling the family silver." Those who have experienced the improvements in service achieved by privatized public companies may be reconciled to the sale of public assets at low prices to international investors.

Prix pied de coupon

French phrase meaning price excluding accrued income.

Profit and loss account

Income statement.

Profitability

Three useful measures are:

$$\text{Pre-tax profit margin (\%)} = \frac{\text{Pre-tax profit} \times 100}{\text{Turnover}}$$

$$\text{Return on capital employed (\%)} = \frac{\text{Pre-tax profit} \times 100}{\text{Capital employed}}$$

$$\text{Earnings per share} = \frac{\text{After tax profit}}{\text{Average number of shares}}$$

Profit-taking

Realising a profit by closing a position.

Program

An agreement, which is not a commitment, between an issuer and a bank concerning the sale, on a best-efforts basis, of debt securities.

Program trading

Most often means **arbitrage** trading between an index and its constituents, but also covers **portfolio insurance**.

Promissory note

An unconditional promise made in writing and signed by the debtor, undertaking to pay a specific sum on a fixed or determinable future date.

Pronti contro termine

Italian phrase for short-term spot and forward dealing.

Prospectus

Document which contains all the necessary information about a public issue of securities and the issuer. The contents are often governed by securities laws as well as by the exchange on which the securities are to be listed. Often a preliminary prospectus is prepared and issued to be followed by a final version when the terms of the transaction are set.

Prospectus liability

In most countries, the authors of a prospectus are liable to investors for any errors of fact or omissions.

Protection

When an issue is being syndicated a firm being invited to join the syndicate as an underwriter will ask for protection, that is to say an assurance that the securities allocated to them will be at least a certain amount. **International Primary Markets Association (IPMA)** guidelines are that an underwriter is entitled to immediate protection on at least half of his underwriting commitment.

Public limited company (PLC)

UK term for a public company which must have a minimum of £50,000 of authorized capital.

Public offering

Offering for sale of new securities to the general public.

Public sector borrowing requirement (PSBR)

Formerly a key figure in the UK government's borrowing plans which now focus on the Central Government Borrowing Requirement, in distinction to the borrowing of local government.

Public sector debt repayment (PSDR)

Used, rather briefly, to mean the net amount of UK government debt repaid in a year. Unlikely to be needed for some time.

Published reserves

A decreasing number of jurisdictions allow some companies, particularly banks, to maintain undisclosed reserves. Published or disclosed reserves are those these companies do make public.

Pune Stock Exchange

Provincial Indian stock exchange in Maharashtra which opened in 1982. Trading takes place on the floor of the exchange with fortnightly settlement.

The exchange has agreed to the creation of a single Indian exchange linked electronically. See **National Stock Exchange of India.**

Punt

The national currency of Ireland.

Purchase agent

Firm employed by a borrower to buy securities in the market in order to meet the requirements of the redemption schedule of a particular issue.

Purchase fund

A purchase fund is an obligation on the issuer of securities to attempt to purchase a certain amount of the issue each year. The issuer is not obliged to purchase bonds above **par.** A purchase fund is therefore likely to support the price of an issue, and may be more investor-friendly than a sinking fund which may redeem by lot at par a set number of bonds each year, irrespective of their market price.

Purchasing power parity (PPP)

A theory that in the long run currency rates are determined by inflation rate differentials. Quite apart from the difficulty of deciding where to start, it is clear that for long periods currencies can diverge from their purchasing power parity levels. Consequently, a foreign-exchange trader could grow old and poor waiting for the theory to prove itself.

Put date

Date on which an investor may exercise the right to put a security back to the issuer for **redemption** at the stipulated put price.

Put option

An option which gives the holder the right but not the obligation to sell a financial instrument, commodity or currency at a specified price on or before a specified date.

Put–call parity

The price relationship of puts, calls and the underlying is governed by put–call parity. There is a relationship between the price of a put and the price of a call at the same strike price. This is because it is possible to construct a synthetic version of the purchase of either option by means of a combination of the other option and the underlying. For example, being long a call is equivalent to being long the underlying and long a put both at the same strike price as the call.

In Figure P1, being long a put establishes a maximum loss which is the pre-

Figure P1

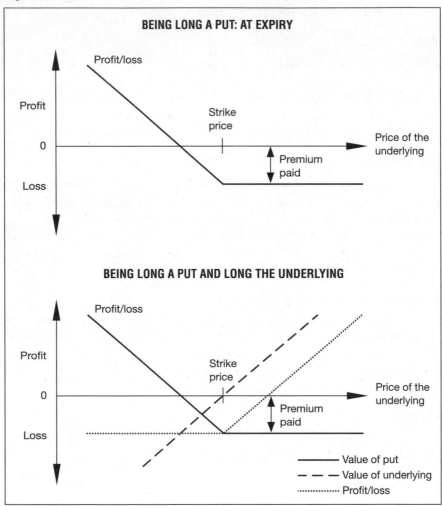

BEING LONG A PUT: AT EXPIRY

BEING LONG A PUT AND LONG THE UNDERLYING

mium paid while being able to benefit from any rise in the price of the underlying. If the price of the underlying falls then the holder of the put will exercise it in order to sell the underlying which he owns.

Being long a call establishes the same maximum loss which is the premium paid and the same potential for profit if the price of the underlying rises. If the price of the underlying falls, the holder of the call will let it expire worthless.

This relationship could be expressed as.

Underlying + put = call.

Which could be expressed as.

Underlying = call – put

or

Put = call – underlying.

The first rudimentary test of an option pricing model is whether it gives option values that are in accord with put-call parity. This test works whatever the option-pricing model being used. If prices diverge from this principal, then arbitrage transactions are possible.

Q

q ratio

Ratio of a company's stock market capitalization to the replacement cost of its assets. A q ratio above 1 implies that a company is worth more than its assets. This ought to encourage investment but does not always do so in reality. The ratio may be distorted by investment in software, systems and brands that are written off rather than capitalized.

Quant

Slang for mathematician employed by a financial institution.

Quanto

A product, such as a swap, where the return is calculated in one currency but converted to another currency at a fixed rate for payment.

Quasi-American option

Another name for a **Bermuda option**. See **American option** and **European option**.

Quasi-subsidiary

Under the UK's draft accounting standard ED49 ("Accounting for the substance of transactions in assets and liabilities"), some special purpose vehicles or quasi-subsidiaries, established solely for off-balance sheet financing transactions, would be consolidated in accounts of the parent group even though they are not technically subsidiaries.

Quetzal

The national currency of Guatemala.

Queue

A formal or informal arrangement regulating the flow of new issues in a market. The purpose of such queues is usually to ensure the orderly conduct of a new or thin market.

Quito Stock Exchange

One of the two stock exchanges in Ecuador, the Bolsa de Valores de Quito was established in 1969. On the exchange a wide range of securities are traded. Private securities are shares, security bonds, bills of exchange, financial certificates, notes, Bonos de Prenda and Bonos de Fomento. Public securities include government bonds, treasury bills, CFN bonds, external-debt bonds, development bonds and Bonos Estabilización Monetaria. Trading is by **open outcry**. An electronic transaction system was bought from the Chicago Stock Exchange. The exchange does not have a clearing house though a clearing house and depository institution are planned in co-operation with the **Guayaquil Stock Exchange**.

Quorum

The minimum number of people at a meeting required for their proceedings to be binding on the organization.

Quota

Capital subscription to the **International Monetary Fund (IMF)** which determines a member country's rights and obligations.

Quotation

(1) The setting of a price at which an instrument may be traded. Quotations may be indicative, that is for information only, or may be firm in which case the price quoted may be dealt at.
(2) Another name for a listing on an exchange.

Quote driven

A market system in which prices are initially determined by quotations of dealers obliged to make two-way prices consistently. Contrast with **order-driven** and other systems.

R

Racketeer-Influenced and Corrupt Organizations Act (RICO)

Bank fraud was added to crimes covered by this act in 1989 by the Financial Reform, Recovery and Enforcement Act (FIRREA).

Raiffeisenbank

German word for farm credit banks, common in Germany and Austria.

Rainbow option

An **option** where the value at expiry is determined by reference to the highest price of two or more specified categories of **underlying**.

Rally

Word used to mean a rise in a market.

Ramp

To ramp an issue is to push up the price above a sustainable level, usually with the intention of forcing short-sellers to cover their short positions at a large loss.

Rand

The national currency of South Africa.

Random Walk Theory

The theory assumes that price changes are independent of each other, and that over time price changes will approximate to a normal distribution. There are not many cases where this seems to happen in reality. There is a better case for arguing that price changes may approximate to a **lognormal distribution** in some cases.

Range forward contract

A range forward contract is a **forward** foreign exchange contract which sets a range of exchange rates within which two currencies will be exchanged at maturity. If at maturity the spot exchange rate is within the range then the range forward contract will be settled at that spot rate. If at maturity the spot rate is outside the range then the contract will be settled at the range price nearest to that spot rate. In essence, a range forward contract offers protection from loss while retaining some possibility of profit.

Range note

A note, with an embedded digital option, which offers a higher yield, so long as a specified price or index remains inside a specified range.

Ratchet option

A ratchet option has a resettable strike price. On specified dates the strike is reset to the then current price of the underlying and any intrinsic value is locked in at each reset.

Rating agencies

There are various rating agencies. Some of the best known in the US are Moody's, Standard and Poor's Corporation, Duff and Phelps, Fitch Investor Services, and McCarthy, Crisanti and Maffei. In Japan, agencies include Nippon Investors' Service, Mikuni & Co, Japan Credit Rating Agency and Japan Bond Research Institute. Elsewhere there is the *Agence d'Evaluation Financiere* in France, Dominion Bond Rating Service in Canada, Korean Investors' Service in Korea and International Bank Credit Analysis (IBCA) in the UK.

Their judgements do not carry equal weight in the eyes of international investors. Moody's (owned by Dun & Bradstreet) and Standard & Poor's (owned by McGraw Hill) are two leading international agencies. IBCA is a leading agency in the field of bank debt.

There are differences of approach between agencies. For example, Standard and Poor's is said to rely more heavily on intensive numerical analysis, while Moody's is said to consider a company and its environment in a broader way.

Inevitably, the agencies do not always agree about individual borrowers. They change their ratings at different times A borrower may have a split rating for long periods, though a split rating more than one grade apart is unusual. The agencies differ, also, in their attitudes to certain types of transaction so that Standard and Poor's may habitually rate, say, a collateralized transaction more highly than Moody's.

No agency is infallible. On 4 April 1994, Confederation Life Insurance was downgraded by Standard and Poor's from A+ to BBB+. On 5 August 1994, the company was placed under the authority of the Superintendent of Financial Institutions pending a request to the Canadian Attorney General to wind up the company. US$490 million of debt was involved. The company did not have a rating from Moody's.

What the agencies rate

Rating agencies give "opinions on the relative ability and willingness of an issuer to make timely payments on specific debt or related obligations over the life of the instrument." The agencies rate long- and short-term obligations of many sorts. In the case of insurance companies, they also rate claims paying ability.

Credit-rating agencies rate individual securities because not all issues of a borrower will have the same structure and therefore the same credit quality. Some issues may be senior debt, others may be subordinated. Some bonds may be issued by different subsidiaries of a group with different levels of guarantee from the parent company or an intermediate holding company. Other bonds may be secured on particular assets. It can be seen that different bonds might easily be rated differently, though apparently issued by the same borrower.

The ratings

Figures B11 and B12 (see pages 35 and 36) show how the two leading agencies, Moody's and Standard and Poor's categorize borrowers. See **Bond rating**.

How the rating agencies work

Country ratings

The starting point for credit ratings is the rating of the sovereign credit which sets a ceiling on the ratings of all borrowers in that country. The rating of a country's obligations in its own currency is often AAA/Aaa and higher than the rating of its foreign debt. The judgement of a sovereign borrower's ability to repay foreign currency debt is based on an assessment of the danger of deficient foreign exchange earnings and of the danger of short-term illiquidity. There is also the question of unwillingness to pay which is a political judgement.

Supranational agencies

The multilateral development banks and the European supranationals are a special case. Their credit ratings rest on their preferred creditor status accorded by member countries together with the financial and political support they receive from member countries. The agencies also have strong capital structures where callable capital is an important element. Generally the agencies are well-run, profitable and subject to prudential restrictions such as gearing ratios. The relative importance of these factors varies from agency to agency. The result of this combination of factors is that in at least one case an agency, the Nordic Investment Bank, has enjoyed a higher credit rating than its member countries.

Banks

The analysis of banks has four components: the role of the bank in the financial system of the country, the bank's market and operating environment, the bank's financial strength and the quality of its management.

The role of the government in maintaining the financial system, in regulating or supporting the banks and in bringing about change, by privatization or deregulation for instance, are important aspects of the first component. The legal environment is a further element in the analysis.

In looking at the bank's business, the agencies will consider the competitive position, likely developments in competition, and the concentration of the domestic banking industry. If the bank has substantial international operations a similar analysis of the international business will be performed.

Financial strength is analyzed under the headings of capital, asset quality, management quality, earnings quality and liquidity. Management analysis is a combined assessment of the strategies being pursued, the quality of the information systems and the influences on management, whether from owners, outside directors or other affiliations.

Bank holding companies are an added complication. The possibility of double leverage, where equity is geared at both parent and operating company level, and the possible barriers to cash flowing up to the holding company must be considered. An international bank may find its operations viewed through yet another lens made up of sovereign risk ceilings in the countries where it operates.

The analytical method applied to securities firms may also be applied increasingly to banks. Here the emphasis is on how market risks are measured and controlled, on the capital of the firm in relation to those risks and on the variability of profits over time.

Industrial companies

This is a wide area where different methods will be appropriate for each segment. Broadly an agency will look at the following five areas: (1) competitive position and the trends within industry and country; (2) financial strength and liquidity; (3) management quality, objectives and appetite for risk; (4) company structure and quality of support for the obligation; (5) risk of unforeseen events.

Ratio analysis

The study of a corporation by comparing recent financial ratios with historical ratios and those of other similar companies. Typically, the ratios used might be measures of profitability, return on assets, return on equity, capital ratios, or liquidity ratios.

Ratio spread

An option spread position where the numbers of contracts bought and sold are not the same.

Rational expectations

The theory that market participants use all available knowledge and infor-

275

mation, so as not to make systematic errors and that market prices reflect fully all currently available information, with the implication that price changes only reflect new information. Egotism and optimism ensure that this theory does not always hold.

Real

The national currency of Brazil since 1994.

Real Estate Investment Trust (REIT)

US mutual investment vehicle for property investments.

Real interest rate

Gross interest rate, less the rate of inflation.

Real rate of return

The nominal rate of return, less the rate of inflation.

Real time gross settlement (RTGS)

In a RTGS system payments are transmitted on a transaction by transaction basis and are settled individually across central bank accounts in real time. Usually there is full collateralization of any intra-day central bank credit extended to participating banks. RTGS eliminates intra-day settlement risk.

Real yield bond

Bond linked to a price index.

Reallowance

A part of the selling concession which may be offered by an underwriter of a new issue of securities to investor clients. In the US domestic market, a reallowance may be offered to recognized professional dealers only.

Receiver

Person appointed to take control of or to sell the assets of a bankrupt concern.

Receiver's swaption

Option on an interest rate swap in which the holder would receive the fixed rate payments.

Recognized clearing house (RCH)

Clearing house approved by the UK's Securities and Investments Board as providing settlement facilities for RIEs.

Recognized investment exchange (RIE)

UK term for exchanges approved by the Securities and Investments Board (SIB). Under UK law, certain investors, such as unit trusts, may only trade futures on RIEs. The seven RIEs are:

London Stock Exchange; LIFFE;
London Metals Exchange (LME);
International Petroleum Exchange (IPE);
London Commodity Exchange (LCE, will merge with LIFFE);
OMLX – The London Securities & Derivatives Exchange;
Tradepoint.

Designated investment exchanges are often foreign exchanges not subject to SIB control but recognised by the SIB for UK regulatory purposes as operating correctly.

Recognized professional bodies (RPBs)

UK term for those professional bodies which, under the Financial Services Act 1986, are empowered to authorize their members to carry on investment business. Generally, this permission is given where the investment business is incidental to their normal professional activities. There are nine such bodies:

Institute of Chartered Accountants in England & Wales;
Institute of Chartered Accountants of Scotland;
Institute of Chartered Accountants in Ireland;
Chartered Association of Certified Accountants;
The Law Society;
The Law Society of Scotland;
The Law Society of Northern Ireland;
The Institute of Actuaries;
The Insurance Brokers' Registration Council.

Reconstitution

The process of recombining previously stripped coupons and principal into coupon securities.

Record date

The date by which the holder of a registered security must have his ownership noted in order to have the right to receive a particular payment of income.

Reddito alla maturità

Italian phrase for yield to maturity. See **Yield to maturity**.

Redeemable preference share

Preference share capable of being repaid by the issuer.

Redemption

The purchase and cancellation of outstanding securities through a cash payment to the holder. Securities called for redemption, but not surrendered, cease to earn interest after the redemption date.

Redemption date

The date when a security may be repaid, not necessarily the same as the final maturity date.

Redemption price

The price at which a security may be redeemed prior to its maturity date. This may vary with time, or according to whether redemption is by exercise of a put or a call.

Reference bank

Prime bank whose quotation is used, usually along with those of other banks, to determine the reference interest rate on a floating-rate instrument. Reference banks were also used in early interest rate swaps, and usually now contribute to a screen page which is used for the same purpose.

Refund protection

Many corporate bonds in the US may not be called for a period after issue if the call is financed by the issue of further securities. This clause does not preclude refinancing from other sources, but does prevent an issuer taking advantage of lower interest rates at the expense of investors in the first bond issue.

Regional Stock Exchange

The Bolsa de Valores Regional is the stock exchange of six states in Brazil with its headquarters in Fortaleza.

Registered options principal

Individual permitted to deal in options by the US Securities and Exchange Commission (SEC).

Registered security

A security, the ownership of which is recorded in a register in the name of the holder. Such securities may exist physically or may exist in book-entry form only.

Registrar

An agent who records the ownership of registered securities. In some markets this function is performed centrally by one organization for all the securities listed and traded in a market.

Registration statement

The statement which must be filed with the US Securities and Exchange Commission before a security is offered for sale.

Règlement

French word for settlement.

Regular way settlement

In the US money and bond markets, settlement on $T+1$ through the Federal Reserve System (Fed). On other exchanges, the regular way settlement method is usually one of a number of possible methods, an alternative is usually cash or same-day settlement. On the Tokyo Stock Exchange, for example, regular way settlement is on $T+3$.

Regulated futures contract

Futures contracts traded on or subject to the rules of an exchange designated by the Commodity Futures Trading Commission and which use the mark-to-market method of determining margin account requirements.

Regulation A

US Federal Reserve regulation governing the operation of the Federal Reserve Discount Window.

Regulation B

US Federal Reserve regulation prohibiting discrimination against consumer credit applicants on grounds of age, sex, race, colour, religion or marital status.

Regulation C

US Federal Reserve regulation which requires mortgage lenders to report on the amount and location of the loans in their mortgage portfolios, so as to ensure that the needs of each community are met.

Regulation D

US Federal Reserve regulation which sets reserve requirements for deposit-taking financial institutions.

Regulation E

US Federal Reserve regulation governing electronic funds transfers.

Regulation F

US Federal Reserve regulation requiring banks to limit their exposure to other banks as a result of payments services and trading activities.

Regulation G

US Federal Reserve regulation, which is one of four governing lending secured on securities or to finance securities transactions, requires loans made by those other than banks or broker/dealers and which are secured on securities to be registered quarterly.

Regulation H

US Federal Reserve regulation setting out the requirements for State-chartered banks to become members of the Federal Reserve System.

Regulation I

US Federal Reserve regulation requiring member banks of the Federal Reserve System to buy stock in its regional Federal Reserve Bank equivalent to 6 percent of each bank's capital and surplus.

Regulation J

US Federal Reserve regulation which, with operating circulars, governs the collection of checks and the settlement of balances through the Federal Reserve System.

Regulation K

US Federal Reserve regulation concerned with the regulation of international banking activities by holding companies and the regulation of foreign banks in the US including the limitation of their interstate banking activities.

Regulation L

US Federal Reserve regulation which prohibits interlocking directorships between member banks, with some exceptions, such as banks owned by minority or women's groups.

Regulation M

US Federal Reserve regulation concerned with consumer leasing and the proper provision of information to lessees.

Regulation N

US Federal Reserve regulation governing transactions between Federal Reserve System banks and between such banks and foreign banks or governments.

Regulation O

US Federal Reserve regulation concerned with loans by member banks to their own executives.

Regulation P

US Federal Reserve regulation which sets standards of physical security for banks and requires the implementation of a security policy.

Regulation Q

US Federal Reserve rule that prohibits the payment of interest on checking accounts. The regulation does not apply to Negotiable Order of Withdrawal (NOW) accounts.

Regulation R

US Federal Reserve prohibition on those in the securities business being employed by member banks with an exception for those involved with government or municipal securities.

Regulation S

US Federal Reserve regulation implementing "right to financial privacy" legislation.

Regulation T

US Federal Reserve rule governing credit extended by broker/dealers for security purchases by their clients.

Regulation U

US Federal Reserve rule that governs credit extended by banks for security purchases by their clients.

Regulation V

US Federal Reserve regulation governing the financing of all those engaged in national defence contracts.

Regulation W

US Federal Reserve regulation concerned with consumer credit which was revoked in 1952.

Regulation X

US Federal Reserve regulation which applies the securities-related regulations (G, T, and U) to foreigners or to those who borrow abroad to purchase securities.

Regulation Y

US Federal Reserve regulation concerned with the activities of bank-holding companies.

Regulation Z

US Federal Reserve regulation concerned with the consumer credit implications of the 1968 Truth in Lending Act.

Regulation AA

US Federal Reserve regulation concerned with the complaints procedure to be followed by member banks.

Regulation BB

US Federal Reserve regulation implementing the Community Reinvestment Act and requiring banks to report on their CRA compliance.

Regulation CC

US Federal Reserve regulation which sets endorsement standards on checks.

Regulation DD

US Federal Reserve regulation which implemented the Truth in Savings Act.

Regulatory arbitrage

The construction of transactions designed to benefit from differences between regulatory regimes.

Reinvestment rate

In the calculation of yield to maturity, the rate assumed to be that at which interest received on a debt security can be reinvested over the life of that security. See **yield**.

Reinvestment risk

The risk that an investor will find actual reinvestment rates to be lower than assumed. See **risk**.

Relit

The French settlement system for stocks and shares operated by Sicovam based on delivery against payment. Its French name is *Système de règlement/livraison de valeurs mobilières contre paiement*. The system for French treasury bills and short-term money-market instruments was the Saturne system run by the Bank of France and now incorporated into SICOVAM. See *Société Interprofessionelle pour la Compensation des Valeurs Mobilières*. As a result of this merger a new system for all debt securities will be formed to be known as "Relit grande vitesse" or RGV (high-speed Relit).

Rendement

French word for yield.

Rendiob

Italian domestic interest rate at which long-term credit institutions borrow term money.

Repo

The word "repo" is an abbreviation of repurchase, and is used to denote a sale and repurchase agreement. A repo is a sale of securities for cash with a simultaneous commitment to repurchase them on a specified future date. The repo market is simply a collateralized money market in which borrowers of cash lend liquid marketable securities as collateral against the loan. In a repo the seller usually delivers securities on a delivery-versus-payment basis and receives cash from the buyer. This money is lent for the period of the transaction at an agreed rate, the "repo rate," which is usually fixed for the term of the deal. When a counterparty lends collateral and borrows cash they are said to repo the collateral. When a counterparty borrows the collateral and lends cash they are said to engage in a "reverse repo." The US domestic repo market has been estimated at about US$1,000 billion. Estimates of the size of the international market are inevitably imprecise, but the non-US dollar repo market is thought to exceed US$300 billion outstanding.

Three variations

Though the term "repo" describes one type of transaction, it is also used loosely to include two other similar sorts of transaction. So there are three separate transaction structures covered by the term.

Sell and buy-back

This is the simplest form. An outright sale of a security is accompanied by an outright repurchase of the same security for value a more distant date. This is sometimes called a "buy-sell" (see Figure R1).

The sale invoice price will include accrued coupon interest to the sale date and the buy-back price will include accrued coupon interest to the buy-back date. The clean price of the buy-back (that is, excluding interest accrued) will be set at such a level as to represent an interest cost. The cost of borrowing

Figure R1

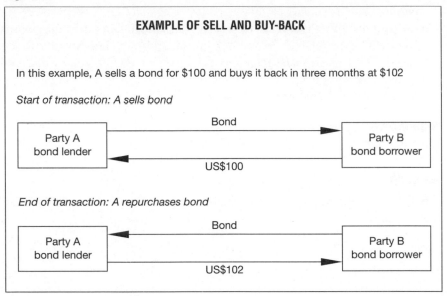

EXAMPLE OF SELL AND BUY-BACK

In this example, A sells a bond for $100 and buys it back in three months at $102

Start of transaction: A sells bond

| Party A bond lender | Bond → | Party B bond borrower |

US$100

End of transaction: A repurchases bond

| Party A bond lender | ← Bond | Party B bond borrower |

US$102

cash by the sale and buy-back transaction lies in this price adjustment. The documentation between the two counterparties is simply the confirmations of the two securities transactions. Sale and buy-back transactions can sometimes be used by institutions which are not allowed to lend or borrow securities, but which are allowed to buy and sell them.

An important difference between sale and buy-back transactions and the two other types described below is in the treatment of coupon payments made during the term of the transaction. In sale and buy-backs, the coupon accrued during the term of the repo is returned to the seller through the repurchase price calculation, an example of which is set out later, but a coupon paid during the term of the repo is not recoverable by the seller because there is no document other than the bond trade tickets governing the transaction. Sellers must be careful to consider this question before entering into trades.

Repurchase agreement (repo)

A repo is merely a more sophisticated sale and buy-back governed by a written agreement rather than merely being evidenced by deal confirmations (see Figure R2). The written agreement, will normally govern all such transactions between the counterparties. The agreement will typically include the right to mark transactions to market, and to ask for variation margin, as well as the rights to terminate transactions in the event of a default, and to set-off one against another, so as to net the exposure of the non-defaulting counterparty. A further difference of a practical nature is that the return to the supplier of cash is quoted separately.

Collateralized lending

A securities lending transaction involves one party agreeing to lend specified securities against collateral delivered by the other party who pays a fee for borrowing the securities (see Figure R3). The supplier of the securities is known as the "lender" and the supplier of collateral is known as the "borrower" even if the collateral is cash and a rate of interest is payable on it. The securities and collateral do not change ownership, and the owner of the securities continues to receive all coupons paid on them. For this reason these transactions are not true repos. Securities-lending transactions may also be structured as "open" trades, in which securities are lent for an unfixed period of time with the fee or interest being reset periodically.

Types of collateral vary from market to market, and may include government securities, Eurobonds, certificates of deposit, commercial paper, bankers' acceptances, mortgage-backed securities and equities. In many markets dealers may specify whether they require a specific security as collateral, or whether they are happy to accept any securities within a general category.

Figure R2

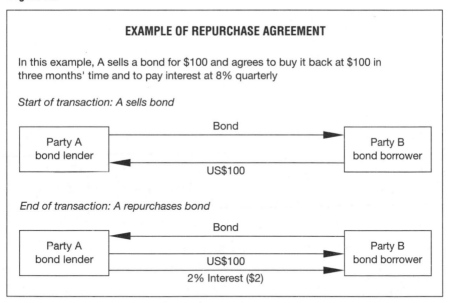

Example of a repo calculation

Trade date	10 May
Value date	12 May
Termination date	15 May
Term	3 days
Security	7.5% Bund 11.11.2004

285

Nominal amount	DM20 million
Clean price (excluding accrued interest)	109.00
Accrued interest	3.770833%
	DM754,166
Invoice price on trade date	112.770833
	DM22,554,166
Repo rate	3.5% pa

Figure R3

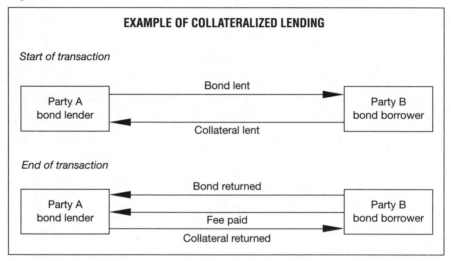

EXAMPLE OF COLLATERALIZED LENDING

Sale and buy-back calculation

If the transaction is to be structured as a sale and buy-back, then the cash flows will be as follows.

Party A agrees to sell DM20 million nominal against the receipt of DM22,554,166 and agrees to buy back the bunds after three days. The clean price at which Party A repurchases the bonds is calculated as follows:

Repurchase clean price = Purchase clean price − (bond coupon − repo rate)

The bond coupon = 7.5% x 20,000,000 x 3/360
= 12,500

Repo rate return = 3.5% x 22,554,166 x 3/360
= 6,578

Therefore the repurchase clean price is
21,800,000 − (12,500 − 6,578) = 21,794,078
or a price of 108.970390

Accrued interest to the termination date is 3.833333% or DM766,666. The invoice price on the termination date will therefore be:

108.970390 + 3.833333 = 112.803723:

or

DM21,794,078 + DM766,666 = DM22,560,744

The difference between the invoice prices on the trade date and the termination date is

DM22,560,744 – DM22,554,166 = DM6,578

During the transaction the coupon of the bond continues to accrue to the benefit of the bond lender or seller while the cash repo rate accrues to the benefit of the borrower or buyer. The difference between the two represents the net benefit to the bond lender or seller.

"Classic" repo calculation

If the same transaction had been structured as a repo, with the benefits conferred by a proper repo agreement, the arithmetic would have been as follows.

Party A agrees to deliver DM20 million nominal value of bonds to Party B against receipt of DM22,554,166, and agrees to take back the bonds from Party B after three days against payment of the same amount, together with an interest payment calculated as the repo rate applied to the cash amount.

In this case, the payment on the value date would be DM22,554,166 and the payment on the termination date would be DM22,554,166 plus interest of DM calculated as

22,554,166 x 3.50% x 3/360 = DM6,578

Uses of repos

Bond lenders

Because repos are collateralized loans, they often represent a borrowing mechanism which is cheaper than unsecured money market borrowing. This is particularly true for financial institutions which do not have direct access to the interbank deposit market. The open-market operations of central banks may also provide low-cost funding to the repo market.

Certain bonds may become scarce when they are described as being "on special." This usually means that there are many market participants who want to borrow a particular bond, and that in consequence the repo cash lending rate is very low for that particular security.

Repos can represent an opportunity for investors holding bonds to enhance the yield on their portfolios by borrowing cheaply through the repo market, and then lending at higher rates so as to earn an interest margin.

Bond borrowers

Bond borrowers may include cash lenders seeking a secured, short-term investment, or central banks, which sometimes use the repo market to add liquidity to the money markets through their open-market operations.

Very often, bond borrowers are traders who use borrowed securities to short the market. Having sold securities which they do not own they need to borrow them to make delivery. It should be noted that while all the cash flows under the repo are agreed in advance, the price at which Party B repurchases the bonds in the bond market is not known in advance. This price may give rise to a profit if Party B has judged the market correctly. It may otherwise give rise to a loss for Party B, if the market price of the bond has risen over the life of the repo transaction.

Repos and tax

The different circumstances of investors and the varieties of regulation make a comprehensive survey impossible. In order to see the sort of transaction which may be useful consider the following example.

Example

A portfolio manager owns a four-year UK gilt on which he has an unrealized loss. He does not wish to recognize the loss for tax reasons, but expects the market to fall further. He decides that hedging his position with the Long Gilt future on LIFFE would not be satisfactory, because of the maturity mismatch between the deliverable bonds (10 years plus) and his own holding of four-year bonds. The investor decides to borrow the same four-year gilt under a repo agreement, and simultaneously to sell the borrowed gilt in the market. If the market falls as the portfolio manager expects, he will be able to buy back the gilt at a lower price, thus offsetting the loss in his portfolio.

Implied repo rate

There is a close parallel between the repo market and the futures market. We have seen above that often the same general objective may be achieved, using futures or repos. We will now look in more detail at what governs the relationship between the two.

> *The implied repo rate is the break-even financing rate for an investor considering a cash/futures arbitrage transaction.*

Example

Suppose an investor was planning to buy a bond and sell an equivalent bond future (known as a "cash and carry position"). The futures contract would allow him to deliver the bond at a known price at the maturity of the futures contract. The investor would sell the future and simultaneously buy the bond, financing the purchase by repoing the bond for a period co-terminous with the future contract. At maturity, the investor would receive back the bond under the repo transaction and deliver it under the future contract. The investor would pay the repo rate to the repo counterparty, and would receive the implied repo rate under the future contract. If the implied repo rate exceeds the repo rate, then our investor can make a profit. This opportunity can be arbitraged away. The reverse condition, when the implied repo rate is less than the repo rate, cannot be arbitraged away, because the investor is not certain which bond will be delivered into the future contract. This is why the implied repo rate is usually less than the repo rate.

The description of the cash flows has been simplified. In practice, for example, there would be margin calls on the futures position, and the amount of the repo financing would be less than the market value of the bond by a sum equal to the margin required.

Calculating the implied repo rate

The starting point is the breakeven concept which can be expressed as:

Cost to purchase and finance bond = receipt from contract delivery plus coupon and reinvested earnings

This can be expressed for cases with no or one coupon payment as:

$$(P + A_1)(1 + rD_1/360) = (DP + A_2) + C(1 + rD_2/360)$$

where

P = bond purchase price
A_1 = accrued bond interest at purchase value date
r = implied repo rate (expressed as decimal)
D_1 = days from purchase value date to futures delivery date
C = coupon received (0 if none)
D_2 = days from coupon date to futures delivery date
DP = delivery price
A_2 = accrued bond interest at futures delivery date

Now this formula can be rearranged into the form

$$r = \frac{DP + A_2 - (P + A + C)}{(P + A_1)(D_1/360) - C(D_2/360)}$$

Risk

We need to consider two main areas of risk: market risk and credit risk.

Market risk

Generally it is the case that market risk on the securities in a repo transaction is borne by the seller/lender of the securities who has contracted to buy them back at a fixed price, whatever the market price of the securities. It is consequently true that the decision of the buyer/borrower of the securities to enter into a repo transaction is not influenced by the market price of the securities, or by their coupon, maturity or expected price performance, provided that the securities represent saleable collateral for an adequate amount in the event of a default by the counterparty.

Credit risk

This may be divided into two parts: counterparty risk and collateral risk.

Counterparty risk is the risk that the counterparty fails to perform on the termination date. If the counterparty fails to return the securities or the cash the risk is that the value of the securities at that point is less or greater than the repurchase price. This might be thought of as contingent market risk. It will be potentially greater with securities of longer duration and in volatile market conditions. This risk can be reduced by agreeing suitable margining arrangements. However there will always be a risk that margin calls are not paid by the counterparty so the risk can not be entirely eliminated.

The second part of credit risk is *collateral risk*, the danger that the issuer of the collateral might default during the term of the repo. This, too, is a contingent risk because the counterparty is still obliged to repurchase the securities whatever their market value. The risk is therefore only crystalized if both the issuer of the collateral and the repo counterparty default during the life of the repo.

Margining

Because the value of collateral will change with market conditions the counterparty looking to the collateral as security will often require a "margin" of value above the amount of cash advanced. This requirement is usually divided into "initial margin," required at the outset, and "variation margin" which is called for if the value of the collateral has fallen by an agreed amount. In order to manage this process in a sensible manner, the repo documentation will often stipulate a minimum amount by which the value of the collateral must change in order for more collateral to be demanded or for surplus collateral to be returned.

In all of these arrangements, it matters where the collateral is held. A "hold-in-custody" repo is one where the supplier of the collateral retains possession and merely segregates it in his books. In some markets, this is pledged to the counterparty, but even so is not always completely secure. The obvious danger is that the same collateral may be used several times over or may not exist at all! The safest form of collateral arrangement is known as a "tri-party repo." It also saves on the expenses of transfering securities between depositaries. Collateral is held by an independent third party which manages the exchange of cash and securities, monitors value and manages margin calls and substitution of securities.

Reserve requirements

The amounts which banks are required to hold on deposit at the central bank, in cash or in certain assets as reserves and calculated as percentages of different types of deposit.

Reserve tranche

Loan to the International Monetary Fund (IMF) by member countries in proportion to each member country's quota to finance lending by the IMF.

Resolution Funding Corporation (REFCORP)

Established by the US Financial Institutions Reform Recovery, and Enforcement Act (FIRREA), REFCORP is authorized to issue debt securities to finance the work of the Resolution Trust Corporation in liquidating troubled savings and loan institutions.

Resolution Trust Corporation (RTC)

US government agency formed by Congress to liquidate troubled savings and loan institutions.

Retail Price Index (RPI)

A measure of retail price changes in the UK which uses a basket of goods and services. RPI-X is the same index less the element related to household mortgage rates.

Retained cash flow

A measure of a company's cash generation defined as gross cash flow, minus common and preferred stock dividends.

Retained earnings

Past profits which the company has not distributed to shareholders. Such profits may well not be equivalent to cash generated.

Retractable bond

Similar to an extendable bond. A retractable bond has a coupon reset date prior to its final maturity date. If the borrower elects to exercise the clause and reset the coupon, the investor has the choice of accepting the new coupon or having his bond repaid at par. An extendable bond has an interest reset possibility on its specified maturity date, with the investor having the same choice of accepting a new coupon or having his bonds redeemed.

Return on assets

Measure of profitability defined as net income divided by average total assets in the period.

Return on equity

Measure of profitability defined as income from continuing operations (after payment of preferred dividends) divided by average common equity for the period.

Revenue bond

US municipal bond secured on the earnings of a specific public enterprise.

Reverse auction

Method by which, for example, the Bank of England used to buy back gilt-edged securities

Reverse barrier

Barrier option set at a strike where a conventional option would be in the money.

Reverse swap

Swap transaction written to reverse the effect of an earlier swap.

Revolving credit

A bank credit facility which continues to be available to be drawn at any time before the maturity date whatever the pattern of drawings and repayments during the life of the facility.

Revolving underwriting facility (RUF)

Type of note underwriting facility. The issue of notes is underwritten by a group of banks. If the tender panel mechanism fails to find investors to buy notes then the underwritting banks are required to buy the unsold notes.

Rho

The price change of an option caused by a change in the risk-free interest rate.

Rial

The national currency of Iran and Oman.

RIBOR

Rome interbank offered rate.

Riel

The national currency of Cambodia.

Riga Stock Exchange

The Latvian stock exchange was established in December 1993. The exchange has been advised by the Paris Bourse and other French bodies on the setting up of a modern order-driven exchange and central depository. The exchange trades shares, bonds and treasury bills.

Right

An entitlement to subscribe for new shares usually allocated to existing shareholders in proportion to their existing shareholdings. Such rights may be traded in "nil-paid" form if the shareholder does not want to take up the rights himself.

Right of preemption

The right of existing shareholders to have the first opportunity to buy any new shares which a company may want to issue. The right is intended to prevent the dilution of existing shareholders' holdings.

Rights issue

An issue of shares to existing shareholders in proportion to their holdings in exchange for payment (and therefore unlike a scrip issue of free shares).

Ring

That part of the trading floor on a futures or options exchange where a particular contract is traded.

Ring trader

Trader in a "ring" or "pit" at the London Metal Exchange.

Ring-out

A procedure under which, in unusual market conditions, an exchange sets an arbitrary cash settlement price for all open positions in a contract.

Rio de Janeiro Stock Exchange

The Bolsa de Valores do Rio de Janeiro is the oldest exchange in Brazil, founded in 1845. Common stocks, preferred stocks, index futures and stock and index options are traded. Trading may be on the floor of the exchange or by the electronic system. Clearing is through the Câmara de Liquidaçâo e Custódia (CLC), an independent clearing house. Trading requires certificates to be delivered on T+1 for settlement on T+2. The main indices are the Rio de Janeiro Stock Exchange Index, the IBV Index a market-weighted index of the most actively traded stocks, and the National Index, I-SENN. which covers the eight exchanges which are integrated by the Sistema Electrônico de Negociação Nacional (SENN), the national electronic trading system. The I-SENN is a value-weighted index of the 50 most-traded stocks on the eight exchanges.

Risk

Risk has been described as the organizing principle of financial institutions. There are many forms of financial risk – several have been identified in this book.

See accounting risk, aggregate risk, basis risk, business risk, call risk, capital risk, collateral risk, country risk, credit risk, currency risk, discontinuity risk, economic risk, event risk, funding risk, Herstatt risk, inflation risk, interest rate risk, legal risk, liquidity risk, market risk, pin risk, political risk, reinvestment risk, settlement risk, spread risk, systemic risk, taxation risk, transfer risk, translation risk, and value at risk.

Risk asset ratio

For capital adequacy and regulatory purposes, a bank's total equity divided by total risk weighted assets.

Rolint

Italian domestic interest rate calculated as the average of Milan interbank offered rate and *Rendiob*.

Romanian Commodities Exchange

Bursa Romậna de Marfuri SA in Bucharest was established in 1992. The market trades in three sections. The first is for grain, flour, potatoes, live hogs, pork bellies, broilers, eggs, alcohol, edible fats, fuel oil, gas oil, scrap iron, non-ferrous metals, cement, timber. The second part of the market is for agricultural and food products, fibres and yarns, fertilizers and chemicals. The third part of the market is for consumer goods, art objects, precious stones and other things. The exchange guarantees the checking and certification of commodity quality.

Rosario Stock Exchange

The Bolsa de Comercio de Rosario in Argentina is grain trading exchange with a futures market and a stock exchange. The futures market is the Mercado a Término de Rosario, the stock market is the Mercado de Valores de Rosario. The securities traded are ordinary shares, preference shares and government bonds. There are futures on Sorghum, Corn, Wheat, Linseed, Sunflower Seed and Soya Bean.

Rouble

The currency of Russia and the Commonwealth of Independent States (CIS).

RTGS

See **Real time gross settlement**.

Rücknahmepreis

German word for redemption price.

Rule 144a

Rule 144a became effective on 30 April 1990. Its principal function was to facilitate private placements made in conjunction with offerings outside the US by streamlining the procedures for initial placement and creating a more liquid market for secondary trading. The rule provides a safe harbour from the requirements of the Securities Act for resales to "qualified institutional buyers" of restricted securities. Such buyers are held to manage at least US$100 million of securities. Foreign issuers generally prefer to furnish to the SEC under rule 12g3-2(b) under the Exchange Act the information that they make public in foreign markets rather than submit to the requirement of rule 144a to furnish certain information on request .

Rule 415

US Securities and Exchange Commission rule allowing the pre-registration of an issue of securities which may then be sold as market conditions allow in tranches.

Run

The series of bid and asked quotes for different maturities exchanged by dealers

Running yield

See current yield.

Rupee

The national currency of seven countries: India, the Maldives, Mauritius, Nepal, Pakistan, the Seychelles and Sri Lanka.

Rupiah

The national currency of Indonesia.

Russian Commodities and Raw Materials Exchange

The trading activities of this exchange in Moscow are commodity trading, currency and commodity futures trading and stock trading.

S

SADC (Southern African Development Community)

Southern African Development Community, established in 1992 by 10 southern African countries (but not Kenya or Uganda) to promote regional economic integration. Based in Botswana.

Safe harbor

The phrase applies to US legislation intended to set out specific circumstances where an action is legal which might otherwise be illegal. There are various cases where the phrase is used.

Foreign issues of securities

There are two specific "safe harbors" which apply to cases where an issue of securities is an "offshore transaction," and where there are no "directed selling efforts." These protect the issue from the full requirements of US legislation.

The first is the "issuer safe harbor," which provides for three levels of control framed around, first, the likelihood that the securities will be bought in the US because a substantial US market interest exists and, second, the adequacy of publicly available information about the issuer. These are known as Category 1, 2 and 3.

A Category 1 issuer is one where there is no substantial US market interest in its debt securities. A borrower is held not to have a substantial US market interest, if its debt securities are held of record by less than 300 investors, less than US$1 billion of its debt securities are held of record by US investors and less than 20 percent of its debt securities are held of record by US investors. (For bearer securities, the issuer must form a "reasonable belief.") In such a case, it is only required that the issue be an offshore transaction and that there be no directed selling effort in the US. Most foreign issuers are in this category.

Category 2 contains issuers who are US reporting issuers, foreign reporting issuers with a substantial US market interest or non-reporting foreign issuers with a substantial US market interest in its debt securities. This category faces additional requirements which include the two following. First, no offer or sale may be made to a US investor other than a distributor during a 40-day restricted period. Second, the issuer must include certain "offering restrictions" in the issue documentation. These should include (1) that each distributor agrees in writing that all offers and sales during the restricted period will be made only in accordance with Regulation S or an available exemption (e.g., Rule 144a), and (2) that the documentation includes statements that the securities have not been registered under the 1933 Securities Act, and may not be offered or sold within the restricted period unless registered or under an exemption.

Category 3 applies to non-reporting US issuers and to the equity securities of non-reporting foreign issuers.

Resale safe harbor
The resale safe harbor is available to any seller of securities except the issuer, a distributor or its affiliates. It allows US investors to resell abroad privately placed securities.

Rule 10b–18
A rule of the Securities and Exchange Commission which allows companies to repurchase their own securities without being accused of market manipulation. It is sometimes called the "Safe Harbor Rule."

Safekeeping repo

Repo where the collateral is not physically delivered but is instead held by a depositary in the name of the lender of cash. See **repo**.

St Petersburg Stock Exchange

The exchange was re-established in 1990, and trades privatization cheques, common stocks, bonds, shares in mutual investment funds, futures and options. Trading is on the floor of the exchange by call-market auction. Settlement is between brokers.

Saitori

Special members of the Tokyo Stock Exchange who act as intermediaries between the regular members and match securities transactions but are not allowed to trade on their own account or with members of the public.

Salam

Arabic word for a form of financing, where a bank buys a commodity for future delivery but pays for it at once.

Sallie Mae

See **Student Loan Marketing Association (SLMA)**.

Samurai bond

Yen bond issued in the Japanese public bond market by foreign institutions.

Sandwich spread

A butterfly spread.

Santiago Stock Exchange

The Bolsa de Comercio de Santiago, Chile was founded in 1893. Shares, debt securities, futures and options are traded. Trading is by both **open outcry** and by electronic system. Infrequently traded shares are traded on the Telepregón computer trading system. Futures are traded on the IPSA Index and on the US dollar exchange rate. Options are traded on individual equities. The exchange's main indices are the Indice General de Precios de Acciones (IGPA), which is made up of 119 shares, and the Indice de Precios Selective de Acciones (IPSA), which is made up of the 40 most traded shares on the exchange.

São Paulo Stock Exchange

This Brazilian exchange was founded in 1890. Bolsa de Valores de São Paulo or BOVESPA lists common shares, preferred shares, debt securities, options and futures. Trading is by **open outcry** and by the CATS electronic trading system. Futures and options on shares are traded. The main index is the BOVESPA index based on the prices of those shares which together represent 80 percent of the trading volume of the previous 12 months. The composition is reviewed every four months.

Sapporo Securities Exchange

Japanese provincial exchange founded in 1950. Trading is by the *Zaraba* method.

Saudi Arabian Monetary Authority (SAMA)

SAMA has encouraged the Saudi equity market. Trading in shares of Saudi companies is restricted to nationals of Saudi Arabia and the Gulf Cooperation Council countries. Trading is through ESIS, an order-driven system run by SAMA and linked to the 12 commercial banks who act as agency brokers but may not trade on their own account. No brokers outside the banking system are permitted. The main market index is the Market Index – NCFEI.

Savings and loan association (S&L)

US institution which takes local deposits and lends primarily for residential mortgages. Savings and loan associations are best-known for the spectacularly expensive rescue they required in 1989. The story is simple. In 1980 the cap on the interest rate they could pay on deposits was lifted, and in 1982, S&Ls were allowed to diversify into direct investments including property development. During the 1980s, a tidal wave of investment in property by domestic and foreign investors financed a property boom and, predictably, led to a slump. S&Ls suffered disproportionately. They had begun the decade with tangible net worth at less than 4 percent of assets, and this figure quickly fell below 1 percent. S&Ls were for the most part small, geographically limited and lacked appropriate skills in commercial real estate. They were, too, vulnerable to fraudulent manipulation and political influence. S&Ls now operate under a tighter regulatory environment created by the **Financial Institutions Reform, Recovery and Enforcement Act (FIRREA)** of 1989.

Savings bonds

US savings instruments with maturities from three to five years which can only be bought by US residents.

Scalping

Trading with the intention of making small profits over a short period of time.

Schilling

The national currency of Austria.

Schuldschein, Schuldscheindarlehen

Loan in the German domestic market evidenced by a promissory letter.

Sconto

Italian word for discount.

Scrip dividend

Dividend paid in shares rather than in cash.

Scrip issue

New shares issued to existing shareholders at no cost, unlike a **rights issue**. A scrip issue involves the transfer of reserves to paid-up capital, but does not change the **market capitalization** of a firm.

Seagull

A position where the holder buys an **at-the-money** or near-the-money call, and sells an **out-of-the money** put and an out-of-the money call.

SEAQ Automatic Execution Facility (SAEF)

The London Stock Exchange's automated dealing system for small bargains in UK equities.

Seasoned

A security which, under US Securities and Exchange Commission rules, is non-exempt, but may be sold to US residents, because it has been outstanding for a period of time.

Secondary market

Trading in securities outside the primary distribution period.

Secondary placement

The placement of securities which are not newly issued. Such a secondary placement has no impact on the entity which originally issued the securities.

Secured creditor

A creditor which has a charge over assets of the debtor. Such a charge may be a fixed charge on specific assets, or a floating charge over the general assets of the debtor. These types of charge may rank differently in a liquidation.

Securities and Exchange Commission (SEC)

Agency created by the US Securities Exchange Act of 1934 to administer securities legislation.

Securities and Futures Authority (SFA)

UK self-regulatory organization formed from the merger in April 1991 of the Association of Futures Brokers and Dealers and the Securities Association.

Securities and Investments Board (SIB)

UK regulatory body established by the Financial Services Act 1986, responsible for overall supervision of the conduct of financial markets and services.

Securities Exchange of Barbados

The exchange was founded in 1987. In 1991 the exchanges of Barbados, Jamaica and Trinidad and Tobago began cross-trading of listed securities as the first step towards a regional securities market. Trading is by a twice-weekly regulated call-over on the floor of the exchange. The exchange publishes the SEB Share Index.

Securitization

The process of creating securities which depend on financial assets which would not otherwise be tradeable.

Securitized option

An **option** embedded in a security.

SEDOL number

UK securities, including gilts, are assigned a Stock Exchange Daily Official List (SEDOL) number. This seven-digit number is incorporated in the 12-digit International Security Identification Number (ISIN) assigned to each security.

Segregated account

Account held on behalf of another by a bank or broker, which is clearly designated as not being the property of the bank or broker.

Self-regulating organization

A professional association or body which has responsibilities for overseeing the conduct of its members. In the UK, the term is defined under the Financial Services Act to be an organization, approved and supervised by the Securities and Investment Board (SIB), which is responsible for writing and enforcing a detailed set of rules governing a part of the financial services industry. The three SROs are the Securities and Futures Authority (SFA), the Investment Management Regulatory Organization (IMRO), and the Personal Investment Authority (PIA).

Selling agreement

Agreement among the managers and underwriters of a new issue which specifies the selling restrictions imposed on it in various jurisdictions and the terms on which the securities may be sold.

Selling commission

Commission paid to members of the selling group in the distribution of a new issue. Selling groups are now rare, the function being performed by the managers.

Selling restriction

A limitation imposed on the placement of a new issue of securities.

Selling short

Selling something which the seller does not own. The **underlying** will be borrowed to make delivery on the sale. The seller hopes to buy the underlying more cheaply at some time in the future. Short-selling has been prohibited in some markets.

Separately traded registered interest and principal security (STRIPS)

Generic name for US treasury securities from which the **coupons** have been detached and for the detached coupons themselves.

Serial expiration

Options on the same underlying futures contract expiring in more than one month. Typically an exchange might have options expiring quarterly (say March, June, September and December) with such other months as necessary so that there are options expiring in the next three calendar months.

Serial loan

A type of mortgage loan, encountered in Denmark for example, which is pre-paid by equal instalments of principal on each payment date. Interest is calculated on the balance outstanding so that each interest payment is smaller than the last. Thus the regular payments in total reduce over the life of the loan.

Settlement date

The date on which a transaction is completed. In a security transaction the settlement date is the date on which the security is exchanged for payment.

Settlement price

Price calculated by a derivatives exchange at the end of each trading session as the closing price that will be used in determining profits and losses for the mark-to-market process for margin accounts.

Settlement risk

Settlement risk, also called "delivery risk," is the risk that in settling a transaction, one party will transfer value to the other without receiving equivalent value. In securities exchanges, delivery-against-payment mechanisms often exist to prevent this happening, but for foreign exchange and other transactions the risk is harder to reduce. See **risk**.

Settle-to-market

Process by which the **variation margin** provisions of swap master agreement are operated. The contracts involved are marked-to-market, (see **mark-to-market**) and the net value is required to be posted as variation margin.

Shanghai Stock Exchange

Exchange in the People's Republic of China which began trading in 1990. Stocks, treasury bonds and 10-year bond futures are traded. Settlement and clearing are through the Shanghai Securities Central Clearing and Registration Corporation. The main indices are the Shanghai Securities Exchange Index (SSEI), a weighted-average market capitalisation index of all shares, and the China Index, an index of all the listed shares on the Shanghai and Shenzhen Stock Exchanges. Towards the end of 1992 trading was very volatile.

Share index

An indicator of price variation of selected shares in a stock exchange. Some of the key indices by country are shown in Figure S1.

Figure S1

KEY SHARE INDICES BY COUNTRY	
Argentina	Buenos Aires Stock Exchange General Index
Australia	20 Leaders Index
	ASX 100 Index
Austria	Vienna Stock Exchange Share Index
	Austrian Traded Index
Belgium	Bel 20 Index
Brazil	Rio de Janeiro Stock Exchange Index (IBV Index)
	National Index (I-SENN)
Canada	Toronto Stock Exchange 100 Index (TSE 100)
Denmark	Copenhagen Stock Exchange Total Share Index
	KFX Index
Finland	HEX Index
France	CAC-40
Germany	DAX
Hong Kong	Hang Seng Index
Italy	BCI Index
Japan	Nikkei Stock Index 225
Malaysia	KLSE Composite Index
Netherlands	Amsterdam EOE-Index
New Zealand	NZSE 40 Index
Norway	OBX Stock Index
Singapore	Straits Times Industrial Share Price Index
South Africa	All Shares Index
Spain	IBEX-35
Sweden	SX-General Index
Switzerland	Swiss Market Index (SMI)
Thailand	Stock Exchange of Thailand Index
United Kingdom	FT-SE 100
United States	Dow Jones Composite Average
	NYSE Composite Index

Shelf registration

US Securities and Exchange Commission Rule 415 allowing advance registration of securities which may be issued at any time within two years of the original registration.

Shenzhen Metal and United Futures Exchange

The Shenzhen Metal Exchange was founded in 1991, and merged with the

303

Shenzhen United Futures Exchange in 1994. The exchange trades base metals, grain, diesel fuel, and sugar. Futures are traded in Copper, Aluminium, Zinc, Lead, Tin, Nickel, Magnesium and Antimony. Trading is by **open outcry**.

Shenzhen Stock Exchange

Chinese stock exchange founded in 1990. A shares, B shares (open to foreigners), treasury bonds, convertibles and funds are listed. Trading is continuous, by an order-driven, computerized matching system. The exchange publishes the Shenzhen Stock Price Index, the Shenzhen Stock Exchange A Share Index and the Shenzhen Stock Exchange B Share Index.

Shibosai

Japanese word for privately placed unlisted securities.

Shogun bond

Public non-Yen bonds issued by foreigners in Japan.

Shokan

Japanese word for redemption.

Shop window

Term used in the UK gilt market. Small amounts of stock acquired in the course of its official operations by the Bank of England are offered to be resold to the market through a "shop window". At 8.30am each day, the Bank posts on its screen pages a list of the amount of each stock available for sale. A necessary condition is that any successful bid must be at or above the current market price.

Short

Selling a financial instrument, commodity or currency.

Short sterling

Slang name for the three-month sterling interest rate futures contract traded on the London International Financial Futures Exchange (LIFFE).

Shout option

A variation of the **ratchet option**. The reset occurs not on specified dates but at the request of the option holder.

Siberian Stock Exchange

Founded in Novosibirsk in 1991, SibEx has eight regional exchange centres in Novosibirsk, Irkutsk, Kemerovo, Ulan-Ude, Novokunznetsk, Omsk,

Tomsk and Barnaul. SibEx merged with the West-Siberian Stock Exchange in 1993. An electronic trading system was introduced in 1993. The exchange trades privatization cheques, ordinary shares, preferred stocks, debt securities, options and futures. Settlement is between brokers.

SIBOR

Singapore interbank offered rate.

Sigma

The standard deviation or volatility of the underlying in connection with an option.

Simple interest

Interest which is calculated on the principal amount without any compounding.

Simultaneas

Spanish word for buy–sell transactions in government bonds similar to **repos**.

Singapore Commodity Exchange Limited

The exchange began trading in 1992, formerly the Rubber Association of Singapore Commodity Exchange. Trading is through a computerized system, NEAT, which provides prices, trade registration, confirmation, and settlement. The exchange's rubber futures are International One Ribbed Smoked Sheet (RSS 1), International Three Ribbed Smoked Sheet (RSS 3) and Technically Specified Rubber (TSR 20). The exchange also trades Robusta Coffee and Cocoa Futures.

Singapore International Monetary Exchange

The first financial futures exchange in Asia, SIMEX was founded in 1984. It also pioneered, with the Chicago Mercantile Exchange (CME), the first mutual offset trading link. All trading is by **open outcry** on the floor of the exchange. Settlement is through the SIMEX clearing house. The exchange lists futures on the Nikkei 225 Stock Average, the Nikkei 300, the SIMEX MSCI Hong Kong Index, High-Sulphur Fuel Oil, Three-Month Eurodollars, Three-Month Euroyen, Three-Month Euromarks, Japanese Government bonds (JGB), Yen, DEM and GBP Exchange Rates, and Gold. There are options on the Nikkei 225 and Nikkei 300 Stock Averages, on Japanese Government Bonds and on Three-Month Eurodollars, and Euroyen.

Single passport

The right of a bank to do business in any country in the European Union provided it is supervised by one of the EU member states. There are seven EU directives which attempt to standardize the conduct of financial business.

Sinking fund

Money periodically set aside by a borrower to redeem all or part of a debt issue as provided for in the issue documentation.

Skewness

The extent to which a sample is asymmetrically distributed. Negative skewness indicates more readings to the left of the peak, positive more to the right. Many equity markets display a positive skewness, reflecting the tendency of share prices to rise over time.

Skip-day settlement

Settlement of a transaction on T+2.

Sociedades de credito hipotecario

Specialized mortgage institutions in Spain and Portugal.

Società di Intermediazione Mobiliare (SIM)

Italian firms authorized to trade and invest in securities, manage portfolios, supervise purchases and sales, give financial advice.

Società per azioni (SpA)

Italian equivalent of a public limited company.

Société anonyme (SA)

French equivalent of a public limited company.

Société d'Investissement à Capital Fixe (SICAF)

Closed-ended investment fund.

Société d'Investissement à Capital Variable de Capitalisation (SICAV de Capitalisation)

Open-ended roll-up investment fund.

Société d'Investissement à Capital Variable (SICAV)

Open-ended investment fund.

Société des Bourses Françaises (SBF)

The French stockbrokers' association, previously known as Compagnie des Agents de Change (CAC).

Société Interprofessionelle pour la Compensation des Valeurs Mobilières (SICOVAM)

Operates a clearing system for French stocks and debt instruments.

Sol

The national currency of Peru

South African Futures Exchange

SAFEX was opened in 1990 in Johannesburg. Trading is by screen and telephone. Settlement is through the exchange's own clearing house, SAFEX Clearing Company (Pty) Ltd, (SAFCOM). The exchange trades futures and options on the JSE Actuaries All Share Index, the JSE Actuaries All Gold Index, the JSE All Industrial Index, Gold, ESKOM L168 Loan Stock, and 91-day bankers' acceptances.

Spanish Financial Futures Market

MEFF Sociedad Rectora de Productos Financieros Derivados de Renta Fija SA, known as MEFF Renta Fija, is based in Barcelona and trades interest rate and currency futures and options. MEFF Sociedad Rectora de Productos Financieros Derivados de Renta Variable, SA, known as MEFF Renta Variable, is based in Madrid and trades stock index futures and options and equity options. Trading on MEFF Renta Fija is automated and is through a combined dealing and settlement system, MEFF-SMART. The exchange lists futures on a three-year notional government bond, a 10-year notional government bond, MIBOR-90, and MIBOR-360. The exchange lists options on all but the MIBOR-360 future.

Spanish Options Exchange

MEFF Sociedad Rectora de Productos Financieros Derivados de Renta Variable SA, known as MEFF Renta Variable, is based in Madrid and trades stock index futures and options and equity options. The exchange trades futures and options on the IBEX 35 Index and options on individual shares.

Special bracket

A special tier in a management group formed so as to give certain firms a larger share in a transaction or to mark their close relationship with the issuer.

Special drawing right (SDR)

Composite currency unit designed by the International Monetary Fund.

Special purpose vehicle (SPV)

Company formed for a single purpose, usually to hold assets or receive cash flows in a financial transaction. Often such vehicles are not formally owned by the company which benefits from the financing transaction and are not, therefore, consolidated in the financial statements.

Specialist

An exchange member who makes a market in a particular listed security and to whom orders in that security are directed. Found on the NYSE and on other exchanges which imitate it.

Spécialistes en Valeurs du Trésor (SVTs)

Primary dealers and market-makers in the French government bond market. The SVTs are authorised to buy new French government securities directly from the treasury and are required to maintain a liquid secondary market.

In the primary market, SVTs are required to ensure that the auctions proceed smoothly, conveying information to the Trésor and bidding for reasonable amounts at each auction. SVTs are required to buy at least 2 percent of the annual volume issued in each of the four categories of security *Bons du Trésor à taux fixe et interêt précompté (BTFs)*, *Bons du Trésor à taux annuel et interêt annuel (BTANs)*, *Obligations assimilables du Trésor (OATs)* and ECU BTANs and OATs. The arithmetical mean of the three percentages relating to French franc securities must be at least 3 percent.

The SVTs are required to trade at least 3 percent each of the total volume traded by SVTs in each category of security in the secondary market (BTFs, BTANs and OATs) and 2 percent of such trading in ECU-denominated securities (combining ECU BTANs and ECU OATs). SVTs are also required to make continuous bid and offer prices in the principal issues and to show the amounts for which these are firm prices.

SVTs have two privileges: the right to make bids in non-competitive bidding rounds and the right to reconstitute stripped OATs.

Qualification for SVT status is earned by serving a period as *Correspondant en Valeurs du Trésor (CVT)*, during which time a firm's competence is assessed. The Minister of the Economy may then grant them SVT status provided the firm meets certain structural and operational requirements. The minimum capital requirement is Ffr300 million. Each SVT must have a stable establishment in Paris from which all trading in French government securities must be conducted for the group to which the SVT belongs. The SVT must have a locally based sales team and appropriate mid-office and back-office resources.

The SVTs at 1 March 1996 are shown in Figure S2.

Specialisti in titoli di Stato

Government securities specialists in Italy who have certain privileges relating to new issues.

Figure S2

```
                    SVTs AT MARCH 1996
Banque d'Escompte
Banque Indosuez
Banque Internationale de Placement – Dresdner Bank
Banque Lehman Brothers SA
Banque Nationale de Paris Finance
Banque Paribas
Caisse des Dépôts et Consignations
Caisse Nationale de Crédit Agricole
CPR – Intermédiation
Crédit Commercial de France
Crédit Lyonnais
Deutsche Bank France SNC
Goldman Sachs Paris Inc & Cie
J.P. Morgan et Cie SA
Louis Dreyfus Finance (Banque) SA
Merrill Lynch Finance SA
Morgan Stanley SA
Société Générale
UBS France SA
Union Européenne de CIC
```

Specials

In the **repo** market, the word refers to securities which are much in demand. Owners of such securities can borrow cash very cheaply against them.

Spot

In foreign exchange and money markets spot signifies prices and trades for settlement on T+2.

Spot commodity

A physical commodity as opposed to the future contract.

Spot month

The contract month closest to the current month

Spot next

The one day period from the spot date (T+2) to the next day (T+3). It is the day after **tom next** which is the one-day period from tomorrow (T+1) to the next day (T+2).

Spot price

The price of a security or commodity in the cash market.

Spot rate curve

The zero-coupon yield curve in which every point represents the yield to maturity of a zero-coupon bond.

Spot week

A period of one week measured from T+2 to T+9.

Spraddle

A **straddle** but with different strike prices.

Spread

(1) The difference between the **bid price** and the **offered price** or **yield**.
(2) The amount above a reference rate used to calculate the interest rate to be paid in a transaction.

Spread-lock agreement

Agreement to lock in a spread (e.g., a swap spread) before concluding the actual transaction.

Spread risk

The risk that the price relationship between two instruments will change. Also known as **basis risk**.

Spread trade

Simultaneous trades in two or more related contracts, where risks are wholly or partly offset made with the intention of exploiting anticipated price changes.

Stabilization

The action of trading in a new issue with the intention of supporting the price in the primary market as an aid to successful placement. Formerly a largely unregulated practice in the international capital markets, now pursued more cautiously. An example of regulation which relates to stabilization is the UK's **Financial Services Act of 1986**. Section 47 of the Act deals with the creation of false or misleading impressions relating to investments. Stabilization of a new issue as traditionally practised in the Euromarkets might have come under such a prohibition. In fact stabilization continues. The exemption is tortuous to explain but in summary is as follows. The Securities and Investment Board (SIB) has Stabilization Rules which are incorporated in the SFA's rules and thus apply to institutions not directly regulated by the SIB. The Financial Services Act (section 48(7)) allows stabilization in certain instruments during certain time periods, provided it complies with the SIB rules. These rules allow stabilization of issues for cash which are dealt on one of nine specified "exchanges" including the International Securities Markets Association (ISMA), but not the Luxembourg Stock Exchange. A manager stabilizing a security must announce the possibility of stabilisation, must be happy that the price is not already artificial and must keep records of the stabilization actions. There is also a time limit which runs from the moment at which the bond's price is announced, until the earlier of 30 days after the closing date or 60 days after allotment.

What has changed in recent years is the habit of making statements about the success of a new issue which were not demonstrably true. While there is no duty to disclose the large amount of a disastrous new issue which remains with the underwriters, the description of such a transaction as a "great success" is now unlikely and probably illegal.

Stack hedge

A **hedge** executed in derivatives, where the matching maturity is not available and so contracts in nearby months are used. A larger number of contracts is needed than in a matching maturity – hence the name.

Stammaktie

German word for ordinary share

Standard and Poor's (S&P)

Credit-rating agency, a subsidiary of McGraw Hill.

Standard deviation

The square root of the mean of the squared deviations of members of a population from their mean.

Standard Portfolio Analysis of Risk (SPAN)

A system of margining for options contracts. SPAN uses a portfolio approach to calculate the overall risk associated with a set of positions by evaluating the profit/loss in a number of scenarios. Developed by the CME the methodology is also used by LIFFE.

Star account

Account with the UK's Central Gilts Office (CGO) which entitles the institutional account holder to receive interest free of withholding tax.

STIBOR

Stockholm interbank offered rate.

Stiftung

German word for a Trust.

Stock

In the UK stock refers to fixed-income treasury debt securities among other things.

Stock dividend

A dividend given in the form of shares of the same company instead of cash. Also called a **scrip dividend** in the UK.

Stock exchange

A physical location where securities are listed and traded. Stock exchanges compete with each other to provide fast price disclosure, safe settlement and clearing and liquid markets. Competence in systems management now counts for more than tradition and antiquity.

Stock Exchange Automated Quotations System for International Equities (SEAQI)

The London Stock Exchange's price display system for international equities traded on the exchange.

Stock Exchange Automated Quotations System (SEAQ)

Screen-based price display mechanism for equities traded on the London Stock Exchange.

Stock Exchange Automated Trading System (SEATS)

Australian screen-based trading system which began operation on 19 October 1987, the day of the 1987 stockmarket fall.

Stock exchange money brokers (SEMBS)

Formerly inter-dealer brokers specializing in stock lending and borrowing in the UK government bond market. No longer separate entities following the introduction of gilt **repos** in 1996.

Stock Exchange of Singapore

Trading is through the Central Limit Order Book (CLOB). The system can be used to trade both Singapore-listed shares and selected shares of companies listed on certain other shares. SESDAQ (Singapore Exchange Dealing and Automated Quotation System) is a market for small and medium-sized companies. Since 1990, main board shares have been included in a central depository system. Options on individual shares are traded. The main indices include the All-Singapore Price Index, the Straits Times Industrial Share Price

Index, the OCBC-30 Index, the UOB Blue Chip Index, and the DBS-50 Index.

Stockholm Stock Exchange

The official market of Sweden which has traded since 1863. In 1991 the exchange opened an electronic trading system for fixed-rate bonds, the Stockholm Bond Exchange (SOX). The majority of trading in interest-bearing instruments is in an inter-professional telephone market away from the exchange. The exchange trades shares, convertible loans, and bonds. Shares are traded under three lists: the official market A list, the parallel **over-the-counter (OTC)** market for smaller companies and the O list for unlisted securities. Trading is through an automated system, Stockholm Automated Exchange (SAX) and share trades are settled on T+3. The main indices are the SX-General Index, the SX-16 Index, the SX-OTC Index and the SX-70 Index.

Stop price

The lowest price accepted at a new treasury auction by the US Treasury.

Stop-loss order

Order which is dependent on a price reaching a given level and is usually used to limit possible losses.

Straddle

The simultaneous purchase or sale of both a **call option** and a **put option** with the same strike price. Straddles are more aggressive than spread positions. Profit or exposure may be open ended.

To be long a straddle (see Figure S3), a trader would buy a call at A and buy a put at A. The underlying is close to A and the trader expects a significant movement but is not sure of the direction.

The maxium profit is unlimited in either direction. If there is a substantial move in the underlying one of the options will expire worthless but the other will entitle the trader to benefit from all the movement in the underlying. Maximum loss is incurred if the underlying closes at A and will be the total premium paid for the straddle. Breakeven occurs at two prices equivalent to A plus the total premium paid for the straddle and A minus the total premium paid for the straddle.

To go short a straddle (see Figure S4) a trader would sell a call at A and sell a put at A. The underlying is close to A and the trader expects very little movement. This can be dangerous. The maximum loss is unlimited in either direction. Maximum profit is achieved if the underlying closes at A and both options expire worthless. It is equivalent to the premium earned on selling the options. Breakeven occurs at two prices equivalent to A plus the premium received and A minus the premium received.

313

Figure S3

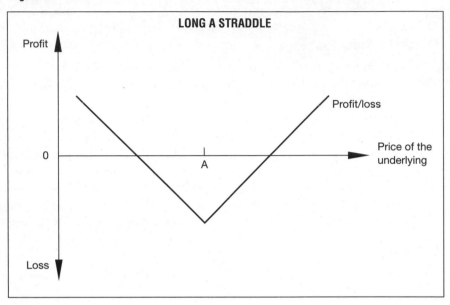

LONG A STRADDLE

Figure S4

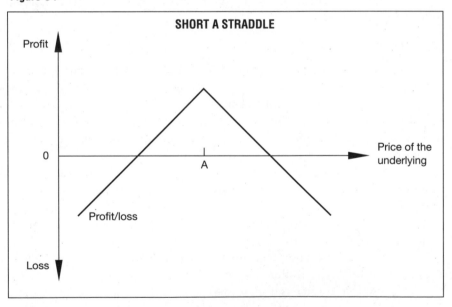

SHORT A STRADDLE

Strangle

A straddle with unequal strike prices but the same expiry date. Strangles are essentially straddles but with different strike prices for each option. Strangles are sometimes called "spraddles".

To go long a strangle (see Figure S5) a trader would buy a call at B and buy a put at A. The underlying is between A and B and the trader expects a sharp movement but is not sure of the direction. Maximum profit is unlimited in either direction. Maximum loss is incurred if the underlying closes between A and B being the total premium paid. Breakeven occurs at two prices equivalent to A minus the total premium paid and B plus the total premium paid.

Figure S5

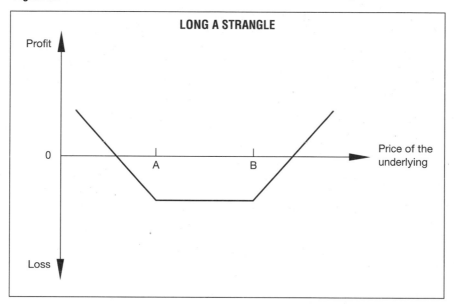

To go short a strangle (see Figure S6) a trader would sell a call at B and sell a put at A. In this case the underlying is between A and B and the trader expects very little movement. The maximum loss is unlimited in either direction. Maximum profit is achieved if the underlying closes between A and B and both options expire worthless. It is equivalent to the premium earned on selling the options. Breakeven occurs at two prices equivalent to A less the premium earned and B plus the premium earned.

Strap

An **option** position, all either short or long, of two **call options** and one **put option**.

Street method

Calculation method where a **yield** is compounded semi-annually regardless of the coupon frequency.

315

Figure S6

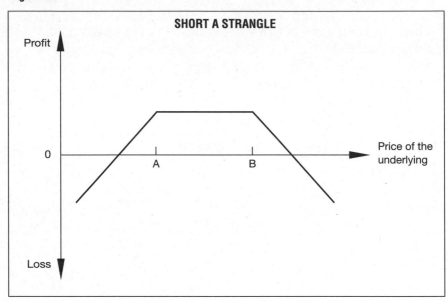

Strike premium

The second **premium** paid under a compound option when the first option is exercised.

Strike price

See **exercise price**.

Strip

The process of detaching the interest coupons from a fixed-rate security so that they may be traded as a set of zero-coupon securities. This practice is frequent in the US and French government bond markets, and is to begin in the UK gilts market in 1997.

Stripped bond

A security which is traded separately from its coupons.

Student Loan Marketing Association (SLMA)

Also known as Sallie Mae, the SLMA is a US federally-chartered shareholder-owned US corporation, which issues securities based on pools of student loans and provides other financial services to educational and financial institutions.

Stuttgart Stock Exchange

Baden-Württembergische Wertpapierbörse zu Stuttgart was founded in 1861. Shares, bonds and **warrants** are traded. It is linked to the other seven German Stock Exchanges by the central exchange Deutsche Börse AG.

Subasta decenal

Spanish 10-day **repo** auction used by the Bank of Spain to manage market liquidity.

Subject

A price which is quoted "subject" is not firm, but indicative

Subordinated debt

Debt which ranks behind other claims in a liquidation. There are numerous varieties of subordination which vary what is subordinated, in what circumstances and to whom it is subordinate.

Subscription agreement

An agreement between the borrower and the syndicate to issue and to subscribe for the bonds respectively.

Sucre

The national currency of Ecuador.

Supranational

Financial institutions, backed by sovereign governments, that act as financing conduits for international economic developments.

Surabaya Stock Exchange

Indonesian stock exchange, PT Bursa Efek Surabaya, re-established in 1977 which trades ordinary shares, preferred stock, rights and bonds. The exchange is linked to Jakarta by the Long Distance Trading System. The main index is the SSE Composite Stock Price Index.

Surf and turf

A **strangle**.

Sushi bond

A non-yen-denominated issue by a Japanese resident in any domestic market.

Swap

(1) Agreement between two parties to exchange payments over a fixed period

of time. In an interest rate swap, the notional principal amount is set and each party pays a different interest rate applied to that amount – typically one is a fixed rate and the other is a variable rate. The **fixed rate** is often set at a spread above a designated benchmark bond yield. The **variable rate** is usually set by reference to a short-term interest rate such as LIBOR (see Figure S7). In a currency swap, there are two contract amounts, and so besides exchanging payments over the life of the contract, the parties exchange principal amounts at maturity. A typical fixed/floating currency swap is shown in Figure S8. The market in swaps is very large and liquid in many currencies. It may be noted that the risk characteristics of the two types of swap are different. An interest rate swap will tend to represent less of a risk as it approaches maturity, while a currency swap may represent an increasing risk until the final exchange of payments has been made. The reason for this is that there is no exchange of principal amounts and no contingent currency risk in an interest rate swap.

Figure S7

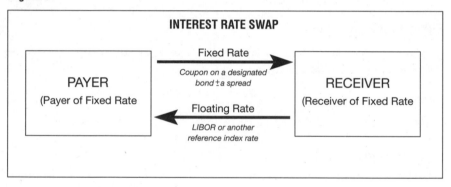

Figure S8

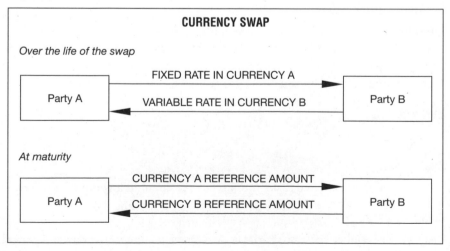

(2) Swaps can also mean the process by which an investor sells a security and buys another similar security in order to achieve a gain in yield. Much of a bond salesman's life is spent trying to identify and execute such trades. See switch.

Swap curve

Interest rate curve derived from the **swap** market. Such a curve is usually above the corresponding government bond yield curve.

Swap rate

The fixed rate payable in an interest rate swap in return for a stream of variable payments. While the variable payments may be calculated in many ways, market convention in many currencies is that swap rates are quoted as a fixed rate against six-month LIBOR.

Swaption

An option to enter into a swap. The buyer of a receiver swaption has the right to receive fixed and pay floating rate. The buyer of a payer swaption has the right to pay fixed and receive floating rate.

Swedish Futures and Options Market

OM Stockholm AB was established in 1985. It is owned by OM Gruppen which also owns the London securities and Derivatives Exchange (OMLX) with which OM Stockholm has close operational links. Trading is by an electronic system which integrates trading and settlement. The exchange trades or clears futures on the OMX Index, two, five and 10-year Swedish notional government bond futures (OMR 2, OMR 5 and OMR 10), 180 day notional Treasury Bills (OMVX 180), two- and five-year notional mortgage bonds (MBB2 and MBB5), two and five-year notional Urban Mortgage Bank of Sweden bonds (CT2 and CT5), a five-year notional Swedish National Housing Finance Corporation Mortgage Bond Future, and three-month STIBOR. Many of the bond futures are traded interbank, but settled through the exchange. Options are traded on individual shares, OMX Index, OMR 5 government bonds and on mortgage bond spreads.

SWIFT

The Society for Worldwide Interbank Financial Telecommunication has operated since 1977 to provide an international payment message service between banks.

Swiss Market Index (SMI)

Index based on the stocks with the highest turnover on the three Swiss stock exchanges weighted according to capitalization.

Swiss Options and Financial Futures Exchange (SOFFEX)

SOFFEX began trading in 1988 in Zurich. The electronic trading system is integrated with the SOFFEX clearing system. Trading is organised as a combined system of order-driven market and market-making with at least three market-makers per product. Futures and options are traded on the Swiss Market Index (SMI), and a notional long-term government bond (Conf). Long- and short-term options are traded on stocks, and there are low exercise price options (LEPO) on 15 selected shares.

Swiss Performance Index (SPI)

Index based on all listed and some over-the-counter stocks in Switzerland.

Swiss Stock Exchange

The Schweizer Börse trades bearer shares (*"inhaberaktie"*), registered shares (*"namenaktie"*), foreign shares, bonds, warrants and options, dividend right certificates (*"genusschein"*), participation certificates (*"partizipationsschein"*), bonds (*"anleihensobligation"*), federal bonds, public authority bonds, convertible bonds, foreign bonds and investment trust units. Trading is by an electronic system, the Elektronischen Börse Schweiz, which has replaced the **open outcry** trading on the floors of the old Basle, Geneva and Zurich exchanges. Settlement is through the Swiss depository and clearing organization SEGA, and is automated. The three main indices are the Swiss Performance Index, the Swiss Market Index and the Swiss Bond Index, with numerous sub-indices.

Switch

The sale of one security in order to purchase another. Usually used in connection with debt securities. Switches are done either because it is possible to obtain a better yield from a security of equivalent quality or because the investor's view has changed and he wishes to change maturity, currency or rate basis.

Sydney Futures Exchange

Originally the Sydney Greasy Wool Futures Exchange founded in 1960. The exchange now trades futures and options on debt instruments, equities, indices and commodities. Trading is on the exchange floor during normal trading hours and by SYCOM, the screen dealing system at other times so that trading continues for 20 hours per day. All trades are cleared through the exchange's subsidiary, the Sydney Futures Exchange Clearing House (SFECH), which uses a SPAN-based margining system.

Syndicated loan

Loan made by two or more banks to one borrower.

Synthetic asset

An asset created out of a combination of other instruments, for example a cash deposit and a derivative. A fixed-rate bond, swapped so as to become a floating rate asset, would be another example.

Synthetic call

A position combining a long put and a long position in the **underlying**.

Synthetic put

A position combining a long call and a short position in the **underlying**.

Synthetic short

A position combining a long put and a short call.

System repo

A US Federal Reserve system (Fed) repurchasing agreement intended to influence short-term interest rates.

Systemic risk

Risk which relates to the banking system as a whole and might arise from a series of interconnecting failures, perhaps in the payments system or as a result of a very large failure in one of the derivatives markets.

T

Tactical asset allocation (TAA)

Mathematical technique used to value and select asset classes. TAA models take account of the returns available on individual asset classes, relevant economic data, measures of market sentiment and past market behaviour.

Tagesgeld

German word for overnight money.

Tail

The difference in government bond auctions between the yield at the average price and the yield at the stop-out price.

Tail hedge

A hedge in a contract of longer maturity than the position being hedged. The opposite of a **stack hedge**.

Taishaku

Japanese bond borrowing market.

Taiwan Stock Exchange

The exchange trades shares, bonds, and certificates. Trading is by an automated order-driven system. Settlement is through the Taiwan Securities Central Depository Co. Ltd. The index is the Taiwan Stock Exchange Weighted Stock Index.

Taka

The national currency of Bangladesh.

Tala

The national currency of Samoa.

Talon

French word for a **coupon**.

Tan Book

The US report on current economic conditions in the 12 Federal Reserve districts. (To avoid confusion, this used to be called the Red Book and is also sometimes referred to as the Beige Book. Together with the Green and Blue Books, it is circulated to members of the Federal System Open Markets Committee.)

Tanshi brokers

Japanese phrase for short-term money brokers.

Tap

A method of issuing securities on an as-required basis, often in irregular amounts. For example, the UK government offers gilts through a tap mechanism in addition to the usual program of auctions. Index-linked gilts are usually issued by tap. Taps of conventional gilts are not intended to be a routine method of financing, but are used as a market management mechanism at times when there is temporary excess demand in a stock or sector, or when there is an exceptionally sudden rise in the market. Tap issues are announced at 10.15am for bids at 10.45am and details of the amount sold at the initial and any subsequent mini-tenders are published.

A variant of a tap is the mini-tender. After an initial tender the Bank of England allows bids to be made either as **blue sky bids** by individual gilt-edged market-makers (GEMMs) or as common price mini-tenders open to all GEMMs for a five minute period. Mini-tenders are held automatically each day between 8.45am and 8.50am with the results published before 9.00am, if sales have been made.

Taplet

In the context of the UK gilt-edged market, a small (£100–£200 million) further issue of an existing bond. Also called "mini tap."

TARGET

The planned euro payment system. It will consist of a real time gross settlement (RTGS) system in each country and an interlinking mechanism to connect them. TARGET's purpose is to eliminate settlement risk in cross-border payments and to ease the operation of the single market. Access to intraday liquidity by non-EMU central banks on the same terms as member banks has not yet been agreed.

Tasso base

Italian phrase for floating rate.

Tasso variable

Italian phrase for floating rate.

Tau

The price change of an option caused by a change in the standard deviation or volatility of the underlying, also known as "Vega."

Taux Annuel Glissant

French phrase for a sliding annual rate.

Taux annuel monétaire (TAM)

French money market rate, calculated as a monthly compounded average of the official overnight money market rate.

Taux de l'Echéance Constante

In March 1996, the French Trésor announced the creation of "Taux de l'Echéance Constante," a 10-year constant maturity yield index. The TEC is published daily in the form of the yield to maturity of a hypothetical *Obligation assimilable du Trésor (OAT)* with a maturity of exactly 10 years. The yield is interpolated from the yields of the two nearest maturities of government bonds based on mid-prices quoted at 10.00am in Paris by OAT market-makers, rounded to two decimal places. There have been issues of 10.5 year OATs with quarterly coupons set in advance based on the TEC. These bonds, like other floating rate bonds, are not very sensitive to absolute rate changes, but are sensitive to changes in the yield curve. They gain in value from any steepening of the curve and will on any flattening of the curve.

Taux de rendement mensuel des emprunts d'Etat à long term (TME)

A French interest rate calculated as the monthly average yield on a weighted sample of 7–30-year bonds on the secondary market recorded over a one-year period. There are variable-rate government bonds *Obligations assimilable du Trésor (OATs)* issued with coupons linked to this rate where the reference period is the 12 months prior to payment of the coupon. The rate is published by the *Caisse des Dépôts et Consignations*.

Taux d'escompte

French for discount rate.

Taux interbancaire offert à Paris (TIOP)

The French name for the Paris interbank offered rate, which is better known, perhaps to the chagrin of the Academie, as PIBOR.

Taux mensuel de bons du Trésor (TMB)

French interest rate calculated as the arithmetic mean of the monthly average of the 13-week Treasury bill (BTANs) auctioned weekly throughout the previous year. There are variable-rate government bonds *Obligations assim-*

ilable du Trésor (OATs) issued with coupons linked to this rate where the reference period is the 12 months prior to payment of the coupon. The rate is published by the *Caisse des Dépôts et Consignations*.

Taux mensuel obligataire (TMO)

French interest rate calculated as an arithmetic average of the last 12 average monthly yields on a specially selected sample of new government-guaranteed issues.

Taux moyen mensuel du marché monétaire (TMMMM)

French interest rate, calculated as the average monthly money market rate.

Taux moyen pondéré (TMP)

French interest rate, calculated as a weighted average rate. It is the official money market rate, published daily at 11.30am by the Banque de France.

Tax anticipation bill (TAB)

US treasury bill maturing on quarterly dates when corporate income tax payments are due.

Tax anticipation note (TAN)

Issued by states or municipalities in anticipation of future tax receipts.

Taxation risk

The risk that the taxation of a business or of the dividends or interest paid by it may change to the disadvantage of the investor. Sometimes only the prospect of such a change is necessary to damage investors' interests. In the UK, the Labour party in opposition in 1996 announced plans to tax utilities companies with a "windfall" tax. See **risk**.

Technical analysis

Price analysis based on graph patterns, moving averages and trend lines.

Technical correction

Change in a market not foreseen by economists and analysts and therefore attributed to factors internal to the market.

Tel-Aviv Stock Exchange

The exchange trades bonds, shares and convertible securities. Trading in the 100 most liquid securities is by the "mishtanim" method. Transactions are concluded in a set order during a number of trading rounds on the floor of the exchange. There is also a computerized market, the CCM. Settlement is through the Stock Exchange Clearing House, a subsidiary of the exchange.

Options are traded on the MAOF-25 Index and on the Shekel/US dollar exchange rate. The main indices are the General Share Index, the TASE (Mishtanim)-100 Index, and the MAOF-25 Index, a capitalization-weighted index of the 25 most liquid shares.

Telefonverkehr

German phrase for the over-the-counter telephone market.

Ten windows

Ten entities in the People's Republic of China allowed to borrow abroad. They are: the Bank of China, the Bank of Communications, China Investment Bank, China International Trust and Investment Corporation (CITIC), Guangdong International Trust and Investment Corporation (GITIC), Shanghai Investment and Trust Corporation (SITCO), Tianjin International Trust and Investment Corporation (TITIC), Dalian International Trust and Investment Corporation (Dalian ITIC), Hainan International Trust and Investment Corporation (Hainan ITIC), Fujian Investment and Enterprise Corporation.

Tender

(1) An unconditional offer of money in a settlement.

(2) An auction such as the weekly auction of UK treasury bills.

Tender panel

A group formed to bid for an issuer's securities in regular auctions.

Tender panel agent

Bank made responsible for the operation of a tender panel auction.

Tenge

The currency of Kazakhstan.

Tenor

Maturity.

Term Fed Funds

US Federal funds for a maturity longer than overnight.

Term loan

Loan made for a term of years, in contrast to a demand facility which may be available for a long period though callable at any time.

Term repurchase agreement (term repo)

Repo for a period longer than overnight, up to one year or more.

Term structure of interest rates

The pattern of interest rates for different periods. This is not the yield to maturity of bonds maturing on different dates, but is the zero-coupon rate for each date. This zero-coupon rate is the the yield of an instrument making only one payment to the investor on a particular date. How are these rates to be calculated?

The formula for the present value of a future payment is:

$$PV = FV/(1+i)^n$$

The present value of a series of cash flows (CF_1, CF_2, CF_3, etc) each discounted at its own appropriate rate (i_1, i_2, i_3, etc) over a number of years (t_1, t_2, t_3, etc) can therefore be expressed as

$$PV = \frac{CF_1}{(1+i_1)^{t_1}} + \frac{CF_2}{(1+i_2)^{t_2}} + \frac{CF_3}{(1+i_3)^{t_3}} + \frac{CF_4}{(1+i_4)^{t_4}} + \frac{CF_n}{(1+i_n)^{t_n}}$$

How do we establish i_1, i_2, i_3 and so on?

This is best answered with an example.

Example

Suppose that there are two annual coupon bonds, both paying interest at 8 percent, one with one year to maturity, the other with two years to maturity. The price of the first bond is 101 and the price of the second bond is 99.

The yield to maturity of the first bond which will make only one more payment is calculated, as we saw above, as:

$$((FV/PV)^{1/n}) - 1$$

which in this case is

$$((108/101)^{1/1}) - 1$$

or $(1.06931) - 1$

which equals: 6.93%

Now, turning to the second bond, we can use this rate as the appropriate rate to value the first coupon payment as follows using:

$$PV = FV/(1+i)^n$$

which gives:

$$8/(1+0.0693)^1 = 7.4815$$

We knew the price of the second bond was 99 and we now know that 7.4815 of that is attributable to the first coupon. So the value of the last payment (108) in two years' time must be 99 − 7.4815, which is 91.5185. Using the implied discount rate formula we can calculate the implied rate as:

$$((FV/PV)^{1/n}) - 1$$

which in this case is:

$$((108/91.5185)^{1/2}) - 1$$

or

$$(1.18009)^{1/2} - 1$$

which equals: 8.63%

So, if we return to the formula which we set out earlier, and apply it to this example:

$$PV = \frac{CF_1}{(1+i_1)^{t_1}} + \frac{CF_2}{(1+i_2)^{t_2}}$$

becomes:

$$PV = \frac{8}{(1+0.0693)^1} + \frac{108}{(1+0.0863)^2}$$

or

$$PV = 7.48 + 91.52$$

which as we would expect = 99

This method of calculating the zero coupon yield curve from the price of conventional bonds could be continued for each subsequent date in the same manner.

In practice this is made both easier and harder in the real world. In some markets it is made easier because there is a liquid market in stripped zero-coupon government bonds. The prices at which these trade can be used to establish quickly a zero-coupon term interest rate structure. However in many markets there is no such short cut, and the choice of which conventional bonds to use for the calculation process is difficult.

The difficulty lies in the tax treatment of bonds. If in a particular country interest income is taxable but capital gains are tax free, then it is likely that low-coupon issues will be more favored than high-coupon issues of the same maturity by investors subject to tax. Such factors distort the prices of bonds and may also distort the term structure calculation.

Use of the term structure

Once we have calculated the two zero-coupon rates, we can also calculate the forward rate which would be offered now for a one-year investment starting in one year's time. To prevent **arbitrage**, this must be the forward rate ($1'2$) which satisfies the following equation:

$$(1 + i_1) \times (1 + {}_1f_2) = (1 + i_2)^2$$

In this example, the calculation would be

$$(1 + 0.0693) \times (1 + {}_1f_2) = (1 + 0.0863)^2$$

which gives ${}_1f_2$ equal to 10.357%

The significance of this figure is that this is the extra return available for extending an investment horizon from one to two years.

One may generalize, and show the relationship of the coupon bond yield curve to the forward yield curve in diagramatic form. If the coupon bond curve is normal or positive, then the forward rate curve will be above it. Conversely, with an inverse or negative yield curve, the forward rate curve will be below the coupon bond yield curve.

Termingeld

German word for short-term money market transactions.

Stock Exchange of Thailand

The exchange in Bangkok trades shares, debt securities, convertible securities, and warrants. Trading is on the main board with a special board for large lots and bonds, and another board for foreign-registered stocks. Trading is by a computerized order-driven system and settlement is through the Share Depository Centre of the Exchange. The main index is the Stock Exchange of Thailand Index, which includes all listed shares.

Theta

The price change of an option caused by a change in the time remaining – time decay.

Third market

US term for trading on the over-the-counter market of exchange-listed securities by brokers who are not members of the exchange.

Third-party repurchase agreement (third-party repo)

Repo where collateral is held by an independent agent who transfers it only against payment of cash. Also called "tri-party repo."

TIBOR

Tokyo interbank offered rate.

Tick size

The minimum price movement of a futures or option contract.

Tier 1 capital

That part of a bank's capital defined by the **Bank for International Settlements** (BIS) as shareholders' equity plus irredeemable and non-cumulative preference shares. It excludes hybrid forms of capital, intangibles and revaluation reserves. The minimum Tier 1 capital requirement is 4 percent of risk weighted assets.

Tier 1

(a) Permanent shareholders' equity (including perpetual non-cumulative preferred shares)
(b) Disclosed reserves and published retained profit or loss of the current year.
(c) Minority interests in permanent shareholders' equity.

Less

(d) Goodwill and other intangible assets.
(e) Unpublished losses of the current year.

Tier 2 capital

(a) Undisclosed reserves/unpublished current year's profits;
(b) reserves arising from the revaluation of tangible fixed assets;
(c) general provisions;
(d) perpetual subordinated debt meeting the conditions for primary perpetual subordinated debt, and perpetual cumulative preferred shares;
(e) subordinated term debt (with an initial term to maturity of at least five years and one day) and dated preferred shares;
(f) minority interests in Tier 2 preferred shares.

Less investments in unconsolidated subsidiaries and associates, including connected lending of a capital nature.

The capital base of a bank is equal to the sum of Tier 1 and Tier 2 elements with the following restrictions.

(i) The total of Tier 2 elements (a) – (f) should not exceed the total of Tier 1 elements (a) – (e);
(ii) Tier 2 element (e) should not exceed 50 percent of Tier 1 elements (a) – (e);
(iii) Tier 2 element (c) should not exceed 1.25 percent of the bank's weighted risk assets.

Time decay

The decline in value of an **option** as it approaches expiry. See **time value**.

Time deposit

Deposit with a specific maturity.

Time option

A contract which obliges the holder to perform under a foreign-exchange contract, but gives the holder the choice of when to do so within a specified period.

Time spread

See **calendar spread**.

Time value

That part of the value of an **option** which reflects the time remaining until expiry. The longer the period of time to expiry of the option, the greater the chance that the option will come to be **in-the-money** before the **expiry date**. Consequently longer-term options are more valuable than shorter-term options, although not proportionately so. For example, a six-month option will be more expensive than a one-month option, but not six times more expensive. The time value of an option decreases as the time to expiry decreases, but falls more sharply as an option approaches its **expiry date**.

TIOP

See **PIBOR**.

Titre de créance négociable

French phrase for a negotiable debt instrument.

Titrisation

French for **securitization**.

Tokkin

A Japanese investment trust fund formed to manage a company's surplus liquidity.

Tokyo Commodity Exchange

Founded in 1984 on the consolidation of the Gold, Rubber and Textile Exchanges. TOCOM is one of the most active precious metals markets in the world. Trading is by the *zaraba* method for precious metals and by the *itayose* method for yarns and rubber. The exchange trades Gold, Silver, Platinum, Palladium, Rubber, Cotton Yarn, and Woollen Yarn.

Tokyo Grain Exchange

Founded in 1952, and merged with the Tokyo Sugar Exchange in 1993. The exchange trades futures in US Soya Beans, Azuki (Red) Beans, Corn, Raw Sugar, Refined Sugar, and options on US Soya Beans and Refined Sugar.

Tokyo Stock Exchange

Founded in 1878. The exchange trades stocks and bonds with derivatives based on them. Stocks are divided between the First Section for the 150 most active stocks and the Second Section. Trading is on the floor of the exchange for First Section stocks, and by a computerized system for all other securities. Settlement is through the Japan Securities Clearing Corporation, a subsidiary of the exchange. Transactions may be settled regular way (T+3), cash (T+0 or T+1), special agreement (up to T+14), or when issued. Futures are traded on the TOPIX Index, 10- and 20-year Japanese government bonds (JGBs), US treasury bonds, and there are options on the TOPIX Index and the 10-year JGB futures. The main indices are the Tokyo Stock Price Index (TOPIX), a market-value-weighted index of all the shares listed in the first section of the exchange, and the Tokyo Stock Exchange Second Section Index. The Nikkei Indices are not computed by the exchange.

Tom next

In money markets, an overnight transaction from tomorrow to the next day.

Tombstone

Summary of a transaction with a list of the firms which were involved published in newspapers to commemorate the transaction and to celebrate the cleverness of the **lead manager**.

Toronto Futures Exchange

The exchange began trading in 1984, having traded before as a division of the Toronto Stock Exchange. Trading is by **open outcry** on the floor of the exchange. Settlement is through Transcanada Options Inc, a clearing house owned by the Montreal, Toronto and Vancouver Exchanges. The exchange has futures contracts on the Toronto 35 Index (TXF), the TSE 100 Index (TOF), and options on those futures (TXO and TOP), as well as options on silver.

Touch option

Form of **barrier option** which depends on the underlying hitting the strike level during the life of the option.

Touch

The best prices quoted by market-makers to buy or sell a security on the Stock Exchange Automated Quotations System (SEAQ) and on the Stock Exchange Automated Quotations System for International Equities (SEAQ

I). Intermediaries are required to deal on behalf of clients at prices no worse than the touch price. Skilled institutional investors would expect to deal regularly inside the touch.

Toyohashi Dried Cocoon Exchange

This Japanese exchange was first founded in 1937 and reopened in 1951. Trading in Dried Cocoon futures is by the *itayose* method.

TRA

The rate is the arithmetic mean of the monthly average of yields on fixed-rate *Emprunts d'État* with maturities greater than seven years. This rate is published by the *Caisse des Dépôts et Consignations*.

Tracker fund

See **index fund.**

Tracking error

The amount by which an indexed equity portfolio fails to replicate the performance of the **index** on which it is based.

Traded option

An option that may be freely bought or sold on an options exchange; *cf.* **traditional option.**

Traditional option

In the UK, an equity **option** negotiated between the granter of the option, called in this context, the taker, and the buyer, called in this context the giver, which may not be transferred. Maturities are up to three months, and the strike price is usually set at the current **bid price** for a **put option** or at the **offer price** for a **call option.** Exercise may be at any time during the life of the option. On exercise, the holder of the option becomes entitled to receive any dividend paid or payable, if the share has been marked **ex**-dividend during the life of the option. The terms of the option contract are not altered for **scrip issues** or **rights issues.**

Tranche

A part of a transaction, as in an issue of bonds, where further issues of the same bonds are contemplated.

Transfer, Accounting, Lodgement for Investors, Stock Management for Jobbers (TALISMAN)

Before the **CREST** system, Talisman was the centralized computer system for the settlement of equity bargains on the London Stock Exchange.

Transfer risk

The risk that an entity wishing to make a payment in a foreign currency might not be able to convert its own domestic currency in a timely manner.

Transferable revolving underwriting facility (TRUF)

A facility where an underwriting bank's contingent liability to purchase notes is transferable. An example of the merging of loan and securities markets.

Translation

The valuation of foreign assets and liabilities for balance sheet purposes. The risk of adverse movements is called translation risk, and is one of the risks requiring foreign exchange exposure management.

Translation risk

That part of currency risk which relates to the treatment of foreign-currency-denominated assets and liabilities at balance sheet dates. See **risk**.

Transparency

The extent to which price and other information in a securities market are disseminated to all participants equally. It is a key quality in a market. As more foreign institutions become involved in markets, it is necessary to make explicit efforts to ensure transparency.

TRAX

TRAX is a real-time trade confirmation system run by the International Securities Market Association (ISMA) which was launched in January 1989. Some 284 offices of securities firms, brokers, fund managers and institutional investors used the system at April 1995. TRAX allows matching and confirmation of trades in equities, government bonds, domestic bonds, **Eurobonds**, **warrants**, medium-term notes and **floating-rate notes**. About 60,000 securities are listed on the TRAX database of which about half are equities from 45 countries. Users of TRAX trade over the telephone. Then within 30 minutes of the trade time, both parties must input details of the trade into the TRAX system. The system then matches the trades input and reports on unmatched trades. The system reduces the risk of disputed trades or unexpected risk positions.

Links have been established between TRAX and the communications networks of **Euroclear** (Euclid 90) and **CEDEL** (Cedcom 2000). Much of the information required by TRAX can be used to form the basis of a settlement instruction. By importing information from TRAX, the need for dual entry is reduced with its attendant risk of clerical error.

ISMA, which operates TRAX, is a designated investment exchange and a International Securities Self-Regulating Organization. ISMA imposes fines on those who fail to meet the TRAX reporting requirements. The trades reported are not published but the process meets the reporting requirements of other regulatory authorities (e.g., the SFA in the UK).

TRB

The rate is reset quarterly as the yield of the 13-week treasury bill auctioned prior to the payment of the coupon.

Treasury bill (T-bill)

Non-interest-bearing discount security issued by governments. Typically issued for three, six or 12 months.

Treasury bond

Long-term government security. In the US, the term refers to a coupon security issued by the treasury with a maturity of 10 to 30 years. See **United States Government Securities**.

Treasury-indexed note

Note with **redemption** value linked to a long-term US treasury bond (usually the 30-year one). See **United States Government Securities**.

Treasury note

US Government fixed rate security issued with a maturity of up to 10 years.

Treasury receipt (TR)

A zero-coupon certificate issued in respect of principal payments on specific US treasury securities. It is a direct obligation of the US.

Trinidad and Tobago Stock Exchange

The exchange began trading in 1981, and began to trade bonds in 1993. The exchange trades shares, preference shares and bonds. Trading takes place on the floor of the exchange. Shares are traded in order by a call-over procedure. The index is the Trinidad and Tobago Stock Exchange Composite Index.

Tugrik

The national currency of Mongolia.

Tunis Stock Exchange

The Bourse des Valeurs Mobilières de Tunis (BVM) was founded in 1969, but was not very active for some years. Shares, bonds and rights are traded. The index is the Indice General BVM which is made up of 16 shares.

U

Undated

A security with no final maturity, also called a **perpetual**.

Underlying

The subject of a derivative contract.

Undersubscription

When a new issue of securities is only partly sold.

Undertakings for collective investments in transferable securities (UCITS)

Open-ended collective investments in transferable securities. 90 percent of assets must be invested in securities listed on a recognized exchange.

Underwrite

To accept a contingent commitment to purchase securities at a fixed price if other investors cannot be found. Also used in insurance to mean the acceptance of a risk to be insured.

Underwriting commission

Fee paid to an underwriter, usually expressed as a percentage of the amount underwritten.

Underwriting fee

See **Underwriting commission**.

Ungeregelter Freiverkehr

German phrase for the unregulated unofficial market in unlisted shares in Austria.

Unit trust

UK mutual fund. Unit trusts are authorized by the SIB under the Financial Service Act 1986. Three definitions are useful to understand the regulations.

Transferable securities are shares, debentures, government securities, warrant, to subscribe for shares, debentures or government securities, certificates representing securities and units in collective investment schemes.

Approved securities are transferable securities which are admitted to an official listing in a EU member country, or are traded under the rules of an approved securities market.

A **derivative** is an option, a future or a contract for differences. An **approved derivative** is a derivative which is traded on a recognized or designated investment exchange.

An authorized unit trust must be in one of the following categories:

Securities fund
The majority of unit trusts are securities funds formed for the purpose of investing in transferable securities. Up to 10 percent of the fund may consist of transferable securities which are not approved securities. Up to 5 percent of the fund may consist of transferable securities, which are units in collective investment schemes, and up to 5 percent of the fund may be invested in warrants.

Excluding government and other public securities, four investments may each be up to 10 percent of the fund, and remaining investments must be 5 percent or less of the fund. If a fund invests less than 35 percent in government securities there is no restriction on how that part of the fund may be allocated. If a fund invests more than 35 percent in government securities there are further rules.

A fund may not hold more than 10 percent of the share capital of a company, of the units of a collective investment scheme or the debentures of a private issuer.

Money market fund
May invest in cash or near cash.

Futures and options fund (FOF)
May invest in cash, transferable securities as limited above, approved derivatives, forward contracts in currencies or gold, units in a collective investment scheme (up to 5 percent of the fund), and gold (up to 10 percent of the fund). All derivatives positions must be covered by cash, securities or other derivatives.

Geared futures and options fund (GFOF)
GFOFs are under similar rules to FOFs, but may borrow no money and derivative activity is limited by a restriction on initial outlay of not more than 20 percent of the fund.

Property fund
May invest in property up to 80 percent of the fund, in transferable securities up to 80 percent, up to 35 percent in government securities, up to 5 percent in collective investment schemes, up to 10 percent in shares in property companies which are not approved securities.

337

Warrant fund
May invest entirely in warrants

Fund of funds
May invest in regulated collective investment schemes with up to 20 percent in any one scheme.

United States Government Securities

The Secretary of the Treasury is authorized under Chapter 31 of Title 31, United States Code, to issue Treasury Securities and to prescribe terms and conditions for their issuance and sale (31 U.S.C. § 3121). The Secretary may issue bonds under 31 U.S.C. § 3102, notes under 31 U.S.C. § 3103 and bills under 31 U.S.C. § 3104.

Since 1 August 1986 Treasury notes and bonds have been issued in book-entry form only. Each Treasury note or bond has a unique CUSIP number. This is a nine-digit identifier (7 numbers and 2 letters) developed by the Committee on Uniform Securities Identification Procedures (CUSIP) under the auspices of the American Bankers Association. When an issue is stripped the principal strip is given another CUSIP number and the coupon strips are assigned a generic CUSIP number common to all stripped interest coupons due on a specific date.

The Treasury, the Justice Department, the Federal Reserve, the Securities and Exchange Commission and the self-regulatory organizations (SROs) have various responsibilities. Brokers and dealers in the secondary market are regulated under the Government Securities Act 1986. Broker-dealers also are regulated by the Securities Exchange Act of 1934 and banks are subject to the banking laws.

US Treasuries are traded over-the-counter by Government Securities broker/dealers and are also listed on the New York Stock Exchange but trading takes place by telephone.

Government agencies (such as the Government National Mortgage Association, the Small Business Administration and the Tennessee Valley Authority) either issue marketable debt or guarantee debt. Government-sponsored enterprises (such as the Federal National Mortgage Corporation, Farm Credit System, Federal Home Loan Bank System and Student Loan Marketing Association) also issue marketable debt, subordinated debt, and guarantee asset-backed securities.

Treasury Bills

Bills are issued with maturities of 13, 26 and 52 weeks. They are auctioned at a discount. Short-term cash management bills are also auctioned when required by the Treasury's cash-flow needs. Bills are in book-entry form held for investors through the Treasury Direct system and by financial institutions and Federal Reserve Banks through the commercial book-entry system. Minimum purchase amount is US$10,000 with larger amounts in multiples of US$1,000.

Treasury Notes

Notes are coupon paying securities issued with maturities of 2, 3, 5, and 10 years. Seven-year notes were issued until April 1993 and four-year notes were issued until December 1990. All notes have fixed coupons and bullet maturities. Minimum denomination is US$1000. Minimum purchase is US$5000 for notes of less than four years to maturity and US$1000 for longer notes with larger amounts in multiples of US$1000.

Treasury Bonds

Bonds are coupon paying securities issued with maturities over 10 years. All bonds have fixed coupons and (for bonds issued since 1984) bullet maturities. Minimum denomination is US$1000 with larger amounts in multiples of US$1000.

Separate Trading of Registered Interest Principal (STRIPS)

At 31 December 1995 there were 65 issues of Treasury securities which were partly held in stripped form. These have been eligible to be reconstituted to their unstripped form since 1 May 1987.

Unternehmensbeteiligungsgesellschaft

Form of German investment company.

Up-and-out option

An option which pays off or expires if a preset price is reached.

Up-tick

A price quoted or dealt at which is higher than the previous quotation or trade.

Uttar Pradesh Stock Exchange

This stock exchange in Kanpur, India has agreed to the creation of a single Unified Exchange for India. See **National Stock Exchange of India**.

V

Valencia Stock Exchange

Sociedad Rectora de la Bolsa de Valores de Valencia was established in 1980. The exchange trades shares and public and private debt securities. Trading by **open outcry** on the floor of the exchange has been largely replaced by trading on the CATS electronic system. Settlement, as on the Madrid Stock Exchange, is through the Central Depository. The main index is the Valencia Stock Exchange General Index, which is made up of 92 shares. There are eight sub-indices.

Valeur

French word for a security.

Valeur compensée

French phrase for compensatory payment.

Valeurs en dépôt

French phrase for a trust fund.

Value at risk (VAR)

There are two main modelling techniques which are referred to as VAR calculations.

(1) Variance/covariance analysis

This uses historic data on price volatilities and correlations within and between markets to estimate likely potential losses. Price changes are assumed to be normally distributed which allows a **confidence level** to be calculated.

This confidence level is calculated by reference to the standard deviation of historic price changes (volatility) multiplied by a scaling factor. If returns are normally distributed, there is a 1 percent chance that the return will be greater than 2.326 deviations from the mean. Thus if we wanted to have a 99 percent confidence interval we would multiply the historic volatility observed by 2.326.

The chief problem with this approach is that the assumption about distribution does not accord with observations in many markets where **fat-tailed distributions** and skewed distributions are frequently seen. The approach implicitly assumes that a portfolio's value changes linearly with changes in the **underlying**, in other words it ignores the effect of **gamma**.

(2) Historical simulation

Historical data is applied to a portfolio to calculate the changes in value of the portfolio which would have occurred if the portfolio had been in existence during that period. This allows the calculation of a 99 percent confidence interval, without assuming a **normal distribution** by calculating the loss which would not have been exceeded on 99 percent of occasions. In this case, the confidence interval is observed, while before it was calculated statistically.

Value date

The date up to which accrued interest is calculated. The value date and the **settlement date** are usually the same

Value Index of Participation (VIP)

Chicago Board Options Exchange (CBOE) index based on the CBOE 50 and CBOE 250 indices.

Value Line Index

Kansas City Board of Trade index which is a geometric average of 1,683 stocks.

Value of a basis point

The effect in dollar terms on the value of a position (or portfolio) of a one-basis point change in interest rates.

Value spot

Price or trade for settlement on T+2.

Vancouver Stock Exchange

Founded in 1907, the exchange is noted for the small and start-up companies whose shares are traded on the exchange. About two-thirds of shares listed are of resource-based companies. Common and preferred shares, rights, warrants, bonds, options and units are traded. Trading is by the Vancouver Computerized Trading system (VCT), which has been bought by several exchanges in other countries. Settlement is through the West Canada Clearing Corporation (WCCC). The Asian Board of the exchange reflects the close links between Vancouver and Asia. The exchange trades options on equities, long-term options (LEAPS™) on equities and gold. The indices are the Composite Index and three sub-indices, the Resource Index, the Commercial/Industrial Index and the Venture Index.

Variable-rate note (VRN)

Form of **floating-rate note** where the spread above the variable reference rate is also variable. Usually, investors have a **put option** to sell the notes back to the issuer on each margin reset date.

Variable-rate preference share

A **preference share** paying a dividend, which changes with changes in short-term interest rates.

Variance

Square of the standard deviation of a sample.

Variation margin

The amount of money paid after the payment of initial margin required to secure an option or futures position, after it has been revalued by the exchange or clearing house. Often paid daily.

Vega

See **Tau**.

Velocity

The rate at which money circulates through the economy.

Vente par soumission

French phrase for a sale by tender.

Verfall

German word for maturity.

Vergleichsordnung

German insolvency legislation which makes possible agreements with creditors instead of outright bankruptcy.

Vertical spread

Option spread position, where the same number of options bought and sold have the same expiry date, but different strike prices. Using two calls or two puts, in a bear spread the option bought has a higher strike than the option sold. In a bull spread, the option bought has a lower strike than the option sold.

Vibor

Vienna interbank offered rate.

Vienna Commodity Exchange

A department of the Vienna Exchange which is more noted for publishing technical guidelines relating to trading in specific commodities than for the volume of trading actually carried out. There is limited trading in hides and leather products, timber, food products and textiles.

Vienna Stock Exchange

The exchange trades ordinary and preference shares, certificates, bonds and warrants. Trading is through brokers (Börse-Sensale), via the computer-assisted trading system (PATS). Settlement is chiefly through the "Arrangement" system run by the Österreichische Kontrollbank AG. The Vienna Stock Exchange Share Index is a weighted all-share index. There are also the Austrian Traded Index, made up of 19 shares, the Participation Certificate Index, the Girozentrale Index, an all-share index, and the Creditanstalt Index of 25 shares.

In November 1996, it was announced that the Vienna Exchange would merge with the Austrian Futures and Options Exchange (OTOB).

Vinkulierung

Right enjoyed by Swiss managers to refuse to register a new shareholder. Can be used to protect the management of a company from an unwelcome takeover.

Virement

French word for transfer.

Vires

Latin for "capacity". In financial transactions *intra vires* means that the transaction is within an enitity's legal capacity, *ultra vires* that it is not. See **Hammersmith & Fulham swap case**.

Vita media

Italian phrase for average life.

Volatility

A statistical measure of price variance over time. Volatility is measured as the variance or annualized standard deviation of the **underlying**. Standard deviation is a measure of variation about a mean or average. It is defined as the square root of the mean of the squared deviations of a sample from its mean. This is a measure of the uncertainty of returns. If, for example, the underlying rose at a constant rate, then the standard deviation would be zero.

A standard deviation in a normal distribution has certain useful properties. The same is naturally true of volatility. Volatility is expressed as a percentage.

An annualized volatility of 8 percent means that over a period of one year, the price of the underlying would be expected to be within one standard deviation (8 percent) of the current price 68 percent of the time and within two standard deviations (16 percent) 95 percent of the time.

The key assumption in most pricing models is that made about future volatility. While most of the other inputs to an option pricing model can be tested or checked, the volatility figure is subjective.

There are three sorts of volatility to be considered.

Historic volatility

Historic volatility may be established objectively by analyzing price movements. However, the choice of period during which it is measured, and the weighting given to each period will both affect the result. For example, if the price of the underlying has moved in a volatile manner in recent weeks after a long period of inactivity, then using a short period of time to measure historic volatility, will give a higher volatility figure, than would be obtained from a longer period.

Similarly, if historic volatility was calculated for a sequence of time periods it might be felt that the recent past was more significant, and that a higher weight should be given to recent periods.

The judgement of which period to use, or how to weight the periods is subjective, even though historic volatility purports to be an objective measure.

There is, too, the problem of how exceptional market shocks should be incorporated. Allowance may be necessary for potential shocks such as the October 1987 stockmarket crash, even though that particular event is outside the time period being used for a particular volatility calculation. There is no simple answer.

Expected volatility

Expected volatility does not claim to be objective. It is simply one judgement of what the future volatility of the underlying might be.

Implied volatility

An alternative approach to the problem is to look at the actual price of other traded options, and to calculate the volatility which must have been used to produce those prices. This is the implied volatility, and may be used to value options in a manner consistent with the pricing of existing options. It has the advantage of being objective, provided that there are traded options sufficiently similar to the OTC option being priced.

Volatility trade

A **delta**-neutral trade where the trader is almost unaffected by changes in the **underlying** but where the trader takes a position in volatility. Neither historic nor implied volatility has any particularly strong predictive value, which is why there will be both buyers and writers of any given options. Inevitably, therefore, option traders will trade volatility by constructing portfolios which are unaffected by small movements in the price of the underlying, but which are exposed to changes in volatility. Some market participants will want to be "long" volatility, and others will want to be "short" volatility, based on their respective expectations for volatilities.

Volksbank

German co-operative bank.

Vorbörse

Trading on the floor of a Swiss exchange in the shares of companies not yet listed on the exchange.

Vorstand

The management board of a company, usually in Germany. The junior part of the two-tier board system. See *Aufsichtsrat*.

Vorzugsaktie

German word for preferred share.

Vostro account

Another bank's **nostro account**.

Voting right share

Share with enhanced voting rights.

Warrant

An option, sometimes of quite long maturity

Warsaw Stock Exchange

Gielda Papierów Wartosciowych w Warszawie SA. The exchange was reopened in 1991, after a closure of 52 years. It trades ordinary shares and treasury bonds, all in paperless form. Trading in shares is order-driven, with brokers acting as specialists to determine a single price at each session. Bond trading is both by the single price method, and by continuous price trading in the block trading market. Settlement is on T+3 with delivery by changes in the National Depository of Securities. The main indices are the Warszawski Indeks Gieldowy (WIG, the Warsaw Stock Exchange Index) and the WIG 20. The former is a capitalization-weighted index of all the listed shares. The WIG 20 Index is of the 20 most traded shares.

Wertpapier

German word for a security.

Wertpapierkennumer

Security numbers on the German Stock Exchanges.

Wertpapiersammelbank AG

German regional agency for the settlement of domestic securities.

West Texas Intermediate

Type of crude oil, a US benchmark.

When issued

Trading in securities which have been announced, but not yet issued. Such securities are said to trade on an "if, as and when-issued" basis. Also called the grey market. (See **grey market prices.**)

Window warrant

Warrant which is exercisable for a certain period begining after the trade date.

Winnipeg Commodity Exchange

Formed originally as the Winnipeg Grain and Produce Exchange in 1887, it is the only agricultural futures and options market in Canada. Trading is by **open outcry**. Settlement is by Winnipeg Commodity Clearing Ltd. The exchange trades futures in Canola, Flaxseed, Rye, Oats, Domestic Feed Wheat, Western Domestic Feed Barley, Canadian Domestic Feed Barley, and options on Canola, Feed Wheat, Flaxseed, Canadian Domestic Feed Barley and Western Domestic Feed Barley.

Winnipeg Stock Exchange

Trading began in 1909. The Exchange trades industrial shares and oil and mining shares. Trading volumes are low.

Withholding tax

Tax required to be deducted at source or withheld on share dividends, coupon payments or bank deposits.

Won

The national currency of North and South Korea.

World Bank

See **International Bank for Reconstruction and Development (IBRD)**.

Worst-of-two asset option

A form of **alternative option**.

Writer

Party which sells an option, and grants a right, but not an obligation to the purchaser.

XYZ

Yakusoku tegata

Japanese promissory note.

Yankee bond

A bond issued in the US domestic market by a foreign borrower.

Yankee certificate of deposit (Yankee CD)

Certificate of deposit (CD) issued in the US domestic market (usually New York) by a US branch of a foreign bank.

Yard

Dealers' slang for a billion. Particularly used with yen and lire.

Yearling bond

A bond issued by municipal authorities with maturity up to one year (in the US) or, oddly, up to two years (in the UK market).

Yellow Book

The London Stock Exchange rule book on listed securities. The Green Book is the US equivalent.

Yerevan Stock Exchange

Armenian stock exchange founded in 1993. Limited trading occurs in a few stocks and in US dollars, Deutschemarks and roubles.

Yield

(1) The yield on a share is calculated as:

$$\text{Dividend yield (\%)} = \frac{\text{Gross dividend per share} \times 100}{\text{Share price}}$$

(2) The return on a security which is the sum of the periodic income, plus or minus any capital gain or loss. Yield is rarely the same as the interest rate. To understand the calculation of yields, it is necessary to start with cash flows and the **time value** of money, leading on to internal rate of return and yield to maturity.

Cash flows

DM100,000 nominal value of a five-year fixed-rate bond, with a 5 percent annual coupon held until maturity will generate the following cash flows:

	DM
At issue	(100,000)
Year 1	5,000
Year 2	5,000
Year 3	5,000
Year 4	5,000
Year 5	105,000

These cash flows are predictable. Discounted cash flow techniques may be used to calculate the return on the investment or to establish a value for the holding.

Time value of money

A sum of money today is worth more than the certainty of the same sum tomorrow. This is the concept of the **time value** of money.

The formula used to calculate the present value (*PV*) of a future cash sum is:

$$PV = FV/(1+i)^n$$

where: *FV* is the future cash sum,
             i is the periodic interest rate, and
             n is the number of periods

Example

To calculate the value of DM100,000 to be received in two years' time when the appropriate discount rate is 5 percent, we apply the formula as follows:

             $DM100,000/(1+0.05)^2$
which is: DM100,000/1.1025
or   DM90,702.95

We can also look at the process in reverse. If the present value of a known future cash flow is given, we can calculate the implied discount rate. The formula is :

$$((FV/PV)^{1/n})-1$$

where: *FV* is the future cash flow,
             PV is the present value, and
             n is the number of periods.

Example

Suppose that $100,000 in three years' time is said to have a present value of $81,060.28. We can apply the formula as follows:

$$((100,000/81,060.28)^{1/3})-1$$
or $\quad(1.23365)^{0.33333})-1$
which equals   0.0725 or 7.25%

So the implied discount rate is 7.25%.

Internal rate of return (IRR)

The internal rate of return is the rate which if used to discount all future pay-ments to present value, produces a sum of present values equal to the price of the bond. It is the discount rate implied by the price of the bond. It can also be described as the rate at which all future payments are reinvested until the final maturity date so as to produce a lump sum which, if discounted back to present value at the same rate, produces a value equal to the price of the bond. Mathematically, this is the same as the first definition.

Example

Let us take the example of a $100,000 five-year 8% bond with annual coupons trading at par (100 percent of nominal value) The IRR is 8.00 per-cent and the calculation (on either definition) would be as follows:

	$ Cash flow	$ Present value	$ Future value
Year 1	8,000	7,407.41	10,883.91
Year 2	8,000	6,858.71	10,077.70
Year 3	8,000	6,350.66	9,331.20
Year 4	8,000	5,880.24	8,640.00
Year 5	108,000	73,502.98	108,000.00
Sum of values		100,000.00	146,932.81

$146,932.81 discounted back over five years at 8 percent produces a present value of $100,000. The price of the bond at an IRR of 8.00 percent is 100.00. In reality the IRR is calculated by a reiterative process.

When the price is deducted from the net present value we have a value of zero as we would expect.

Yield to maturity

In the above examples the running yield of the bond, expressed as the coupon divided by the purchase price, was the same as the IRR. In fact this is rare. Most bonds will not be bought or sold at exactly 100 percent of their nominal value. Yield to maturity is the same calculation as that for the inter-nal rate of return.

Example

We would like to buy a five-year bond with an IRR or yield to maturity of

8.5 percent. We are offered the same bond as described above. How much would we pay for it?

	$ Cash flow	$ Present value at 8.5%
Year 1	8,000	7,373.27
Year 2	8,000	6,795.64
Year 3	8,000	6,263.26
Year 4	8,000	5,772.59
Year 5	108,000	71,824.91
Sum of present values		98,029.67

So we would be prepared to pay 98.03 for the bond.

The second definition of IRR above highlights the reinvestment risk which this calculation may encourage us to overlook. Only with an instrument which returns only a single payment to the investor (e.g., a zero-coupon bond) is there no reinvestment risk. Otherwise the yield to maturity will be achieved in fact only if it is possible to reinvest each of the coupon payments at the same yield until the maturity date.

Yield basis

Quotation of a security not in price terms, but in yield terms. A bid yield and an offer yield may be quoted.

Yield curve

Graph produced by plotting yield against maturity. If the line slopes upwards from left to right, the curve is said to be positive: if downwards from left to right, the curve is said to be negative.

Yield curve option

Option on the shape of the **yield curve**.

Yield maintenance agreement

Part of a **repo** agreement which provides that the collateral given back at maturity need not be the same securities lent at the outset, but must have the same yield and credit quality.

Yield to average life

The yield of a security when the average life is substituted for the final maturity date

Yield to call

The yield of a security when the first **call date** and **call price** are substituted for the final **maturity date** and par **redemption price**.

Yield to maturity

The yield of a security calculated as an internal rate of return (IRR). Assumes that any interest payments received over the life of the security are reinvested at the IRR.

Yield to put

The yield of a security when the first **put date** and **put price** are substituted for the final **maturity date** and par **redemption price**.

Yokohama Raw Silk Exchange

Japanese exchange re-established in 1951. Trading is by *itayose* method on the floor of the exchange. The exchange trades a raw silk future.

Zagreb Stock Exchange

Revived in 1991, the Zagrebacka Burza in Croatia trades shares and bonds. Trading is by rolling call-over, **open outcry** and is partly electronic. Settlement is directly between brokers.

Zaibatsu

Japanese informal business conglomerate, usually centred on a bank.

Zaiteku

Japanese term for financial engineering.

Zaraba

Japanese term for a form of trading on an exchange based on the principle of open auction.

Zero-cost collar

A collar where the price of the sold component is the same as that of the one bought so that the net cost is zero.

Zero-coupon bond

Security issued at a discount to its nominal value and paying no interest. The return to the investor is the amount by which the redemption value exceeds the purchase price. The yield-to-maturity calculation for a zero-coupon bond does not involve any reinvestment rate assumptions. The duration of a zero-coupon bond is the same as its maturity.

Zero-coupon swap

Swap in which one party makes a zero-coupon payment, against some other form of interest. The party receiving the zero-coupon payment runs a considerable credit risk on the counterparty. One solution to this is to have a rising notional principal amount over the life of the swap, with the zero-coupon-paying party making cash payments equal to the periodic increase, rather than a single payment at maturity. The party paying the variable rate therefore pays it on the rising principal amount.

Zero-coupon yield curve

The yield curve formed by zero-coupon bonds of different maturities. It is a more precise than a yield curve formed by coupon bonds where the maturity dates are plotted. A zero-coupon yield curve plots yields for duration.

Zero strike price option

A method of circumventing restrictions on the transfer of securities, which gives the holder full participation in the price movement of the underlying.